Ev

Marjorie Klemme Jranan

THE ROAD FROM SPINK

A RETROSPECTIVE ON GROWING UP IN THE RURAL MIDWEST DURING THE GREAT DEPRESSION AND WORLD WAR II

BY

MARJORIE KLEMME FLADOS

authorHOUSE™

1663 LIBERTY DRIVE, SUITE 200
BLOOMINGTON, INDIANA 47403
(800) 839-8640
WWW.AUTHORHOUSE.COM

First published by AuthorHouse 11/10/05

ISBN: 1-4208-5871-8 (sc)

Printed in the United States of America
Bloomington, Indiana

http://www.authorhouse.com/BookStore/SearchCatalog.aspx

This book is printed on acid-free paper.

DEDICATION

Written in loving memory of my parents, Anna and Emil Klemme, who by their example of honesty, trust, decency, kindness and respect for hard work, instilled a little of each of those attributes in me as I sauntered and sashayed my way through my formative years.

I dedicate this memoir to my siblings, Leverne, my brother, and two sisters, Lu Ida and Agnes, who between the three of them always knew when to grab my kite string if I began to soar, sail or rattle out of control.

And to my husband, who through the years encouraged my intellectual development and supported my varied efforts to do new and interesting things.

And to our three children, Fara, Mark and John, whom we parented to adulthood without serious heart-breaking problems along the way.

FOREWARD

There were people and events in my life that I wanted to remember forever. To maintain those memories, I often wrote my thoughts and feelings on yellow legal pads which would subsequently be forgotten and disappear among stacks of accumulated keepables. Relying on the snippets of my writings, in some cases tucked away for decades, this retrospective records the events of my life against the backdrop of the Great Depression, World War II and the culturally jolting 1960 s and 1970 s. As I began to write, the scenes, sights, smells and emotions associated with my childhood rushed into my conscious memory, recalling one incident often renewed a recollection of another.

Many hours were spent with my siblings discussing and verifying events of the past. Interestingly, we often remembered things differently. The Internet and especially Google provided access to historical verifications. I am grateful to Esther Lykken for making segments of Peter Norbeck's manuscript available to me. Special thanks to Marion Aaker for providing me with a copy of her mother's painting of the Spink Store crossroads. (Myrtle Twedt, artist.)

I have made a special effort to be factually accurate and these recorded events and their influence on my life up to and including the year 2005 are as I perceived them.

Growing up in a rural setting, surrounded by the homogeneity of the upper Midwest, I believed everyone was like us. With maturity, I learned that when compared with the population in general, we were wonderfully unique and that I had been given a gift beyond value: good parenting in a wholesome, healthful, Christian environment.

Growing up Norwegian and Lutheran was a double whammy, but because of, or in spite of this circumstance, I always felt that God loved and approved of me. I felt confident that He would protect me when I needed Him. Truth be known, I needed Him a lot.

TABLE OF CONTENTS

INTRODUCTION

COUNTRY ROADS

Why a chapter on country roads? Because I spent much of my young life walking, riding, coasting or sledding on them. The crossroads community of Spink was the hub around which our lives revolved. The roads in the immediate vicinity of our farm were dirt roads and they could become deep rutted quagmires after a rain. During the drying out process, automobile tires would create narrow pathways as smooth as a sidewalk that provided an ideal place for coasting down the hills in a wagon or sled. On the icy roads of winter, the downhill speed of our sleds would reach a momentum that could carry us partway up the next hill.

When riding horseback, it was on the nearby roads that I would let Polly have her head, lean forward over her withers, letting her long mane whip against my face as I rode like the wind. These spurts of speed were of short duration for Polly's favorite gait was plod, not gallop. In winter snow we would tie a rope to the saddle horn and she would pull us along on skis.

My second hand bicycle provided me with "wheels" and I ranged far and wide. It was precarious riding on a 15-inch wide path of hard packed dirt bordered on both sides by rough, crusted, deep furrows, knowing that one swerve of the front wheel could cause a big tumble. I took a few.

Unless obstructed by river or stream, the Township was divided into grids, 640 acres to a square mile. A country road bordered each square in the grid and each section contained several farmsteads. There were rural one-room schools, named and numbered, in close enough proximity to each other so most children could walk to and from school. We lived one and one-half miles from Pleasant Hill School, District # 57, and we walked the distance both ways daily. We left home at 8 A.M. each morning; we would hear the 8:30 A.M. bell ring when we were at the half way mark, arriving before school started at 9:00 A.M.

During extreme weather Dad would take us or pick us up after school but that didn't happen very often. Usually we walked and everyone else did too. Putting a pencil to it, 3 miles a day x 170 days (# of school days in a year) = 510 miles each year, multiplied times 8 years (grades) = a distance of over 4080 miles that we walked during our first eight years of school. That does not include the countless times we walked to our friends' homes or walked the one-half mile to and from our mailbox to pick up our mail each day during the summer months.

We walked along, dreaming our childhood dreams, watching the ever-changing shape and character of the clouds in the sky. We heard the trilling song of the meadowlarks as they sat atop the fence posts along the way. I practiced imitations of the individual bird songs and can still do an almost perfect imitation of a meadowlark.

Each season had its unique sights, sounds and smells. In spring we were well aware of the crawling insects, the bumble bees, the rodent tracks, the sounds of farm animals, the putt-putt of farm machinery and the smell of the various crops and hay fields as we walked past farmsteads to and from school each day. In fall we noted the tall sunflowers with their yellow blossom-faces nodding toward the sun and we walked to the accompaniment of the staccato tattoo of ears of corn hitting the farm wagon bang-boards as neighborhood farmers handpicked the fields of corn. In winter the landscape was white, the snow crunchy and we usually took our sleds so we could coast down the hills along the way. We rarely carried books home from school.

The pasque flower would be one of the first blossoms of spring, so fragile and beautiful and so hidden away in a favorite blooming spot. We could anticipate finding them up on a road bank at the intersection north of our farm. Squatting down to admire their pink petals, we felt they were so special and the very best harbingers of spring and summer days to come. We never picked them; we just searched for them and admired them. (Note: the pasque is the state flower of South Dakota.)

Because the roads would become deeply rutted, the township hired a "maintainer" to grade and scrape them with an enormous, bladed road-grader pulled by four horses. Our "maintainer" was a neighbor who had most unusual speech habits. He spoke in epithets laced together with pertinent nouns and verbs. Whenever Dad stopped to talk with him on the road, he would astound us with the number of extraneous mild swear words he would utter.

"Hello, Emil," he would say, "G---d--it-to-hell, by Jiminy Christmas, the corn, by dang, may never, for hell's sake make a crop, by golly. I know, by hell, a gol-darned rain, by damn, Jiminy Christmas would do the whole dratted area some good, for gosh sakes. Yessir, by god." He was a decent man and a good neighbor; interestingly, he spoke in normal language when in the presence of women.

Since ample grass grew along roadsides during the summertime, when pastures were over-grazed the cattle would be driven out onto the roads, once in the morning and again in the late afternoon, to eat the grass. Herding the milk cows was considered kids' work. We would open the farm gate, urge them on their way down the driveway to the road, then head them south (or north) to start them on a grazing path. They would walk and graze and we would keep abreast or slightly ahead of them so if they strayed too far we could turn them around and head them back toward home. Graze, walk and turn them around….graze, walk and turn them around; this was the routine for at least an hour.

Usually these herding exercises were uneventful, but at other times the cattle would be restless and ornery and try to stray down a neighbor's driveway or through a field gate. They would stand in knee high grass and stick their dumb heads through a fence to eat from the other side.

A cow's tail normally hangs straight down, and it isn't a pretty tail, at best. But when they stuck their tails straight up in the air, it struck terror in my heart for I knew they were going to run away and scatter far and wide to who knows where. I hated the sight of the dumb beasts running off, tails in the air, hell-bent in the wrong direction. When this happened I would have to walk back home to get help rounding them up.

I often wished my folks had armed me with a cannon or a sawed off shotgun to use during these times. Our farm dog helped some, but only up to the point when the tails were hoist in defiance of my control, then it was overwhelming for the dog and me. Herding was not my favorite pastime during the summer months, but I did a lot of it. Circumstances required that we spend time alone while herding along the roads and of necessity we learned to consider our own company worthwhile, a valuable lesson in itself.

In winter the roads could be treacherous and impassable, requiring hours of snow scooping to get to an open gravel State road. Everyone growing up in the '30 s has a story about life threatening experiences in winter. One of the severest winters in memory was in 1936 and it was followed by one of the hottest summers.

Dad and 15-year-old Leverne had driven the corn-shelling rig to a farm five miles from our home. During the afternoon, a late February snowstorm blew in, fast and cold and as the storm rapidly worsened, they decided to head for home. Leaving the rig in place, they hitched a ride on a truck loaded with shelled corn and headed for Spink, 1½ miles from our farm. By this time it was necessary to scoop a path through the snow for the loaded truck. It took them 3 ½ hours to go 5 miles. They arrived in Spink, long after dark and a resident with a pickup truck agreed to take them to the intersection ½ mile south of our farm; from that point the roads would be impassable for his truck and they would have to walk the rest of the way. The wind was howling, snow was blowing, the temperature was 15 below zero; it was a total whiteout.

Earlier that afternoon the school children, and Agnes and I, were caught in the same set of weather conditions. Facing a threatening blizzard, the teacher dismissed school early; parents could not be notified for there was no phone at the school and all the kids headed for home, post haste. Agnes was about seven years old and I was ten, and as we trudged along in the snow and bitter cold, she kept asking to sit down and rest awhile. All children who live in the cold north are warned never to sit down to rest if they feel cold. Never, never, never, for when the body cools down, resting and sleeping soon become the most appealing of ideas. It is also a sign of hypothermia and impending death by freezing. I knew that.

When Agnes kept asking to rest, my mind clicked into an "I-must-save-my-sister-from-freezing-to-death" mode. I told her she would probably die if she sat down and that she had better keep walking! So on we trudged. It became scary when I, too, felt like resting awhile. As we reached the hill near our farm, we   saw

Mom walking to meet us with extra clothing to keep us warm, for the remainder of the way. She had no way of knowing we had left school early and were on our way home.

Supper was prepared and the lamps were lit, for it became dark very early. As the evening wore on, I noticed Mom kept looking out the windows toward the road. It was the only time in my life I ever saw my mom show fear. She did not verbalize her concern, good, stoic, Norwegian mother that she was, but as we busied ourselves with our usual evening activities, her apprehension and unease permeated the room, without a word spoken regarding it.

Since one's sense of direction is absent in a whiteout, Leverne and Dad were making their way home from the intersection by following the fence line. Dad was still quite lame with painful arthritic feet and walking in snow was particularly difficult for him. When they arrived at the base of the hill south of our farm, Dad told Leverne he could go no further, and asked that he go on ahead, and bring Polly to carry them home. Leverne headed out alone, following the fence line for as far as he could, eventually having to leave it due to ditches and steep banks; he made his way to the driveway and into the house.

He arrived covered with snowflakes and two frozen cheeks and a frozen chin. Frozen cheeks or not, his tasks were not finished. Mom accompanied him to the barn, they bridled Polly and Leverne started south down the road to where he had left Dad.

In the meantime, I am sure Dad also realized he should not rest for fear of freezing, so he struggled on. Riding Polly, Leverne crested the hill and almost collided with Dad weaving from side to side in the snow. Visibility was zero and he didn't expect to find him at the top of that long hill for he had left him at the base of it.

Leverne said it was a miracle that they met as they did, for if Dad had fallen in the snow or had veered from the center of the road, he could have passed him by. Dad was too weak and tired to mount Polly so he wrapped his hands in her long mane and they slowly walked the remaining distance to the barn and home. By this time, Dad too had frozen spots on his face.

When they entered the warm kitchen where we had been waiting, the relief we all felt was palpable. My mom was a praying Christian and I know her fervent prayers prevented that day from ending in tragedy. A week later, Dad hitched the team to the bobsled and we all went to where the shelling rig had been left. What we saw on our arrival was a mound of snow completely covering the corn sheller with only the grease cups at the very top protruding through the snow bank.

When the spring thaws arrived and the frost left the ground, the roads were a mess; that was the time when young Leverne liked to "plow mud." He wasn't alone, I think my dad enjoyed it too.

Approaches to the wooden bridges would sometimes cave in and a plank would be placed across the open hole until it could be repaired properly and these crossings became challenges to my brother and my dad. Riding in the back seat of our car, I would look down at the hole and be scared to death. My dad would laugh and think it was great fun to drive over those dangerous spots. It affected me seriously. To this day, my heart pounds on an approach to a muddy spot in a road or places that fall off steeply on the passenger's side of the car. One time while traveling in California, I got out of the car and walked because I couldn't stand the sight of drop offs on my side of the car.

As the road network was up-graded and improved, more of them were graveled, made into all-weather roads and major highways were constructed. The nearest major highway was referred to as the K.T., which stood for "King of Trails." It wouldn't impress anyone today, but we thought it was a great road.

When we drove across the state to visit grandparents we traveled the distance on two-lane gravel roads, a two-day trip. As the major highways became paved and more and more of the country roads were graveled, the dirt roads became fewer in number. Now an honest-to-goodness dirt road is a rare thing.

For a land so green in the summer that it astounds the eyes, in winter if there is no snow, South Dakota is a brown and dreary scene. There are few flecks of color; even the evergreen trees are not green but rather a frozen shade of green-gray. Yet so obvious in the barren landscape is a land lying in wait for spring, hunkered down to withstand the onslaught of snow, ice and below zero temperatures, ready to burst forth into a riot of sprouting green when spring arrives and the fertile soil is planted in neat rows of corn, soybeans and grain.

After living away from the State of my birth for decades, it was on a visit in November of 1989, driving on the Spink Township roads that I saw them through different eyes. Once so familiar and locked in my memory, the roadways of my childhood had undergone many obvious changes. The old peaked-roofed houses had been replaced by neat homes with aluminum siding and appeared to be snug and cozy inside. There were very few of the old wood-frame houses, so well remembered, that generously invited the cold air in, in winter and the hot air in, in summer. Painted barns and sheds added patches of color to an otherwise colorless landscape. It was then that I felt compelled to write about the roads of my youth.

Now the countryside was intersected with paved roads that were kept open to traffic at all times. On the mailboxes along the roadsides, I noted the familiar names: Ronning, Sveggan, Stene, Lykken, Oie, Isackson, Swanson, all good Norwegian names whose families I knew two generations ago. These people were my people, with their flat Nordic faces, prominent brows, blue eyes and their unique area accent. South Dakota was pronounced "Soud D'koda"...the heavy R sounds, the sentences so often ending in "then". ("Well, are you feeling better, then?")...the hissed S that gives the letter S its true sound.

During this visit I stayed with Leverne and LaVonne on the home place and in the room I had occupied as a child. The big silver poplar had grown many feet higher and much larger in diameter and it still hovered outside my south window. It was bare and stark, but I gazed at it in wonder, finding beauty in its knotty trunk; I could easily recall the pleasant quaking ripple that was its unique leaf-sound in summer. Because I could hear it as it flowed through the branches, as a child I thought that tree made the wind.

The people who settled this rugged land converted the rolling hills and prairies into fertile farms, an awesome challenge. They turned their hearts and faces toward their newly adopted nation and seldom looked back. That their children learn English was important to them and to accomplish this, they enrolled them, young or old, in the first grade at the local school. Their willingness to work in heat and bitter cold through good times and bad made the land blossom. These sturdy immigrant people of the Heartland lived, loved, married and inculcated in their children the virtues of respect for hard work, love of God and Country, frugality and decency.

When I visit South Dakota, I have a warm back-home feeling and a deep yearning to remain there. But the rational side of me knows that my place is with my husband and family in Texas. Although it is pure pleasure to return to the places and people of my childhood, I look forward to slipping back into my comfortable niche in Harlingen, Texas on my return.

I will always cherish the memories of my journey on the road from Spink, my life-road. I will continue to find pleasure in remembering a time when it was great fun and quite safe for children to spend countless hours riding, sledding, walking or coasting on country roads.

SECTION ONE

THE CHILDHOOD YEARS

1926 -1939

While reading the Sioux City Journal, my mother was attracted to a theater notice announcing the appearance of a singer/dancer named Marjorie Lorraine. She told my father that if their expected baby was a girl, she would like to give her that name. I was indeed a girl and I have been Marjorie Lorraine ever since.

The entertainer would never know that fifty miles away, on a farm near Alcester, South Dakota a ten pound baby girl, born to Anna and Emil Klemme, on Saturday, March 13th, 1926, would bear her name.

My earliest memories predate my 4th birthday, before we moved from the Nora community in 1930, six miles south to Spink Township. I vividly remember falling down the back stairs all tangled up in the family's soiled laundry, how my head hurt, how I cried and was comforted by my mother.

I remember opening the little door on the oat bin with the intention of feeding some oats to our Shetland pony, Nibbles, then watching in horror as bushel after bushel came pouring out of the opening. Totally powerless to stop it, I stood screaming until my dad came to my rescue and closed off the stream of grain pouring from the bin. Every detail of those events is etched in my memory, including how the sky appeared on those memorable days. These recollections are my earliest. The next three years are a complete memory blackout.

My mom and dad had lived on the Nora farm since they were married in 1919. It was wrenching for my mom to leave her Norwegian friends and the Roseni Church where she had been baptized, confirmed and married, to move into a different community to a house and farm owned by my grandfather. The house was much bigger and much nicer, but she knew that the stress of her father-in-law's observing her care of it, would remove some of the joy she should feel living in a spacious, five bedroom home.

We continued to attend church in the Roseni Community for a time, before finally making the break and joining the Brule Creek Lutheran Church near home. We attended Sunday School, Mom sang in the choir, became active in Ladies Aid and my folks gradually made new friends whom they came to know and enjoy for the rest of their lives.

By the age of four or five, we were allowed to carry morning lunch at 10:00 a.m. and afternoon lunch at 4:00 p.m. to our dad working in the fields. Mom would send a sandwich, a piece of cake or cookie, fill a thermos with coffee and place all in a lunch pail that we would carry to Dad wherever he was working. We would wait for him to come to the end of the field row; he would halt the team of horses, (or later, the tractor) and we would sit cross-legged in the freshly turned soil and have our lunch together. Mom would have put something in the lunch pail for us to eat, as well, and after our lunch was eaten, we would be allowed the traditional "ride a round" with Dad.

We would ride one circuit of the field perched up on the steel cross piece of a cultivator or whatever piece of equipment he was using. Some of those seats were quite precarious, but it was a thrill to sit and watch the horses as we rode high on our perch.

One day as I was carrying afternoon lunch to my dad in the field south of the orchard, it was necessary to crawl through a fence. In so doing, the lunch bucket dropped to the ground, the lid flew open and Dad's sandwich rolled out onto a patch of thick dust. Blowing on it failed to remove any of the ugly brown coating. There was a livestock well with a hand pump nearby, and I carried the sandwich over and held it under the spigot and began pumping water to wash it. The sandwich became soggy so I hurriedly put it back in the lunch pail and went on my merry way to the top of the hill where I saw my dad approaching the end of the field row.

We sat down in the dirt; Dad opened the lunch pail, poured out his coffee into the metal lid cup, reached in and picked up the sandwich, now a soggy mess that fell through his fingers. He said, "What's this, Margie?" I said, "I dropped your sandwich in the dirt and I tried to wash it off down by the pump." To my surprise, he burst out laughing. Then he said, "Margie, didn't you know you can't wash bread?" I remember how foolish I felt, but my dad had a wonderful laugh and a great grin and I was so thankful he wasn't angry. There was one half of a cookie in his lunch pail that was suitable to eat. I don't think we ever told my mom.

My memory kicks in again after I started school at Pleasant Hill, District # 57, a one-room school where one teacher taught all eight grades. The building was neither centrally heated nor insulated from the severe cold winters of South Dakota. As in most rural schools ours contained a large metal heating stove that the teacher was expected to keep stoked with wood or coal. Those in the front of the school were quite warm; those in the back of the room were not so cozy. Strangely, because we dressed for the conditions of the north central plains, I do not recall being cold. Cold was a normal state of being in the wintertime.

In winter, my mom would occasionally place a pint jar full of homemade soup in my lunch pail. I would place the jar on a shelf at the top of the stove and by lunchtime it would be nice and hot. Sometimes she would send a mixture of homemade ice cream, which I would place outdoors in a snow bank, making certain to stir it during 10 o'clock recess. By noon I would have some tasty homemade ice cream.

Miss Ringsrud was my first grade teacher, and it was her last year of many that she taught in our country school. Olive Ringsrud was a legend in her own time and seventy years later people still remember her as the most remarkable teacher they ever had. She was tall, rawboned, rather masculine, opinionated and energetic. She was a masterful teacher who could inspire any child to learn.

3

To my little 1st grade eyes she seemed a titan, so tall with her hair pulled back in a hairnet and knotted at the back of her head. But under the brusque exterior was a kind heart.

Everyone in the District has an Olive Ringsrud story to tell if they ever attended Pleasant Hill School. The room had several rows of desks in graduated sizes and the alphabet in large, cursive letters covered the front wall above the blackboard. There was a piano, a wood box, and on the walls pictures of George Washington, (Stuart), the Gleaners (Millet) and The Horse Fair (Bonheur).

There were two cloakrooms, one for the girls and one for the boys. Along the back wall hung our individual drinking cups on metal hooks, and we drank water from a large, spigotted crock, which was filled daily from our cistern. Everyone brought noon lunch from home and placed the lunch pails neatly on the shelves in the cloakrooms.

Miss Ringsrud didn't have a discipline problem because everyone knew she could beat them up with one hand tied behind her back. When she made a rule, it stuck. There were two outhouses behind the schoolhouse and in winter it was the coldest place in the world to drop your pants. Only one person was allowed in the toilet at a time and if two kids ever entered together there was always a knock on the door and the teacher would tell one of them to come out.

One day when the sun was pouring in too brightly through the south windows, Miss Ringrud asked me to pull down the window shade. I tried to grasp the little finger ring at the end of the pull-down string, but I wasn't tall enough to reach it. She was watching. I meekly said, "I can't reach it." She said, "Well stand there until you figure out a way." With everyone in the room enjoying my discomfiture, no one saying a thing, just waiting and watching, I stood there with my face in my hands. She walked over and asked me what I thought I might do when things were out of reach. Then it dawned, and I meekly said, "I could climb up and reach it, I think." She smiled and said "That's right, Margie, when you can't reach something, you just climb UP and then you will find you CAN reach it." So I placed my knee on the windowsill, pulled myself up, grabbed the finger ring and lowered the shade. She patted my head and went back to teaching her class. I felt as if I had climbed

4

Mt. Everest....down deep in my mind, I also had a valuable lesson imprinted on my brain.

She was big on music and rhythm bands. My brother, Leverne, rather prided himself on saying, "I can't sing." He made the mistake of saying that to Miss Ringsrud, and it went something like this. "What do you mean, you can't sing! Everyone can sing." Then she proceeded to stand him up and place her hands on his chest and back, told him to say, "aah," banged a key on the piano and told him to make a sound that sounded like it. This went on for some time, but sitting there watching, I could see the stubborn look on Leverne's face and I knew he was not going to sing in spite of her efforts. And he didn't. Nobody can make another person eat, pee or sing. I knew that.

We had marvelous rhythm bands and I usually played the wooden sticks, Lu Ida played the drums, but the position I coveted was that of director. We wore capes and little paper hats when we performed on a program. Sooner or later we progressed through the various instruments and those who showed a talent for it were eventually allowed to lead the band. I thought the status instrument was the jazz horn, (kazoo) because it carried the tune. I do not remember a child who was not able to hear the beat and keep time with the music as she banged it out on the piano. Or do all Norwegians have rhythm? We were also expected to master two-part harmony.

She would preach to us about eating fruit and vegetables and would frequently announce that it was time for our iron. She would then give each child 10 raisins to eat. We were told to chew each bite of food we put into our mouths 20 times...and many times we kept chewing, to get to 20 long after the food had disappeared down our throats. By the count of 8 my mouth was usually empty! Leverne was not feeling well the day he was scheduled to attend a Field Day in Alcester so she insisted that he eat six oranges, her personal get-well therapy. No one remembers if he won any competitions that day, but he had a jolt of Vitamin C, for sure.

She disliked snuffling, snotty noses. She made us blow our noses, and those who forgot or were too poor to have hankies would receive a square of torn bed sheet that they were expected to use for that purpose. We saved our hankies for indoors and when we were

5

outside, we blew our noses into the wind, one nostril at a time. We were all good at that.

Miss Ringsrud demonstrated her ability to control a situation during one of our school programs, when a neighborhood teenager pulled the school bell rope that hung from the rafters in the entrance hall. When the bell began to toll, Miss Ringsrud went into action. She marched down the aisle amongst students and parents, walked up to the errant fellow, grabbed him by the scruff of the neck and seat of the pants and dragged him out onto the front porch of the school and told him to go home. He did.

She called me "Little Miss Dutch Cleanser," because she said I smelled clean. (Dutch Cleanser was a cleaning powder much like the Comet used today.) After her retirement from teaching she entered politics and was elected Secretary of State for the State of South Dakota. In later years she spent time in California teaching remedial reading, no surprise since I witnessed her teaching of remedial singing.

Pleasant Hill School was the center of my world. It was where I learned to love reading, where the teacher read to the entire school from books of adventure and derring-do. It was where I learned Palmer penmanship. On Fridays we practiced our writing skills doing concentric circles, push-pulls and cursive examples of our script. When our example was as good as it could get, the teacher would submit it to the Palmer Penmanship Company to be graded and if warranted, we would receive little blue and gold pins to reward our efforts. To this day, I can identify handwriting that resulted from the teaching of Palmer Penmanship.

We had a fifteen-minute forenoon and afternoon recess and an hour for lunch and play at noon. The play was active and very competitive, Simon Says, Oley, Oley, Oxen Free, softball in warm weather, sledding and Fox-and-the-Geese during the snowy winter. Sometimes play became quite rough and tumble.

My second grade teacher was a young, pretty woman, named Miss Holmquist, who looked like an angel to me. I believed she was perfect and would never be capable of passing gas rectally or anything as vulgar as that. The younger children were not allowed outside at recess if the weather was severe; we would remain inside and play blackboard games or sometimes, Hide and Seek. During a Hide and Seek game on a very cold day I crawled under the teacher's desk. She was sitting at the desk at the time, and I remember looking up her skirt to see if she wore bloomers like I had to wear. She didn't.

I hated my bloomers. Mom made them from flour sacks and sometimes she dyed them, but usually they were white. They were longish and we tucked our stockings up under the elastic. In October we would start wearing our long legged underwear, the kind that buttoned up the front and had a drop down seat in the back. We pulled on our stockings, wrapped the leg of our underwear around the back side of our leg, just above the ankle, pulled our stockings up over it, leaving a big knot in the back of our leg and ripples in our stockings all the way up.

Winter underwear was worn until May 1st. Even if we had an early spring, the long legged underwear stayed on until that magic point in time. When we were allowed to leave off the underwear I felt like a chrysalis escaping the confines of my pupa. I felt so unconfined that I suspected I could fly. On one nice May day, the underwear had just come off, I arrived at school and yelled, "I FEEL NAKED TODAY!" After I said it, I wasn't sure I should have.

We had wonderful school programs at Pleasant Hill School and it was the only time that parents showed their faces at school. We would set up a stage made of 2 x 10 inch planks and string a stage curtain on wire across the front of it. We would sing, the rhythm band would play and we would present plays or skits with occasional guest performances.

When Agnes was three she was placed on a chair at the front of the room and she sang the song, Little Bird in a Cherry Tree. She was plump and cute as a button and I remember her in her little green dress with the red flowers on it, singing "A little bood in a chey-wee twee, tweet, tweet, tweet, tweet, tweet, etc." She couldn't pronounce her R s and there were a lot of R s in that song. A classmate and I once stuck our heads and hands through holes in a sheet and did a dance on a tabletop to the tune of The Arkansas Traveler. We thought we were ready for Broadway or at the very least, Major Bowes Amateur Hour.

7

We had booths, where we charged a nickel to see a Side Show or Go Fishing. I remember one advertised as the MONKEY BOOTH, and upon entering, there was a mirror on the wall to look at one's own reflection....and someone there to say, "Did you see the monkey?" Then there was the BOXING MATCH booth, and it contained 2 matchboxes facing each other. The schoolhouse would be filled with people for these program/fund raisers and they willingly bought the cookies and cakes donated by our mothers.

Our neighbors, the Abrahamsons, occasionally gave us clothing their adult daughters had outgrown or had chosen to discard. Mom would rip the garments apart and make us dresses and coats from them. We were grateful for the serviceable clothing.

Mom made me a pretty wool school dress from a hand-me-down garment, which not only kept me warm but was a pretty shade of light green set off with a little satin collar. One day when I was wearing this favorite of dresses, I took my # 2 pencil and drew two big circles on my chest, one around each small breast. As I turned in my seat after doing this strange deed, a seventh grade boy noticed my "circles", who could miss them, and he smirked.

Sitting there with my breasts outlined by penciled circles, plainly visible from across the room, I knew it was only a matter of seconds before others would notice. What could I do? I felt compelled to remove them, at first unsuccessfully with an eraser, and then with the only cleaning solution I had...my spit. I would pull the front of my dress up, put a segment of the circle in my mouth and slobber and suck on it with every hope of slurping the lead ring circle away. Mom believed spit would remove anything, even rust! It may indeed, but it doesn't remove lead pencil marks.

After sucking and slurping my way around the two circles, I ended up with the pencil marks slightly obscured by two wet circles on my chest. And if I found my tormentor's interest embarrassing when he first saw the original art work, his reaction to the wet circles made me wish for death.

I considered this boy a pervert, because one day he drew an outline of a naked woman, folded the paper in quarters and bit out the folded corner and chewed on it. Then with a flourish unfolded the paper and waved this picture at me, a picture of a naked woman

8

with nothing but a hole where her private parts should be. No doubt, he chewed his little paper wad 20 times.

Once a week we presented oral reports on a news item as described in the local newspaper. This Friday morning segment was called Current Events, usually pronounced "Curnt Events." Some gave short ones, some gave long ones, but the entire school was expected to listen, even if they were too young to participate.

As we matriculated through the grades we were expected to become active in the Young Citizens League. We learned Robert's Rules of Order and everyone was expected to know how to conduct a proper meeting. With only three in my class, competition wasn't very stiff, and in 8th grade I was elected a delegate to the county Y.C.L convention, and at the county convention, I was elected a delegate to the state convention. While attending the convention at Pierre, South Dakota's state capitol, Governor Harlan Bushfield addressed the delegates and I had my picture taken with the governor, just him and me. I still have the picture.

At this convention a choral director lead us in singing. It was the first time I had heard or had to sing music composed for children. We had always sung songs from the Civil War such as Marching Through Georgia, Carry Me Back to Old Virginny, Lead Kindly Light, Flow Gently Sweet Afton; World War I songs, such as Tenting Tonight, Over There, Long, Long Way to Tipperary, or old spirituals like Swing Low Sweet Chariot, and Massa's in the Cold, Cold Ground. When I heard these light, cheerful songs about birds, sunlight and caring for one's friends, my thought was that they were the silliest most tuneless songs I had ever heard. I was more into Massa's in the Cold, Cold Ground than Say Hello With A Smile Today.

Did we ever need a grief counselor in our schools? Probably not. We sang about death! We sang dirge-like songs about sorrow, yearning and dying. We were accustomed to animals and pets dying and birds occasionally falling with a thud from the sky. Animals were butchered to provide food for our family and watching one's mother wring a chicken's neck to provide meat for Sunday dinner did not distress us. Death happened all around us and except for our own, we didn't give it much thought. We were expected to cope with disappointing events.

After Miss Holmquist, my teachers were Astrid Anderson, Miss Steensland and Gladys Bennett. Miss Steensland had a temper and kicked the coalscuttle one day in a fit of anger. As junior Norwegians, emotion of any kind was seldom exhibited or encouraged so we were scandalized and had great times thereafter imitating "the kick," in private of course.

Miss Bennett was a great teacher. I liked her feet. She wore pretty shoes; up until then our teachers all wore sensible, laced up brogans. Miss Bennett occasionally wore red shoes and on red shoe days my spirits soared. I loved her red shoes! I thought I learned better when she wore them.

At the Alcester County Field Day the year I was an eighth grader, I was fourteen years old, had a waistline, some breasts, was tall for my age and on the lookout for good-looking boys. This was before the time of specialized clothing for specific sporting activities, and for this sports event I foolishly decided to wear a dress with a dirndl waist and my little black, church pumps. I felt grown up and glamorous. But not for long. Miss Bennett made me compete in the foot races.

In my dirndl dress and my Sunday shoes, there I was, lined up at the start line with twenty-five or more 8th graders making ready to sweat my way down the course. The starting gun went off and we pounded down the field. First one little squirt passed me, then another, then another, until all had passed me by. I was the tallest and my legs were the longest, but I couldn't seem to move as fast as those fat, little, stumpy-legged Norwegian kids zipping past me. I came in last. My hair was a mess, my shoes were dusty, and I felt like a dolt. Anyone with Lykken blood can't run fast, I knew that! I would have rather been shot, than run that foot race in my glamorous finery.

A family moved into our community who were not Norwegians or Lutherans, we thought they were Holy Rollers, what they really were, no one ever knew. The girls didn't cut their hair, and the boys wore what we called a "heinie" haircut. There were eight kids and the mama stayed pregnant. They were different and they were

10

very, very poor. Kids can be cruel and the kids of Pleasant Hill were no exception. I was too kind hearted to be overtly cruel but I have always felt guilt for not trying to stop some of the meanness I witnessed. They would bring homemade bread smeared with lard for their lunch, or a gallon pail of popcorn, nothing else, just popcorn.

I walked into the cloakroom one day when the oldest girl was opening her gallon bucket containing popcorn. I felt sorry for her. I knew she would never accept part of my lunch, they were too proud to do that, so I lamely said, something about how I loved popcorn and how lucky she was to have all of it she wanted. She gave me an odd look. She quickly closed her pail and went out to the playground. I always felt I could have done better than that. These were the depression years and we were all very poor, but somehow my mom saw to it that we had an apple or an orange in our lunch bucket. I remember envying those who had white grapes to eat. My mom considered them too expensive for school lunches.

Some of the kids in that family were very bright, and I understand in later years they prospered and did well. But they must have felt ostracized and sad at times. I hope in their maturity, they have forgiven us for not being more tolerant and accepting.

One year we all caught "the itch", scabies. I knew whom I caught it from because I had observed who was scratching between their fingers, a sure sign. Catching the scabies in those days presented a daunting challenge to mothers, especially if it was wintertime. It was also pretty rotten for us kids. The cure was worse than the condition. Since scabies are very contagious, if anyone came home with it my mom would click into her scabies mode. First a quick run to town for a grainy sulfur-based salve that was as malodorous as a cesspool. We called it "PRRUUP" salve.

At night, off came the clothes, the underwear, everything, and the salve was rubbed all over our bodies. It was so grainy that it hurt when applied. Then back into clean underwear and nightclothes. But the next day, we wore that stinking underwear to school under our school clothes. We reeked to high heaven. No mistaking when someone was taking the cure. We kept the salve on for several days under our underwear and when Saturday came we got to wash it off. In the meantime, Mom was boiling and washing bedding, doorknobs and clothing everyday. I never remember getting scabies when the weather was warm when it would have been easier to cure. With Mom boiling everything in sight and slapping "prrup" salve on any thing that moved, we didn't keep "the itch" for long.

As I walked to and from school each day, there was lots of time for youthful dreams. I decided that someday I wanted to wear beautiful clothes, I wanted to go to exciting places, I wanted to have fun in high school, I wanted to make lots of friends and I wanted to be Homecoming Queen. An ad in a periodical caught my eye; it stated, "Be Popular...Join the Compliment Club.....Give as few as one compliment a day and see how your friendships grow".... and on and on. I sent in the registration fee of one dollar and waited for my Compliment Club kit. In about 10 days it arrived; there was information describing the program and documents on which to keep records of the compliments given during a 3-month period. After the pages were completed they were to be sent in to qualify for the official membership seal. I fulfilled the requirements, recorded my compliments, filled in my blanks and in due time applied for my membership seal. When I received my certificate of membership with its gold, embossed seal, I knew I was ready to meet the future. Looking back, that little exercise made quite an impression and I learned quickly that saying something nice to someone brought surprising benefits.

A new family, Roman Catholics of French extraction, moved into our district and I thought they were very glamorous. They played bridge; everyone I knew played Pitch, Rummy or Five Hundred, and their kids took tap dancing lessons. One daughter became my good friend and she taught me to tap dance. A son was in my grade and I considered him very handsome; they didn't wear long-legged underwear and I wondered why they hadn't all died of pneumonia.

One spring Saturday afternoon I went over to play at their farm, and for some reason we three, Joan, Teddy and I were left at home to play by ourselves. We collected a sack of small stones, took sling shots (Y shooters) and went to the barn where there were a great many pigeons. We fired stones at the pigeons, killed three of them, skinned them, cut them up and fried them. Then we sat down at the kitchen table and ate them. When their parents came home about 4 o'clock, they were shocked at what we had done. Being soft hearted about animals and not one to mistreat them, I marveled at how I could have participated in that Saturday afternoon slaughter. It was totally out of character for me, but the pigeon was rather tasty, as I remember.

An advertisement stated that a beautiful red wagon could be mine if I sold three shipments of White Cloverine Salve. This ointment was reported to cure many things. I sent for my first shipment of nine metal containers of salve. I then walked all over the neighborhood selling my "product." The first batch went rather quickly, but when faced with selling a second shipment, the sales went a bit slower. By the time I had to peddle my third shipment, everyone had about as much White Cloverine Salve as they could handle in a lifetime. One neighbor bought three tins from my last batch, probably to prevent me from making another house call. I eventually received the beautiful red wagon and it had battery powered headlights that actually lit up. Agnes and I would take it on the road and with both of us sitting in it, coast down the hills lickety-split. One year I pulled my wagon home, full of day lily bulbs, given to me by a neighbor, and I presented them to my mom on Mother's Day. Some of those day lilies still bloom where they were planted sixty-six years ago.

Like most farm children, during our grade school years my sister, Agnes, and I enjoyed having pets, she loved animals, as did I. My mom raised chickens and one year she presented me with a few hatchlings to raise and I was excited about the possibility of selling them when they were grown and making MONEY! No chickens on the planet had more tender loving care than those fifteen chickens. They had their own pen and shelter away from Mom's flocks and I was so chicken-oriented that I learned the names of the different varieties of chickens extant in the neighborhood and who raised which kind. There were Plymouth Rocks, Rhode Island Reds, Buff Orphingtons and Leghorns. Mine were Plymouth Rocks and they died like flies and were dead as rocks before they reached maturity, in spite of my care and attention. Even my mom couldn't figure out why they all perished.

As a rule farmers do not keep runts in their herds and my dad was no exception. When a runt was born in a litter of piglets it was removed and killed. This touched my tender heart, but my dad explained that runts eat like the others, but never thrive. I didn't want to believe that. One day, when a runt piglet was born, I pleaded with my dad to let me have it, he finally agreed and I was given the little white pig for a pet. I thought with all my attention and the good food I would provide, he would grow into a sleek hog that I could sell for big MONEY!

That sorry pig was regularly brushed, bathed, ate like a king and grew a little but not much. His head didn't match his body, he had a scraggle-tag look to him and his tail was a disgrace to hogdom. It hung like a "U" instead of an inverted "E." Mom decided one day that maybe if we wormed him he would grow faster. She stood him on his hind legs in a corner of the hog shed and forced some medicine from a bottle down his throat. When he had swallowed it all, she stood up to turn away. We stared in awe, as that stupid pig just continued to sit there, squashed in the corner with his front feet up in front, dangling in the air, looking confused but obedient.

During my "pig phase," we had a Pleasant Hill School Fair; we were to bring our pets to display them and compete for a prize. A parade was held and the contestants were judged by visiting parents. Agnes brought Spot, our terrier, and of course she had her tied up prettily and Spot behaved beautifully. I brought my pet pig, and as we walked in the judging parade, he dug in all four feet and I had to drag him around the entire judging circle with him squealing at the top of his lungs every step of the way. I felt like butchering him on the spot. My pig and I didn't win a prize and we didn't deserve one. When he was grown, and I use the term loosely, I sold him to market for $5.00 and I had a sneaking suspicion my dad contributed part of that sum to make me feel better. I used the five dollars to buy a second hand bike that my dad repainted and repaired.

I had good luck raising my goat. Nanny was given to me when she was quite small and what a wonderful pet she was. She would romp with us, climb and follow us about. Dad made a double hitch for my red wagon, Mom made a harness out of leather straps and braided twine, and we hitched True Heart, our German Police dog, and Nanny to my red wagon and they pulled well as a team.

One afternoon when mom was at Ladies Aid, Agnes and I took Nanny upstairs and she jumped on the beds with us, leaped around on the balcony and ate the matches that were sitting on a chair by my bed. Jumping on the beds was a no-no and Mom could always tell if we did it. This time was no exception. We had not only done it, but with a goat joining in the fun. We were in big trouble and were made to understand that Nanny was not welcome in the house, ever! Nanny was a tyrant when among the cattle and would butt them and overwhelm them with her assertiveness. They gave her wide berth in the barnyard.

Many of our activities revolved around our membership in the Brule Creek Lutheran Church, ALC Branch, which was a white, wood framed building with stained glass windows. It had a fine pipe organ and a beautiful altar. We Lutherans enjoyed good music. The minister sang the church liturgy; there was a choir and we had many soloists and several accomplished pianists in our congregation.

We went to Sunday School and Church every Sunday, and I carried my nickel or three pennies for the collection plate tied in the corner of my handkerchief. The Sunday School Christmas program was a highlight of the year, we spoke a "piece" or had some dialogue to say and for the nativity scene roles we had some tired looking costumes. I also had what in later years I referred to as my "poinsettia" cold sore on my lower lip each and every year in time for the Christmas program. I do not remember a Christmas program when I wasn't burdened with a fat lower lip. As poor as we were during those years, my mom somehow managed for us to have a new Christmas dress each year. She usually sewed them and we thought they were very pretty.

Babies were baptized soon after birth and young boys and girls began "reading for the minister" at the age of thirteen in preparation for confirmation. Confirmation was a time to re-state the vows of baptism, for it was believed that children at the age of fourteen had reached the age of accountability and should take the baptismal vows with their own voices. Preparation for confirmation required one year of study and every Saturday morning was spent with the church pastor as we learned and memorized the tenets of the Lutheran faith. The Catechism contained every thought Martin Luther ever had in his head, and we had to memorize them. And memorize we did: the Commandments, the Articles of Faith, the Petitions, the Sacrament of Baptism and the Sacrament of the Altar. WHEW!!

The format of the Catechism was a series of statements, many of which ended with the words, "This is most certainly true," followed by questions, such as, "What is meant by this?" We not only were obligated to learn what was "most certainly true," but had to memorize the answers to "what is meant by this" or "how is this done" and countless questions that began with "Who" or "Why."

We had one fellow in our class who was a bit of a renegade and he challenged our minister in many ways. He spread pepper around one time and had us all sneezing. There were times the minister would just have us bow our heads and silently meditate on how naughty we were.

On the Friday evening before the Sunday of our confirmation the congregation was invited to witness the catechization exercise. The confirmands, there were eight of us, sat in the choir pews in the front of the church and the minister stood before us and asked us questions at random from the book of Martin Luther's Catechism. We were expected to give the verbatim answers. It was a stressful, hair-raising exercise. Some members of our class were very bright and some were not and I felt sorry for those who might miss a question. I felt sorry for myself, too. Many years later when my husband was studying for his PhD. and faced his Orals, I felt no sympathy, for I had faced "Orals" every bit as challenging at fourteen years of age.

Confirmation was very special and we wore white dresses for the occasion. Our families invited relatives to dinner and gifts were given to the confirmands. It was a milestone event in a Lutheran child's life. The preparatory classes were very meaningful to me. It was made very clear to us how we were expected to lead our lives. To our minister, things were black or white, there was no gray and we were expected to make wise and discerning decisions as adults. We knew exactly what sin was and we knew the penalties of a sinful life. As a child I had always dreamt of being a singer, dancer or entertainer in nightclubs, but was convinced during this year of study that I could not follow that path and stay in the good graces of my Lutheran beliefs. This year of training for confirmation left me with a desire to walk the walk of a godly person, and I know the Lord protected me many, many times when throughout my life I foolishly put myself in harm's way. After confirmation girls were expected to be active in Lutheran Daughters of the Reformation. It was at an L.D.R. convention at the age of fifteen, that I first tasted Coca Cola.

During this period of their lives, girls were expected to begin saving household linens for their Hope Chest. This cedar-lined chest, usually gifted by the parents, provided a place for young girls to store their hand embroidery work, "fancy work," as well as those items received from their mothers, aunts or grandmothers. By the time they married, many girls had extensive collections of very nice bed and table linens. Me, I never had a Hope Chest or wanted one, and my embroidery work was pretty sloppy compared to some.

There were fall bazaars and church picnics, some held in the Larson cow pasture, a nice shady place with plenty of room for a soft ball game. Everyone knew to be watchfully alert to avoid stepping in the cow pies. There was lots and lots of food; buns were always buttered before putting any meat on them and the butter had better reach to all the outside edges or someone was being "scimpy!" We were served ice cream from a tall 5-gallon container that arrived wrapped up tight in an insulated, canvass bag with flaps tied across the top.

I enjoy returning to Brule Creek Church on my trips back to South Dakota. It is still a beautiful church and although it has lost some of the vibrant energy of sixty years ago, it continues to be a comforting place of worship. I have since internalized the fact that I could probably have become a singer or a dancer (perish the thought) and not gone straight to hell. The absence of exceptional talent in those areas saved me from having to put the concept to a test.

Until the advent of modern equipment and mechanization most farms had horses, hogs, chickens and cattle. We always milked cows and I learned how to milk, but never enjoyed it. All those pails of milk had to be carried to the house to a room off the kitchen, where a De Laval Separator would separate the cream from the milk. After pouring the milk in a big round container at the top, the crank handle was turned causing the milk to spin through disks. The cream came out one spigot and the skim milk came out the other. Cream was a salable commodity and the skim milk was fed back to the young calves or mixed with ground grain to make mash for the hogs. To clean the disks after each use, hot boiling water was poured in the bowl after the milk was run through. Every few days, the disks required cleaning, one by one, washed and rinsed and placed back in line. Oh hateful job!

Listening to the radio was a big part of our evening entertainment. We listened to Orphan Annie, snorfed our Ovaltine, saved our coupons and sent in for our Orphan Annie Code rings. There was The Shadow, Jack Armstrong-All American Boy and Leverne wouldn't miss Jimmy Allen, a program about a young man who flew airplanes. He would run from the barn to the house carrying a full pail of milk in each hand, timing it to the minute so he could sit transfixed with his ear pressed against the radio. If he was late Lu Ida was instructed to listen for him and tell him every single thing that had happened.

My mom would send cream, eggs and homemade butter to the local store where they were bartered for food staples. Sometimes she would send live chickens for barter as well. While the hens were at roost, she would press three fingers of her hand against their backsides to determine if they were producing eggs and if they weren't, off they went to the store to be sold. The chickens and eggs were what provided us with money for groceries during the depression years when there were poor crops because of grasshoppers and drought. They sustained us.

We looked forward to local celebrations such as the Old Settlers Picnic, Fourth of July, Labor Day, Pancake Festivals and the annual Sunday School Picnic in Vermillion when we would rent bathing suits and go swimming, a once a year event.

On very cold mornings when the snow was deep, Dad would take us to school in the bobsled, a spring wagon to which he had attached runners converting it into a sleigh. Before our departure, Mom would have heated bricks in the oven; we would all hunker down in the bobsled with horsehair blankets and rugs over us, and with the warm bricks placed on the floor of the sled, we would be very cozy. My dad in his thick wool overcoat with the sheepskin, woolly collar turned up beside his ears, would stand in the front of the sled like a Roman charioteer and expertly drive his team of horses over the snowy countryside.

Because my grandparents had moved to the Black Hills in the western part of the state, we took several trips out to visit them. The trip took the better part of two days, the roads were mostly gravel, two-lanes, bumpy, and we packed all our food and slept in the car or in town parks along the way. There were no motels in central South Dakota. Visiting our grandparents out in Hill City was a wonderful experience, for the Black Hills offered new and different scenery. We saw Mount Rushmore when it had but one face on it.

On one trip to the Black Hills, driving through the barren, sparsely populated, central part of the State, Agnes and I had to go potty. Really bad. What to do? Mom spotted a farmhouse in the distance with an outdoor privy behind it and she felt the people would gladly let us use it. Dad left the highway, approached the house and Agnes and I knocked on the door. A woman who looked the typical dust bowl prairie wife in her plain dress and apron answered our knock. We asked if we could please use the toilet. Unsmiling, she said simply, "yes." We turned to head for the toilet when she called, "Wait a minute," disappeared inside the house, returned and thrust a Sears Roebuck catalog into our hands. She said, "Here, you will need this." And so we did.

In preparation for this trip my mom had dyed feed sacks and made Agnes and me each a matching slacks and jacket outfit, a red set for me and blue set for Agnes. They were beautiful. Chicken feed and flour came in sacks made of plain or figured muslin. The figured sack material was quite attractive and was used to make dresses and underwear. Many of the clothes we wore were made of feed sack muslin.

While at Grandma's house we had picnics in the surrounding hills and canyons; the kids slept on the glassed-in front porch and we had lots to eat and wonderful times.

In the year 2000, Leverne, LaVonne, Lu Ida and I visited Hill City, and Grandma's house still stands on Main Street, looking much the same as it did sixty-five years ago. We had our pictures taken on the rock wall in front of the house, and after talking to the owner in the back yard, we were invited into the house, and to our surprise discovered it looked much the same as we remembered it.

Spink was a crossroads community made up of a grocery store, garage, feed store, barbershop and a beer parlor. There were tall, red gas pumps near the store front filled with pink colored gasoline and after a gas tank was filled, the glass receptacle at the top had to be refilled by a push-pull action on a vertical handle attached to side of the pump.

On Saturday evenings families would gather at Spink to shop and visit. The young people would mingle as they sat in, on and among the parked cars. The adults would do their shopping, visit with each other inside the store and I would play with my good friends, the Twedt twins. Since their father owned the store, they would often work in the basement transferring eggs from the private crates into shipping crates and I would help them when I could.

On summer nights we would sit on wooden plank benches and watch black and white third-rate movies projected against the exterior south wall of the store building. The sound system undulated, wavered and ootched along with interruptions to change reels. We thought the movies were great.

Spink had competing ball teams for all ages. I played on a girls' kitten ball (soft ball) team, the men and boys played competitive baseball. There were regularly scheduled horseshoe pitching competitions, as well.

A traveling theater group called the M & M Tent Show would arrive in summer and put up their tent in a nearby field. For three consecutive nights a small company of actors would present dramas with comedy skits between acts. The company would arrive on an afternoon and local people would assist in erecting the tent in exchange for a free ticket to a performance.

Admission was 35 cents for adults and 15 cents for children. We could afford to attend one night only, and to my childish eyes it was the most exciting experience of the year. I thought the actors were leading a wonderful life and I dreamed someday of doing the same, performing and traveling. Looking back it must have been a hand-to-mouth, hard–scrabble life on the road for these traveling thespians and I never have figured out where or what they used for a toilet since they pitched their tent in a nearby field.

Children had the usual illnesses, but there were home remedies for most of them. Vapor Rub was a standard cure for anything respiratory; it went on the neck, on the chest, up the nose and down the throat. There were poultices for various things, for an earache you got the heated core of an onion inserted in your ear. Castor oil cured many symptoms, and anything from boils to menstrual cramps brought my mother's medical ingenuity to the fore. The only time I was ever taken to a doctor was when I had my tonsils out at the age of 4 ½ and my dad paid for the surgery by giving the doctor a heifer calf. Dr. Kerr had purchased a farm to hold all the farm animals taken in payment for his services.

We were almost self sufficient as far as our basic needs were concerned. Mom sewed our clothes and made our soap. We raised our own meat and vegetables, rendered lard, churned our butter, cut our firewood. We had warm clothes, sturdy shoes, which Dad repaired by replacing heels and half soles. We each had two pair of shoes: school/work shoes and Sunday shoes. Our clothing was of three varieties: everyday clothes, school clothes and Sunday clothes and we rarely mixed the categories. If we attended a special event on a weekday, Friday, for instance, we wore our "Sunday" clothes!

We entertained ourselves with pets, played with dolls and we always had a swing; sometimes a tire swing, sometimes a bag swing. We played cards, we visited relatives or received visitors on Sunday. We sang, harmonized, played the piano, read books and listened to the radio. With solid family relationships in our home, I did not feel deprived and if I had only 15 cents to spend at the carnival, I made it do; it bought a candy bar and one merry-go-round ride.

In spite of growing up during the worst depression in this nation's history I do not remember being overly concerned about it, as we were no richer or much poorer than any of our neighbors. Providing for a family of four children must have been a challenge for my folks, but I was blithely unaware of how difficult their struggles must have been. The Christmas that my mom remembers as a tough one for them was the year when there was no money for gifts. She made new doll clothes, re-furbished our dolls and tried to make the holidays as special as she could. Underprivileged was not a term we would have ever embraced to describe ourselves.

The events of the times shaped the attitudes and values of my generation, a generation steeped in the need to be frugal, to save for emergencies and to avoid the squandering of one's resources. We were content to dance, sing, picnic, go to the movies, watch or participate in competitive sports and worship in our respective churches. We coped.

I owe a debt of gratitude to my parents for the pleasant memories of my childhood. No blessing surpasses that of growing up in an atmosphere of security and loving kindness.

SOME THOUGHTS ON THE DEPRESSION YEARS

Following on the heels of the stock market crash of 1929, the thirties ushered in extreme heat in summer and dire cold in winter coupled with drought, dust storms and swarms of grasshoppers, making survival tough for the entire nation. Dad left his jacket in the field one day, went back to retrieve it and found that the grasshoppers had eaten all but the double stitched seams. On occasion dust storms would obscure the sun, making visibility near zero and lamps would be lit in the middle of the day. Years of poor crops, depressed grain and livestock prices and the need for manufactured products no one could afford to buy created a nation of people struggling to survive.

Although we had plenty of food to eat, not a morsel was wasted. What we did not consume was sold for cash or bartered for the staples of life. Somehow we managed.

Mine was the only age group that could say the first twelve years of their schooling took place under one president. Franklin Delano Roosevelt was elected to the presidency when I was in 1st grade and was still president when I graduated from high school. He shepherded the nation through a period of unemployment, poor crops, low wages, bank failures and an economy in ruins. He did this in very innovative ways.

I remember how my dad detested the New Deal programs; my mom on the other hand, thought they were necessary for the people to survive. Ultimately, one out of every ten farms changed ownership. Many farmers could not support their families and were forced to leave the land to their creditors or accept foreclosure and move to the cities to find whatever work was available.

It wasn't an accident that the Great Plains states became a dust bowl. Poor land management practices, some done at the behest of government experts, had farmers plowing the prairies and making few attempts at soil conservation or crop practices that would have held the soil in place. Pile on drought, extreme heat and cold, a sluggish economy and the result was disaster.

They were jokingly referred to as Democrat alphabet soup. Programs such as the C.C.C., W.P.A., P.W.A., N.Y.A. and N.R.A., to name a few, proliferated like so many weeds in an unplowed field. My dad hated them all.

President Roosevelt said, "I propose to create a Civilian Conservation Corps to be used in simple work....more important, however, than the material gains, will be the moral and spiritual value of such work." Three million unemployed young men jumped at the chance to join the C.C.C. to live in the boonies in tents or cabins, charged with the task to replant and refurbish the forestlands of the nation. Their pay was meager and those living in close proximity to the camps wondered about the spiritual and moral values that were supposed to be garnered from this experience, but the nation's forests still bear the fruits of their labor.

I remember the jokes and political cartoons which depicted someone in the W.P.A. leaning on a shovel, doing nothing. Truth be known, in spite of confusion, waste and political favoritism, the Public Works Administration (P.W.A.) and the Works Progress Administration (W.P.A.) programs reached many millions of the unemployed and resulted in successful slum clearance, improved highways, new public buildings, new and repaired bridges and rural improvements. Interestingly many 8-hole golf courses were built in small towns throughout the country, many still operating today as local Country Clubs.

Grateful for the wages paid to them by the government, men with horses and wagons cleaned out ditches and opened waterways and during one very bad year when he found all his neighbors were taking advantage of work offered by the W.P.A. for cleaning out local waterways, my dad finally capitulated and contributed a team of horses and a wagon to a ditch cleaning project nearby. As men worked with shovels on both sides of the road, the men moving dirt with teams and wagons would have to drive their horses through the phalanx of shovel wielders. To the frustration of the driver, a favorite trick was to keep yelling "Whoa" and laughing as the team of horses would stop in its tracks. The driver would keep urging the horses forward on their way only to have more resounding "Whoa-boys" halt them again and again. My dad took great pride in the fact that his team would flatten their ears back toward him on the wagon seat and he would make his unique sounds to them as they drove through the line. His team would not hesitate, but keep flicking their ears at him listening for his commands as they pulled their load of scooped soil. Since contour farming was not generally practiced, most of the soil hauled out of the waterways would return with the next few hard rains.

The youth of the nation had their own unique challenges. Perhaps the most controversial of the national programs was the National Youth Administration created to help the 18 to 24 year olds stay in school. The program was still intact when I was in high school and the disadvantaged did indeed benefit. For part time work, a high school student would earn about $6.00 a month and a college student about $20.00 a month. Seems a pittance today, but it made staying in school possible for many.

With national unemployment at about 29 % and school drop out rates of over 50 %, the nation's youth who were idle and unable to improve their prospects became very disenchanted with democracy and capitalism and blamed these systems for their sad plight. One poll of college students during the time previous to World War II found that 80 % of those polled stated they would not fight for their country if it went to war abroad and 16 % said that they would not fight even if the country was invaded.

It was considered a disgrace to be "on the county" which translates into, someone who would accept welfare. Anyone who accepted county assistance had their names published in the local papers. Truth be known, the entire nation was on welfare.

Because a working woman might be taking a job away from a head of household who may have a family to feed, widowhood was about the only acceptable reason for women to seek employment outside the home. The positions of secretary, nurse and elementary school teacher were the exceptions to this, since men rarely entered those fields.

During this time, my parents had the added stress of Dad being bedridden with arthritis for months at a time and my mom and my 14-year-old brother having to run the farm without his help. Never one to malinger, my dad used crutches then progressed to a cane as soon as physically possible. With no known cure for his disability, local doctors removed his teeth, appendix, gall bladder and two thirds of his stomach (bleeding ulcers) searching for solutions for the arthritis in his feet. Endured for so many years, his arthritis pain gradually subsided as his ankle joints froze into a state of immobility. Although he always limped, he was relatively pain free for the last thirty years of his life.

It is still being debated today, whether the New Deal of the thirties jump-started the economy; was it the advent of world war or a combination of both. Just as many factors brought on the Great Depression, I suspect that many factors brought about its end. When World War II began, the nation heaved itself into a driving force of arms and industry that was nothing short of phenomenal. With national mobilization, the economy recovered, the rains came, crops flourished and even the grasshoppers were fewer in number. By the mid-forties, in the rural areas of the Midwest people began to install indoor plumbing and receive rural electrification.

Facts concerning the depression years of the thirties are readily available in the history books for all to read, but I lived through these times and the events described affected me and my generation in very telling ways. A generation of Americans was forged during the depression years, preparing them for the challenge of the forties. Their disenchantment and bitterness fell away and with a restored economy and a national challenge, the men and women of our country provided the manpower, sustenance and courage to fight and win a World War. Those same young men and women who so vehemently criticized their country during the thirties, flocked to enlist and serve it during its time at war, justifiably earning the respect and admiration of the nation and the sobriquet "the greatest generation."

ON GROWING UP NORWEGIAN

The early immigrants sought out communities containing fellow settlers with whom they shared a culture and religion. Over many decades this created small, rural enclaves of people of similar nationality and faith. There were the Irish Catholics, the French Catholics, the German Lutherans, Swedish Lutherans and various other nationalities and faiths whose community life centered around their churches and schools. We were members of a Norwegian community.

Ecumenical and multi-cultural agendas in church and school had yet to be promulgated by the self-anointed few in the halls of academia. As Norwegian Lutherans we concerned ourselves with our community and our church and gave short shrift to any other. The insular nature of our attitudes encouraged a feeling of security and complacency that remained unchanged until the advent of World War II, which played fruit-basket upset with the entire nation, socially, culturally and economically.

I remember my childhood years as being very pleasant. I was aware that money was scarce, but I didn't feel deprived because the people we knew didn't have money either. Because Mom raised chickens, always had a large garden and Dad raised cattle and hogs, we had plenty of meat and vegetables to eat. Even during the leanest times in the thirties there were always pleasant things to do that compensated for the lack of material possessions.

My parents were typical representatives of their time and culture. They seldom verbalized their affection. I do not remember hearing the words "I love you," however I knew that my parents loved each other and us unconditionally. I never questioned their love for me or my siblings. I didn't hear quarreling, arguing or loud voices raised in criticism. My Dad was known to lose his temper at times when things went wrong with his work outdoors and he would cuss to vent his frustration; hearing him swear uncontrollably would concern my mom. I never heard her say so much as darn or dang. She used expletives but they were a "pzzsst" of disdain, "by hookity," "dirty pup," "snukerut" or "dumb cluck!" My Grandpa Lykken was remembered for two rather unusual expletives: "By Jibbers" and a Norwegian expression that translated into English as "Fire Rag."

Norwegians are a stoic, hard-working, unemotional people. Only "weenies" shivered in the cold and any excessive show of emotion made them uncomfortable; Norwegians consider crying a sign of weakness. To their credit they love to laugh at their own foibles, and take great pleasure in hearing Ole and Lena jokes.

The Thirties was the era of dance halls and ballrooms where local bands would play for community wedding dances and the touring big dance bands would make regular appearances. The Arkota and Skylon ballrooms could easily accommodate the large crowds that gathered to dance to the music of Lawrence Welk, Ted Lewis, Jan Garber, Tommy and Jimmy Dorsey and Blue Baron.

Children oftentimes accompanied their parents to the dances held in the rural halls such as the Ritz, Hamilton Hall and River Sioux, to name a few. Between dances kids would be allowed to run and slide on the dance floor, which was made slick by a generous sprinkling of dance-floor compound.

I was about nine years old and had accompanied my folks to a community dance at the Ritz hall when a neighbor asked if I would perform during the time when the band was on a break. I had a meager talent, but I could carry a tune and I could tap dance. Once on stage, I began singing the song, Wahoo, and two bandsmen quickly came in softly on the accompaniment as I sang, "Oh give me a horse, a great big horse and give me a buckeroo, and let me Wahoo, Wahoo....Wahoo." After I sang the song, I did a tap dance and ended with bent knee, arms outstretched and a loud "WAHOO!" The audience applauded, and to the embarrassment of my mom, a neighbor passed the hat and presented me with $2.65. Ever after, the

Ritz held a fascination for me; I considered it my first step toward a Broadway career. I wanted to go back to re-live my "stage moment," but my mom said when I reached 16 I would be allowed to go to the Ritz hall on a date, but not before. She meant it and I didn't.

People enjoyed dancing in those days and I loved to watch my mom and dad dance. One of our neighbors who had a large house with hardwood floors would hold community dances in their home; take up the rugs, haul out the furniture and hire a three-piece band. They would dance until the wee hours of the morning. During the evening the fiddle players in the community, my dad among them, would take a turn at playing with the band, the fiddlers would each have a go at playing their favorite dance tunes. There was no overt drinking of alcohol at the private dances, however, my dad said there were bottles of whiskey stashed outside behind the trees; if anyone drank, they did it out of public view.

They danced waltzes, two-steps, polkas, schottisches and at intervals someone would call a square dance. I had learned how to waltz and two-step when I was quite young, and occasionally the young adults would ask kids to dance. That was always a proud moment. Sandwiches, cake and coffee would be served around midnight and then the dancing would resume until very late.

At home in the evenings my dad would play the fiddle and Lu Ida and I would take turns accompanying him by chording on the piano. He would begin tuning his fiddle and call, "Come Margie, chord for me." I recall my dad dancing with us while mom played the piano, teaching us how to waltz and how to "follow." He was a smooth, nice dancer. Most families had pianos and most were players-by-ear regardless of what instrument they played. Our nearest neighbors had sons who were musicians and we could hear them playing trumpet, saxophone, banjo or violin on summer evenings when the wind was wafting in from their direction. Both became professional musicians, neither ever had a lesson on the various instruments they played.

My mother was raised to subject her thoughts and actions to the will of her husband, which she did, uncomplainingly. She was invariably jolly, good natured and I never heard her complain about being poor or having to do without things that I know she must have wanted or needed. I remember her buying a new dress with a little red scarf. Even though the dress would have looked better had she worn the scarf, she never wore it because, as she said, "Daddy doesn't like me to wear red."

My dad did not abuse his special standing in their marriage. He was an innately kind and gentle man who never criticized my mother, at least where we children could hear it. Later in my life, I realized he had a few passive aggressive tendencies, that his will would prevail by virtue of his not verbally opposing the point in question. And if he expressed no opinion, my mom would equate that to disapproval and that ended it, once and for all.

I felt thankful for my parents and thought it must be great to never disagree with one's spouse. With maturity I realized that circumstance is the result of one member of the team habitually giving in to the other and may not have been as admirable as it seemed. My mother opposed my dad on the subject of educating their children, however. Mom prevailed in her quiet way, but I remember detecting an undercurrent of disagreement when they were deciding if Lu Ida should go for further schooling. She did, of course.

Leverne, being oldest, was unable to attend high school after graduating from eighth grade because my dad was very ill with rheumatoid arthritis, unable to walk, and Leverne had to run the farm with Mom's help. In lieu of attending high school and to compensate him in some way, my mom sent off for a crystal set kit from which he was expected to assemble a radio. He did. Later when he was 17 years old, and Dad's health was somewhat improved, he started to high school and proved to be an excellent student and athlete. He joined the Army Air Force in 1942 and became a pilot instructor of four engine aircraft until the end of World War II. He was called back into service in 1951 during the Korean War and flew 35 missions over North Korea as pilot commander of a B-29 Super Fortress.

Leverne married LaVonne Hornstein, his high school sweetheart, and they had two children, Glen and Donna. He farmed the family farm and his own farm, until his retirement. He has always demonstrated leadership ability and because he shouldered responsibility at a very early age, I suspect he has never had a frivolous, impulsive thought in his life.

30

Leverne was the one that set the pace when we were children, and demanded that we not drag our feet if we were going to walk with him!!! He would check our overshoe tracks in the snow and look for signs of "dragging." He was the one who coasted the farthest on his sled and set the scholastic example. A prodigious reader, he became very knowledgeable and a good conversationalist. He was a successful farmer and served on advisory boards at the county, state and national level.

My sister, Lu Ida, was a dutiful daughter and seemed to do everything my folks expected of her. The summer she turned sixteen, she was expected to "work out" to learn how to make her way in the world. She worked at a motel in Vermillion, cleaning rooms and doing laundry, and it was very hard work indeed. One summer she worked as a live-in "hired girl" for a family in Sioux City. Affluent families in the city preferred hiring girls from the country because they "knew how to work" and work they did, with Thursday afternoons and alternate Sundays off. Whether this practice taught work habits, or not, it was quite a humbling experience. As Norwegians, we really didn't need much more humility than what was inculcated by our parents.

In 1941 after attending a nine month term at South Dakota State Teachers Normal in Springfield, South Dakota, which cost a total of $300.00 for tuition, room and board, Lu Ida began teaching in a nearby one-room country school with a beginning salary of $80.00 a month. She was a dedicated teacher and greatly respected by her students and their parents.

She married Olaf Abrahamson who lived on the farm next to ours, and they had three sons, James, Larry and Curtis. Lu Ida taught school for a total of twenty-six years during which time she continued to work toward her degree, graduating from the University of South Dakota in 1970. She is greatly loved for her caring ways and her wonderful hospitality. Her husband, Olaf, who farmed until his retirement, was accomplished on the saxophone and trumpet and played as a dance band member for 45 years.

Making Lu Ida laugh has always been one of the joys of my life. Her twinkling eyes brought out my silly side and her merry laughter was music to my ears. We still love to laugh together and being in her company recharges my battery.

My younger sister, Agnes, three years my junior, was pretty and popular in school and a bit of an enigma. She had a very high I.Q. and was a speed-reader who read five or six books a week during most of her adult life.

She married Berdell Kinsley and they had three children, Lesley, Deborah and Kermit. Both were schoolteachers and taught for the Bureau of Indian Affairs in South Dakota and in Alaska for many years. She received a Masters Degree in Psychology from the University of South Dakota and after many years of teaching was the clinical testing psychologist for Todd County, South Dakota until her retirement. She, like her older sister, became a teaching legend in her own time. She was a great cook and gracious hostess; I loved being with her.

Agnes worked hard, accomplished much, was a published author and lived her life marching to her own set of drums. On one of my visits to South Dakota many years ago, she showed up in her school clothes. She was wearing beaded moccasins, her hair in two long braids banded on the ends with beads, and a beaded headband with necklace to match. She looked like Little Red Wing instead of my sister. When I asked about her clothes, she answered, " I teach first graders, they are Lakota Sioux Indian and what I am wearing is "very Sioux." These children need to know they have a heritage!" That is one of my fondest memories of her.

In spite of all those smarts, she was capable of making impractical decisions. She loved a challenge and met it head on; she was a fearless, caring person, with a tinge of self-destructive behavior that she refused to address. She demonstrated individualism, yet had an inhibited streak to her nature. I have always felt that had we lived in the mid-19th century, she would have willingly and enthusiastically driven a team of oxen across the nation's prairies to seek her spot in the developing west. On the other hand, Lu Ida and I would have stayed behind where it was more comfortable.

My dad shaved once a week, and used a straightedge razor which he sharpened on a leather strop. Always hanging in its usual place, after lathering his face, Dad would grasp the end of the leather strop and hone his razor before shaving. That strop held a fascination for us, because it was what we got smacked with if we were naughty enough to deserve it. When we were small my dad would gather us in his arms and rub his whiskers on our forehead or cheeks and we would protest, squeal and kick, but we loved it. Coming in from working in the fields I remember how he smelled of grain, leather, fresh air, soil, mild perspiration and tobacco, a wonderful smell.

Working in the fields without a watch, he could tell the time of day by the sun and would arrive back at the house each day at five minutes to twelve and leave the fields each day in time for supper at six o'clock. He was very adept at predicting which clouds would deliver rain and which wouldn't, which had wind and which didn't. It was uncanny.

In the spring my dad would cut potatoes into sections making sure there was an "eye" or two in each piece. He would plow deep furrows. Then carrying a bucket in the crook of his arm, he would drop the potato sections into the furrow, step on each one, pressing it down into the soft soil as he walked along. It was considered important that potatoes be planted on Good Friday, for what reason, I know not.

Dad considered being in debt or paying interest two things to be avoided at all costs. Being a courteous man, it was hard for him to forgive discourtesy. No one in our family ever sassed my father or spoke to him in anything but a respectful manner. Criticism from our dad was something we avoided. I think I can recall each and every time he ever chided me about anything.

Probably because I was the kid that resembled his side of the family more than the others and had slightly different behavior habits, I felt that I was the apple of his eye. And my siblings didn't let me forget it. If we needed to ask Dad for permission to do something about which Mom had said, "Let's see what Daddy says," I was the one selected to seek his approval, which I willingly did.

Dad was tall, slender and from the pictures of his youth appeared to have been a fine featured, handsome man with thick auburn hair, blue eyes, straight nose and beautiful skin. I can understand why my mom was attracted to him. His parents spoke German and until he started school, my Dad did too. It was in 1917 when Mom attended a barn dance where Dad was playing the fiddle that he noticed this smiling, lively girl. Mom related that she had made up her mind, early on, not to marry a Norwegian, and her folks nearly disowned her when they learned that she had fallen in love and wanted to marry a full-blooded German boy from outside their immediate community. They teased her and asked how she could ever like a skinny guy with such a long neck. This was understandable since the stocky Lykken family and many other Norwegians don't have necks, their heads sit right smack on their shoulders. Her folks changed their opinion of him when they learned that he and his family operated custom threshers and corn shellers, skills they considered admirable. When Mom and Dad took the train to Sioux City to buy their wedding clothes, Mom said the salesman who sold Dad his wedding suit made sure he had a tall shirt collar that would flatter his long neck.

Dad was drafted into the Army during World War I and did his basic training in Florida. He developed the Spanish flu prior to his scheduled departure for France and was not shipped out with his unit; consequently, he never saw overseas service. His former outfit was gassed during their battlefield experiences and many came home with compromised lungs. Thousands of people, young and old, stateside and overseas, died during the flu epidemic of 1917 and 1918.

He and my mom had become unofficially engaged before he left for the army. I asked her about those long horse-and-buggy rides and if they did a lot of "smooching" in the moonlight as they rode along. Her answer was to laugh and say, "Oh yes, Daddy loved to kiss me, but I didn't kiss him back until we were engaged."

After his discharge from the army, he and my mom were married in a formal ceremony at Roseni Lutheran Church. During the wedding reception and dinner at her parents' home, a blizzard came blowing in and many of the guests, as well as the bride and groom, were unable to leave. The bride and groom were given a private room but many of the guests spent the night sleeping "all over the house." (Mom's quote.)

My mother had a tremendous influence on her children. Under the façade of submission to my dad's ideas and thinking, down deep, where she lived and thought, she was a strong, progressive woman.

34

I doubt that my dad ever suspected just how strong or progressive! She read a lot, and had very sound opinions, on everything. Her thinking processes were more that of a college graduate than someone who hadn't graduated from 8th grade. She and her older brothers were needed to harvest the crops every fall, so they missed the same portion of the school term each year making them unable to complete the requirements for eighth grade graduation. Had she been able to finish her education and gone on to advanced study she would have been a wonderful nurse or teacher. Instead, she quietly nurtured her family, encouraging them to read, cope, assume accountability and hold onto the basic high standards of decency and achievement. Her unique spirituality served to anoint her children and grandchildren in a very special way that they feel, experience and share to this day. She was a joyful, cheerful person, had a marvelous smile and believed all things happen for good reason. She believed the Lord was in control and she gracefully accepted what transpired throughout her life, be it good or bad.

One of her younger brothers, Louis, whom my grandmother felt "owed something to the world" was educated and received a Ph.D. in Chemistry from Iowa State University. He had international credentials and an illustrious career, retiring as Professor from the University of California at Berkeley. Educational levels differed greatly in that family of seven children, not an uncommon thing in second generation Norwegians. My mom learned to speak English after she started school. She never lost her gentle Norwegian accent.

Serving food was a holy calling to a Norwegian mother and in the realm of life's necessities; coffee was surpassed in importance only by the air we breathed. Even little children drank coffee, albeit usually laced generously with cream. Mom made everything from scratch and setting a meager table would have been an unbearable indictment. So she always cooked too much of everything. We used to think she was the most marvelous cook in the whole wide world. I didn't learn until I was an adult that she wasn't; her bread and rolls were beyond compare, however. She cooked Norwegian. There is an old joke that asks, "How do you cook a beef kidney?" The answer being, "Put it in a kettle of water and boil the pee out of it." Well, my mom boiled the pee out of everything, mainly to ensure that all the germs were dead.

She even boiled the laundry. After she washed the clothes, she would place each load in a copper tub of boiling water on the cook stove, and boil the germs out of them; then she lifted the clothes out with a stick before placing them in the rinsing tub. All this boiling must have had some effect for we were seldom ill.

Norwegians tend to be blonde and so is their food: bland, bulky and blonde. They eat potatoes, corn, rice, macaroni, noodles, eggs, cheese, bread, carrots, chicken, pork, all blonde food. Any vegetables that were not blonde, were smothered in cream sauce and became blonde in the process. Potatoes were served at every meal and they ate lots of Jell-O. Aha! But Jell-O is red! No! It was inevitably smothered in whipped cream or Dream Whip and therefore, blonde. Dream Whip was a staple item, right up there with flour, sugar and salt. No one will ever see a billboard advertising Norwegian cuisine. Those two words are contradictory.

Mom served a supper meal called Krap Soup (said with a soft "a" and a rolling rrrrr) It was a creamy dumpling Norwegian soup, quite tasteless but we thought it was good. My dad used to refer to it as "crap soup," in fact we all did. I do not remember my mom taking exception to the name we gave it, but I am sure she thought we forgot to make the "a" say "ah" or use the proper Norwegian rolling "rrr." HA!

After I left my family home, I quickly grew fond of Italian, Mexican, Indian, Cajun, Chinese and most ethnic foods, the spices and flavors were happy on my tongue. Not so Norwegians of my generation, spices could burn out one's innards, give you ulcers and blister the tongue....they were to be avoided. Two generations later, this is no longer true, I might add.

Our family would sometimes go visiting on Sunday afternoon, we called it "going away" and if we didn't, we hoped that someone would come to visit us, for we were "to home." Mothers were always prepared to serve an ample 4 p.m. lunch without any prior notice. It wouldn't have occurred to anyone to call before they arrived. Relatives or friends just showed up.

Whether in afternoon or evening, when a family had visitors, it was customary to serve a lunch, which usually consisted of coffee for the adults, Kool Aid for the kids plus sandwiches, Jell-O, cake and cookies. This was standard fare. These items were usually on hand for such occasions, but there was an interesting dialogue that went with this custom.

Mom would say, "I will make some coffee and we will have some lunch, then."

The visiting mother would say, "Oh you don't have to do that. Don't go to any trouble for us, we don't need to eat. We had a big dinner just a short while ago."

Mom would then protest and say, "Oh yes we've got to have some coffee, it's no trouble."

Visitor, "Just something simple, we don't need much."

Mom, "It will be just what I have here, we have to eat, you know."

Visitor, "Well don't go to any fuss for us, now."

This crazy exchange happened each and every time people visited each other, anywhere, anytime, knowing full well that 1) lunch WOULD be served or the world would stop turning on its axis and 2) if lunch were NOT served, it would be the scandal of the community. Interestingly, on a visit with my siblings in the year 2004 this interesting exchange was still taking place on a regular basis. And I might add, I loved every morsel of the Norwegian food that I was served.

My mom used to say she was never pretty, yet pictures taken in her youth showed her to be very attractive with a small waist, curly hair, twinkling eyes, straight teeth and a big ready smile. Her Norwegian upbringing would never have allowed her to feel she was pretty. She was still pretty as a very old woman with pure white wavy hair and smooth beautiful complexion.

She told of the time she disgraced herself and her folks, when on a Sunday afternoon, in the presence of aunts, uncles and cousins, she vaulted over the railing on the back porch of their house, showing a little too much leg in the process or so it was thought at the time.

Mom wore a corset at all times; I never saw her with her hair uncombed and she always wore an invisible hairnet over her hair to keep it from looking "mussy." When she emerged from her bedroom in the morning, she was totally dressed including hose and sensible lace-up shoes with Cuban heels. When she worked outdoors, she enveloped herself in coveralls, rubber boots and headscarf, all of which were removed when she entered the house.

Oddly, these people of the soil, born and bred, felt there were certain words that shouldn't be spoken in polite company. Mom called a boar, a "he-pig," a bull was a "he-cow"…boar and bull being off limits. Pregnant was referred to as "in the family way" and when discussing calves unless it was in the privacy of the family, one avoided the term "suck." Animals were not castrated, they were "fixed" or "cut." Menstruation was your "monthly" or "sick time" and menopause was "the change of life."

Looking back, my mom was one of the most disciplined people I have ever known. She found pleasure in work and I remember her saying to me when I was young, "learn to like work; it is good for you. I hope I never reach a stage in my life when I can't work." Up at 5 a.m., seldom needing more than 5 hours sleep, she took great joy in the duties of homemaker and farm wife. She raised chickens, had a large garden, maintained a beautiful yard, cooked three square meals a day plus 2 or 3 lunches, canned all the food the family ate, including the meat from butchered animals. She kept a clean house, washed her inside windows every week, washed clothes on Monday, ironed on Tuesday, waxed the kitchen floor on Saturday, sewed our clothes and was active in the church. She wasted nothing; she considered waste a sin against nature. She sewed our clothes on an old treadle sewing machine and I remember hearing the rhythmic sound of the treadle machine going late into the night. And she still had time for us when we needed her.

She was one of the first women in the neighborhood to have a fenced lawn and flowers around the house and yard. She loved flowers. Her houseplants thrived and she grew beautiful gloxinias, which are very temperamental houseplants. However, I never remember her ever cutting an outside flower to bring inside the house. I think she felt she was doing the flower a disservice, removing it from its natural habitat.

How my mother coped with a sick husband, failing crops and the responsibility of a family during the thirties, I shall never know. During the time my dad was bedridden with arthritis, she moved him to a second floor bedroom so he could watch the activities on the farm. In the mornings, I would help him put on his socks and slippers before he was helped to his chair by the window. As soon as he could hobble about, Dad was up on crutches doing what he could. He would drive the car to the fields to watch Leverne in case he needed assistance. He spent years dealing with disability caused by his painful feet. The years of stress, drought, crop failures and illness took its toll; an over-whelming feeling of responsibility and helplessness caused a relapse, physically and mentally.

Each day Mom drove Dad twenty-eight miles to visit the local chiropractor who encouraged my dad to verbalize his concerns and worries as he massaged his back. This good man must have been a fine psychologist, as well, for my daddy regained his health, which continued to improve through the years. His feet became relatively pain-free and he never showed signs of depression or mental breakdown again. Mom persevered, maintained a cheerful attitude and gave little indication to her young family of what must have been incredible worry and stress for her. A very strong Norwegian woman, my mom.

Our home was a spacious, wood-framed, two-story, five-bedroom house with two stained glass windows and it provided ample space for a family of six. It had a second floor veranda, a columned porch on the side facing the road and a sizeable entry with four windows on the back side, the side we used. It had a full basement with a cement floor that provided a wonderful place for us to roller skate and play in relative comfort during the cold winter months. The basement also served as a root cellar, was a place for storing canned goods, coal, wood, corncobs and held the big floor furnace that provided heat for the rest of the house. We rarely used the front porch, in fact the door to the front was seldom opened and the upstairs veranda was used only for shaking rugs when cleaning the second story bedrooms.

A boyfriend who lived in a nearby town came to take me out on a date late one afternoon. We saw him drive up but couldn't figure out where he had gone until he began knocking on the west (front) door. The door was so seldom opened, it stuck and I had trouble getting it open. I said, "Hi, what are you doing back here?" He said, "I thought this was your front door." I said, "It is, but we never use it!" He found that amusing.

The summer that I was 17, while working as a live-in baby sitter for a Jewish family in Sioux City, this same fellow came to take me out on my Thursday afternoon off and he parked in the front, walked all the way to the back and knocked on the back door. I went to the door and said, "Hi, what are you doing back here?" He said, "I thought since you were domestic help, that I should pick you up at the back door!" I said, "I am hired help but next time, front door, please!" Humility was never one of my long suits. Poor fellow, it must have been confusing. But I digress.......

My Grandpa Klemme built our house in 1919 and paid $9,000.00 for it. He owned two farms and when Grandpa and Grandma retired in 1930 and moved to LeMars, Iowa, our family moved onto the farm by Spink and my dad's brother lived two miles away on the other farm. Upon the death of their parents, each son inherited the farm on which they lived.

We did not slam doors or abuse this home because Grandpa made us all aware that we were really just tenants and that he owned it. I know it bothered my mom at times because she felt that when Grandpa visited he seemed to be looking for signs of wear and tear. My dad paid cash rent for the privilege of farming this 80-acre farm, and cash rent was hard to come by during the terrible depression years. Dad eventually bought another 160 acres adjacent to our farm.

After my mom and dad retired from farming, they built a new home in nearby Spink. They painted it pink and it was known as the "pink house in Spink." My brother and his wife moved unto the home place and farmed the land and his adjacent farm until his retirement. The family home site was eventually sold and my brother and his wife now live in Akron, Iowa near my sister.

Grandpa Klemme was a typical German of his day. He was chauvinistic to a fault and felt women and children should be seen and not heard. I was a little afraid of him. He could play the violin and when we visited them, he would insist that anyone who had talent, however meager that might be, should perform. There would be a little jam session with those who could play violin, piano or whatever instrument was available. I could chord accompaniment on the piano when my Dad played violin but I wasn't very bold with my playing. Lu Ida likewise would be called upon to provide chord accompaniment during these impromptu musical interludes. My grandpa would jig to the music and when he learned that I could tap dance I would have to tap dance for him.

During World War I, first and second generation Germans were occasionally suspected of lacking the expected patriotism for the times. Many a German farmer awoke to the sight of a barn or farm building smeared with yellow paint, the work of some over zealous bigot. Never one to express criticism of the Kaiser, Grandpa felt it prudent to declare that he was a Finn, not a German. En route to America, from the Klemme ancestral home in Sabbenhausen, Lippe Detmold, Germany, his brother had indeed been born in Finland, so he changed his nationality to suit the times. As far as I know he never ended up with a yellow barn.

My grandpa showed disapproval of my mom at times because she wasn't quite meek enough and, in fact, he once intimated something to that effect to my dad. My mom sensed that feeling of criticism and I felt she never was too fond of Grandpa. But when he became terminally ill and needed someone to care for him, he didn't ask for his quiet favorites, he asked for my mom to care for him and she did, until his death.

When he visited us, he would take a long leather pouch out of his pocket and dig around until he found a penny and give us each one. In his own way, he intimidated us, and my dad never quit trying to seek his approval and admiration. When my dad was in his 70 s he told me that he still had a recurring bad dream in which he had done something that displeased his father.

My grandma was a kind, caring and giving person, but had played the role of submissive wife so long she had lost all individual thought of being herself. I think she suffered from depression because she often mentioned feeling "blue," and as a child I wondered what feeling blue was all about.

On one visit when we were playing in her spare bedroom we found a stash of True Romances and Love Story magazines under her bed. I remember how shocked we were, but as I grew older I realized she may have been a romantic soul in spite of the dark cotton stockings, sensible lace-up shoes, long mother hubbardy dresses and hair pulled back into a gigantic knot at the back of her head. She was greatly loved as a kind and caring woman and her hobby was making quilts and crocheting. As she grew old and disoriented, she continued to crochet endlessly; creating pieces of various lengths and sizes, which could be put to no use.

She lived to the age of 88 and my mom and my Aunt Hilda took care of her when she became bedridden before her death. Because of senility she was not an easy patient to care for toward the last years of her life. She must have received excellent care, for the funeral director who prepared her body for burial, stated that in spite of being bedridden for a long time, her skin was in perfect condition and he wondered how my mom and my aunt had accomplished that.

I always remember my Grandpa Lykken as being a bit dotty, but in his younger days he was a successful farmer and retired quite young. He and Grandma moved out to the Black Hills of South Dakota where he worked as a park ranger at Custer State Park and they later moved to Hill City. He made some real estate investments that supported them nicely in their later years. As a young man he attended the University of South Dakota for a time and studied science and math. The pressures of farming during that time required that he return home before he finished his first year. He wore a mustache, was slow and deliberate in speech and movement and was dominated by my Grandma Lykken who had a sharp wit and a high intelligence.

My Grandma Lykken was much revered by her children and grandchildren. She was witty, loved to laugh, was well read and good humored. She loved picnics, nature and believed in re-incarnation, once having been quoted as saying she hoped to "come back as a chipmunk, so she could run free, running and jumping from one rock to another." I can think of lots of things I would rather be than a ground squirrel in South Dakota!

42

She was short and stout with sallow skin and snapping eyes. She had a strangely Oriental look. As a young woman, she arrived from Norway and worked as a domestic helper for my Great-Grandmother Lykken until she could defray the expense of her passage. She had a meager third grade education but she became a prodigious reader.

She had an unfortunate childhood; her mother died at her birth and her father died three months later. Raised by relatives who couldn't afford to keep her, by the age of five she was made to herd sheep in the foothills of Norway. She was kidnapped by Gypsies and lived with them against her will for many years. We always wondered about that period of her life. She wouldn't speak of it, except to say that her sojourn with the Gypsies was one of mistreatment and abuse. She was eventually rescued by a member of the Salvation Army and given the chance to emigrate to America. She spoke of a brother, Albert, but little is known of her family.

My great grandmother never forgave my grandmother for having the temerity to fall in love and marry her eldest son. Their marriage didn't heal the rift; there were bad feelings between the two of them for as long as they lived. I remember my mom saying how sad it made her feel knowing that her grandmother whom she loved so dearly, disliked her mother.

When my great-grandmother developed cancer, a disease not discussed openly in that day and time, my mom, a young girl in her teens, would willingly stay and care for her. One day, the doctor told my mom's parents that they must keep my mother at home, because as she sat at bedside and held Great-Grandmother's hand the strength was being drained from her young body. How sad. How far we have come from those superstitious and unenlightened medical ideas.

When my Grandma Lykken was ill with cancer, my mom nursed and cared for her until her death. My grandpa was like a fish out of water without his wife. I remember them speaking to each other in Norwegian and sometimes the conversations were quite heated. He missed her terribly. Mom and her brothers took turns caring for him until he died of a blood clot, while staying at Uncle John's home in Chicago.

As a third generation Norwegian with a sizable infusion of German genes, unlike my siblings, I had never accepted the mantle of humility and modesty that our folks expected of us. There is a Norwegian word for it, which literally means that it is inappropriate to make an exhibition of wanting to stand above others in any respect. It makes one wonder how Norway developed all those world-class skiers! We were discouraged from showing pride of self, or taking excessive satisfaction in feeling pretty. As a child I overheard my mom receive a compliment on a new coat she had worn to church and her comment was, "It's just a coat." My childish thought at the time was, "No it isn't, it is new and it is very pretty!"

One Easter, Mom had bought my sister, Lu Ida, a gray straw hat with a flower on it, a new dress and ¾ length coat, which made her look very pretty. Upon arrival at the church, I ran over to a neighbor family, who had just driven up in their green Model A Ford and I said, "Come look at Lu Ida's beautiful hat and outfit!" I felt like shouting this to the roof tops and then I remember feeling embarrassed because I knew by their reaction, that what I had done, (calling attention to something that made me feel proud) was unseemly for a good Norwegian girl.

In most situations our behavior was predicated on that tired old criterion, "What will the neighbors think?" We were made to be very concerned with what they would think. Many times as a child I felt guilt because I didn't give a fig what the neighbors thought, but certainly my parents and my siblings did care. I secretly harbored the thought that someday, I would not let "the neighbors" decide what I would do or how I would behave.

Looking back with the wisdom of my years, I understand that the constraints placed on us to conform to the expectations of relatives and neighbors were probably the reasons that immoral, uncontrollable and disorderly conduct were uncommon among teenagers. The penalties were too great; misbehaving offspring were an embarrassment parents chose to avoid.

It is interesting that in spite of the self-deprecating attitude expected of young Norwegians-in-training during their formative years, my siblings all became leaders and take-hold-type adults. My leadership abilities, though latent, became apparent later in my life, many would say to a fault. Somehow I garnered the nickname

"Marge, the Sarge, in Charge" along the way and I suspect it wasn't due to my being a shrinking violet.

I grew up Norwegian because of the strong influence of my mother and the community in which we lived, but I had the added blessing of an infusion of German genes. It was a positive blend! Genetics cannot be ignored, but generally we are what we are because of the attitudes and behaviors of our parents and grandparents. Their legacy, their earthly immortality lives on in the generations that succeed them.

GREAT-GRANDPARENTS

Ole Johnson Lykken - Born: 4-27-1843 - Died: 10-17-1929
Ane Kongsvik Lykken - Born: 6-24-1847 - Died: 5-1-1917

Family histories have provided me with interesting information regarding some of my female ancestors who were known to have great strength of character. I have included information about my great-grandmother, Ane, and my great-great-grandmother, Berit, because they seemed so like my mother and other members of our family. They were women of strength and courage and after reading about them, I began to feel a genuine kinship. I am grateful to be a member of this clan of strong Norwegian women.

Although my brother and older cousins remember my great-grandfather, I have no memory of him. I appreciate those who have delved into the history surrounding my great-grandparents' arrival in the United States as immigrants from Norway. In 1871 Ole Johnson Lykken boarded a steamship at Trondheim, Norway and sailed to America to make his home in a new land that offered something more than his hardscrabble existence in Norway. The cost of his passage was 59 Kroner, 60 ore, approximately $12.00, American. He was 28 years old and had recently been released from the army. His wife, my great-grandmother, Ane (Kongsvik) Lykken, and their son, Lars Olson, (my grandfather) stayed behind in Norway until he could provide a place for them to live.

The previous year a neighbor in Norway named Olav Johnson Stein (now Stene) had come to America and laid claim to land in Union County, South Dakota. When Ole Lykken arrived in Sioux

City in 1871, he made his way to the Nora community and filed his claim ½ mile from Olav Stene's claim, the same distance as had separated them in Norway.

The first order of business was a place to live; he dug a hole in the ground and lived in it. He acquired 2 oxen and drove them twenty miles, across streams and prairie, to the young settlement of Vermillion, South Dakota where he purchased cottonwood lumber from a sawmill on the Missouri River. After returning with the lumber, he then drove his oxen to Sioux Falls, South Dakota, a distance of 50 miles, to secure rock from a quarry in order to have a solid foundation on which to build a 14' by 14' one-room cabin. This wood framed, cabin had an unfurnished second story room with one tiny window on the east side. Anyone sleeping upstairs would sleep on the floor. It took several years and long days of hard work before his cabin was built and his farm established. Not until then did he bring his wife, Ane, and son, Lars, over from Norway.

This little cabin, still stands today on the Isaac Lykken farm and has its original windows and doorframes. Later another room measuring 8' by 14 ' was added and a lean-to was built to provide a dry place for the storage of wood. That first small home served many purposes. At times it was used as a post office, a place for church gatherings and housed their family as well as a few newly arrived immigrant men who worked as farm hands.

Ole and Ane were first cousins. Marrying cousins was a common practice in rural communities in Norway and because Norwegians clustered together as they settled in this country, the practice continued after immigration to America. Settlements were small, isolated, transportation was difficult and young people married within their own communities. If they were related, they accepted it as a practical solution to finding marriage partners.

Ane was a strong, capable woman, short and stout with light brown hair and hazel eyes. She loved her family and bore 13 children, 5 of whom reached adulthood, however, John died at the age of 27, and young Betsy drowned in a stock tank as the result of an epileptic seizure. The three remaining children were Lars (my grandfather), Isaac and Sigvold all of whom married and raised large families within the Roseni community.

Ane was a dedicated planner and her capacity for looking after details and completing the essential work of a pioneer wife and mother was well known. She not only managed the household, but also made the clothing for the family and kept track of all family activities on the 500-acre farm. She was familiar with the merits of every horse, the milking capabilities of each cow on the farm, as well as the market value of the products the farm produced. In addition to the dairy work she was in charge of the poultry as well.

Because they worked very hard, they prospered. She was known to be very willing to offer sound suggestions. (bossy, perhaps?) She was a generous contributor to her church and participated in Ladies Aid and other church activities. In 1883 a larger home was built and the small cabin was used as a summer kitchen. Because wood-burning stoves propel tremendous amounts of heat into a room, it was common practice to utilize a summer kitchen for baking, cooking and canning purposes in order to keep the main house cooler during the summer months. The use of summer kitchens has long since been discontinued, but the little original cabin still stands as a place of storage.

My mother spoke of walking to her grandparent's house on Saturdays at which time she would polish all of her grandmother's copper cooking kettles. Ane would have prepared a supply of soured, clabbered milk with which to clean the copperware and my mom would rub and polish the pots until they sparkled.

In 1884 a large barn was built and is still standing and in use today. Metal siding has replaced some of the exterior walls and galvanized metal roofing has replaced the original shingles. Later a second barn, hog house and other farm building were added to the farm. This farm has always been bisected by a road, which is now a state highway. A tornado did serious damage to one of the barns in 1949 and more of the buildings were moved across the road. Today there are several buildings on both sides of the highway. The two-story home that was built in 1883 is now the home of a great-great-grandson of Ole and Ane Lykken. It has been remodeled and a full basement built under the house.

In Ole and Ane's time, the barn housed as many as 25 to 30 milk cows and the cream was sold to a nearby creamery located at Nora, and the milk was fed to the young calves. During recent times, the farm continued to be a dairy operation, milking many more cows in a modern facility that sold in bulk to Land 'O Lakes Processing plant. Interestingly, cows have been milked on this farm since it was homesteaded in 1871.

Unlike now, in early years there was manual labor and horses to provide power and this sizeable farm kept the three sons busy as well as hired immigrant men from Norway who came to America at Ole and Ane's expense and worked on their farm until they paid off the cost of their trip to America. For many years, Ole and his sons operated a large threshing machine powered by a steam engine and when I was growing up, many people in the community recalled having the Lykkens thresh their grain.

The U.S. Government granted Ole a 40-acre tract of land in payment for planting a 5-acre tree claim. In 1914, another house was built on the farm which was to be the retirement home for Ole and Ane (the other home was turned over to son, Isaac and his family of seven). On his retirement, Ole dug up 5 bull pine trees from the tree claim and planted them near his house. Although two were destroyed by the tornado of 1949, three of the trees still stand, stately and tall as sentinels of a bygone day. There are 320 acres remaining of the original Ole and Ane farm and it is still owned and operated by their descendents. In 1971 the farm was designated a Historical Century Farm by the State of South Dakota.

My brother remembers Grandpa Ole as a very old man with a long white beard. He must have been an honorable man. He arranged passage to America for his first-born son, Ole Lykken Wevik, whose birth predated his marriage to Ane. He could have left him behind but chose to recognize him as his son and give him a much- needed chance for a better life. The Wevik son married and raised a family in the Roseni community and the Wevik descendants continue to participate with the Lykkens at the annual Lykken family reunions.

Ane and Ole are buried near the church in the Roseni Cemetery, 10 miles south of Beresford, South Dakota.

GREAT-GREAT-GRANDPARENTS

Berit Stene Lykken   Born: 2-19-1820 - Died: 1891
Lars Olsen Kongsvik   Born: 1814- Died: 5-31-1864
Married: 7-24-1845

BERIT

Gleaning what information was available to me from histories and verbal accounts, my maternal female ancestors appeared to be resourceful women who married kindly, decent men and tended to dictate the standards and activities of their families. Ane's mother, Berit, fell into the mold most comfortably.

Genealogy in Norway can be confusing since names can differ in families. Husbands sometimes took the names of their wives if they owned land, and sons took their father's first name and added "sen" or "son" to it, hence Lars' sons were Larsens and Lars was Olsen from his father, Ole, until he was given Kongsvik at which time he was known as Lars Olsen Kongsvik. Daughters would take a father's name and add "datter" (daughter) and become Larsdatter etc. A very confusing system and long since discontinued in Norway.

Kongsvik, (King's bay or cove) the family farm in Norway, was supposedly named after a petty king who temporarily occupied the vik or bay at some time in history. The farm near Bynesett Sor Trondelag, was a few hilly, rock-strewn, wind-swept acres, but it contained some grassland which could be utilized for summer pasture or even hay, once cleared of brush. Back in the early part of the eighteenth century the family cut the willows off this land and sold them in Trondheim for barrel hoops, bringing them a very meager amount of money, but enough to purchase Kongsvik. This inhospitable, wilderness land was not considered suitable for farming. Lars Olsen Lykken was given Kongsvik by his father, Ole Johnsen Lykken, who had managed to give each of his three sons a small parcel of land. Land ownership in that time carried with it some distinction and some advantages, for instance, exemption from certain military responsibilities and in Lars' case, a new name, Lars Olsen Kongsvik

In 1845 Lars Olsen Kongsvik married Berit Stene, a neighbor girl from a large family, and they moved their meager belongings to Kongsvik. Their worldly belongings consisted of a wheelbarrow load of clothing, produced by Berit on her spinning wheel and loom, and some tools and utensils made by Lars. In past years many attempts had been made to make this piece of land produce, but all had failed. Berit and Lars wondered if they could survive on this farm that nobody wanted, now even devoid of its virgin willows. In Berit's mind there was no thought of failure; she knew it was a matter of hard work and good management. She is quoted as saying, "We can produce more than we can eat and so we gain---don't worry about that---since this is the best place we can get; the best is good enough."

The place was small and uninviting, but Berit's plans were big and already well developed. There was only brush, stones and grass on Kongsvik but grass was important; it meant hay. Some land must be cleared for cultivation and would have to take priority, but the removal of stumps and stones would be a slow on-going process until they could afford a horse. And slow it was. They would need a cow stable, a horse stall, workshop, smokehouse (a stabur) and a house to live in. However, Berit had in mind more of a factory than a residence, she insisted the house must have places for the following activities:

1. A place for carding and spinning wool
2. A place for weaving cloth, sewing and repairing garments
3. A place to make lye for the lutefisk and soap
4. A corner for the use of the itinerant leather worker to make shoes, harness or saddle.
5. A place to tan leather and cure furs

6. A place to make cheese

7. A place for making linen fabric from flax

8. A place for preparing malt and brewing of "ol", a mild ale

9. A large kitchen and living room with a good fireplace for preparing food.

When they butchered they would need space, but one fireplace must suffice; two fireplaces would be ideal but would require far too much wood. Norway winters are long and bitterly cold, but except for the fireplace the house was unheated. Berit knew that during the day they would keep warm by working and at night the heavy quilts would keep them from freezing.

Berit wanted a modern house, not a traditional one with low doors that made it necessary to stoop over to enter. Stooping to enter houses was an ancient practice since an unwelcome visitor, bending low to enter a door was in perfect position to be hit on the back of the head by the homeowner. She said the day was past when they had to worry about neighbors rushing in too rapidly. The upper floor would consist of one large, unheated bedroom for hired help or guests, with only an outside entrance. The children could sleep there after they had been confirmed, as was the custom of the day. They would have good bedding, eliminating the need for heat. Never one to make things too easy, Berit thought everyone would dress more quickly in a cold room.

She also wanted a full-length bedstead, not the old style five-foot bed. It was no longer necessary to sit upright when one slept as was done in the past, sword in hand, ready to protect hearth and home. There was still a weapons house at the local church but it was no longer used for weapons; it now served as a place for placing overcoats. Times were changing.

Berit insisted on wood flooring in part of the house. She felt earthen floors were too dirty and when the time was right, two men with a saw could make twelve boards a day, enough each day for one room, so why not have board floors? All this would take time, but they would do what they could, each year. Lars was a good and willing worker and she knew it was all a matter of obtaining the logs and the work would progress more rapidly when they owned a horse!

She had it all figured out. They must have complete farm units, and if they planned for it, eventually they would have an income. They must produce more than they needed and sell some of the following articles:

1. Wool, woolens
2. Linens
3. Goat Cheese
4. A little salmon in good years
5. Cow's milk and at times some meats or fats

They could not afford to eat salmon or much meat. Certain fishing rights on the Bay netted them a few salmon, but they would sell the salmon and buy herring and cheap fish. They borrowed a milk goat from Berit's parents and when the goat produced a kid, they were allowed to keep it as their own.

After providing a shelter, Lars cleared a small area of land for cultivation, which provided a place for growing potatoes and garden vegetables the first year and the following year they added an acre of barley. They, in fact, produced more than they needed for meals and ale. Berit's plan was already in operation. Rye and oats would be planted, for sure, but first a little plot for flax so Berit could begin making linen fabrics.

Soon they owned a few goats and some sheep and the numbers increased with the years. They secured a cow, then another until they had three and they purchased a "cheap horse." It was all working out fine for Berit, but she urged Lars not to overlook the logs for making her floors.

Their first baby was a girl, which they pushed in a wheelbarrow three miles to attend their church. When other babies arrived they too were placed in the wheelbarrow and when the wheelbarrow could hold no more, Lars carried them. The church was a stone building, with no stove or fireplace, a cold place to worship in the cold Norway winters.

At the age of 5, the children were expected to help by herding the sheep and the goats and children developed a healthy respect for the old Billy Goat or Ram that would sometimes bump them to the ground on the steep hillsides. Barit and Lars had five children: Karen (Norbeck), Ane (Lykken) (my great-grandmother), Ole, who called himself Ole Larson, Marit (Bodeberg) and John who called himself John Larson. Karen and Merit were dark-haired with dark complexions, but Ane, Ole and John were blondes.

Berit was very insistent on cleanliness and good order, but maintained the family could keep clean without the use of soap, which was permitted only on Saturday evenings. She is quoted as saying," If you will scrub harder, you won't need soap." Their soap was homemade but it took valuable tallow and fat to make it and such products were scarce and saleable if you had extra.

Lars, a very quiet, hard-working man, was of medium stature said to be blue-eyed with brown, curly hair. He was willing for Berit to assume a strong leadership role in their family.

Berit was blonde, strong, quick, resourceful, original, and kindly but always assumed the lead. Her neighbors and later her family gave her full credit for the success of Kongsvik. Her advice was sought and her sayings were often repeated. Her farsightedness and good judgment were always commended. She was active even in her older years and at the age of sixty she enjoyed demonstrating her strength and agility.

Berit's main objectives in life were to keep Kongsvik on a balanced budget, be debt free, and raise children who would be honest, healthy, law-abiding, respected members of the community. She was generous to the hungry who came to her door, and they were numerous under the hard conditions then existing in Norway. However she refused to lend money to anyone. She was known to close an interview with some very "unconventional" remarks when people asked her to loan them money, and their demands were not repeated.

Flax was grown to provide linen for towels, for underwear and several other purposes and the flax fiber was put through five or six complex processes where the crudest of tools were used to make good linen from flax straw. Until it was softened by multiple washings and wear, underwear made of woven linen fabric was torturous to wear because of its needle-sharp roughness

A well-managed farm was supposed to have on hand a year's supply of food consisting mostly of grain, flatbread, cured meats and fish stored in a separate building. It was not long before Lars and

Berit could point with pride to their food supply, which insured them against distress in years of scarcity, should unseasonable weather bring on crop failures.

Kongsvik did not have building timber, any required timber had to be bought in Buviken across the bay and for years in the dark of cold winter days, Lars' biggest job was to fetch logs, first with a borrowed horse, and later with his own "cheap horse," but logs and more logs had to be hauled every winter.

The land of Kongsvik, long famous as poor, unproductive land began to yield returns for labor expended and according to the views of the time and place, the family prospered, though they still enjoyed only the barest necessities of life. They had wholesome food, all necessary clothing and Berit and Lars were able to send their children to school where they learned to read, write and be confirmed in the church, educational advantages which had not been fully available to their parents. Berit could not read or write.

Tools and utensils for the home and the farm were produced by Lars in the workshop. Only the wealthiest farmers used dishes and their use was reserved for holiday occasions. Most farm people, as did Berit, served food on a flat piece of board, which after each meal was scrupulously cleaned and scoured with sand. Kerosene oil was unknown; candles or pine torches were used for lighting. Matches cost a penny each so they were unknown among the peasant people who would borrow fire from their neighbors in the event their fire went out---hence the saying to those who seemed to be in a hurry, "are you carrying fire?"

At the age of fifty, Lars died as the result of a cancer that started on his hand. He refused to have his arm amputated and it metastasized and spread quickly. In Berit's words, "he went fast." Later Berit married a bachelor from their parish and she continued to be the boss of the household. The second husband was kind and decent but proved to have even less to say than Lars.

The farm was now productive and doing well, more land had been reclaimed and fertility had greatly improved. It provided all that was needed and eventually even a few luxuries such as a Sunday carriage, a fine saddle and a set of table silver, used only when the pastor or other "important" people paid a visit. The cow barn had running water; the house did not. The reason being, cows provided the income, the house did not. It was decided that what water was needed in the house, they would carry.

Berit provided the means for all but one of her children to come to America, as an "advance" on their share of the estate. These voyages were not easy; they took from eight to thirteen weeks, depending on weather, wind and ports of call. Food was not provided on these ships of passage, each immigrant having to carry his own "kuffert" or ration box. The ship furnished only water to drink and a bunk in which to sleep. There was no refrigeration, no milk and no vegetables, nothing fresh. Those who became ill were not separated from those who were well. Many children died during these long voyages. The immigrants carried clothing and what utensils they would need upon their arrival, such as pots and pans. These were transported in wooden trunks, stenciled with their name and the traditional rosemaling decorations. Marit, the youngest child, was expected to remain in Norway to help care for her mother in her old age. This she willingly did. She married and raised a family some of whom still live on and near Kongsvik.

It must have been difficult for Berit to bid her children goodbye, one after another, so they could seek a better life in America, a life better than Norway could provide at that time. She accepted the possibility of never seeing them again. For reasons of economics, illness or family responsibilities, only one daughter ever returned to Norway for a visit. Her two sons returned to visit her in the company of a son-in-law, George Norbeck.

Berit dreaded to see her youngest son leave for America, and she was heard to say, "They all promise to return, but they don't." John replied, "But I will." And he kept his promise, making several trips back to see his mother. It was a momentous occasion for Berit in 1882, when two strangers appeared at her door, one was a tall, red-whiskered, pleasant but dignified Norwegian of about thirty-one years of age, the other about ten years older and a smallish man. The first had to tell his mother that he was her elder son, Ole. She said, "Can this be little Ole?" She was remembering a small, young man of nineteen who one morning left home on foot for Trondheim to take the boat to America...so happy, that he whistled all the way and attracted the attention of the people along the roadside. Ole had been a wild boy then. He shocked the neighborhood with his behavior that anyone could be so happy about leaving his home and the Motherland, but now he had traveled, seen and experienced much, and was a different man, certainly different in appearance. He had always been small for his age, now he was much taller and had a beard.

He had been converted and was a devout Christian. The other man was George Norbeck, her son-in-law from America. She called him neither Goren nor George, just Norbeck. She was so pleased over Ole's development. She said, "Who would have thought it? He is now married, in business and successful, and is converted and does some work as a lay preacher. They are to preach at the prayer house before they leave---he and Norbeck." She liked her son-in-law because he was so quiet and nice. She was quoted as saying, "While Ole and I visited for hours about everything and everybody in Norway and America, he just sat there and looked pleasant. He made no attempt to break into the conversation. I could tell he was a Swede; he was so well mannered. They are going to Sweden from here to see Norbeck's folks and also do some preaching. Is it not strange? Some people in this parish have had a lot to say about that boy, but now they can see for themselves. They will not say much after this, I am thinking." Ole, her wild son, had out-grown his wild ways, and she was proud of him.

(Note: Later that same Norbeck returned to South Dakota and was elected to the first South Dakota State Legislature. His son, Peter Norbeck, was elected Governor of the State of South Dakota and later became a United States Senator. The information about Berit and the verbatim quotes are excerpts from a very old and tattered family history written by Peter Norbeck who went back to Norway several times and became very interested in learning everything he could about his grandmother, Berit. Peter Norbeck's mother was a sister to my great-great-grandmother.)

CORN

To the farmers of southeastern South Dakota, Cornliness was next to Godliness. They felt pride in producing the best yields of corn in the State and according to my dad, any area that didn't grow corn could be shrugged off as worthless and unimportant. Corn was "knee high by the Fourth of July" or things weren't going right. We ate canned corn and cornbread but never acquired a taste for hominy, grits, corn pudding, pone or many of the other corn dishes enjoyed in other parts of the country.

Dad prided himself on his straight corn rows and even when debilitated and unable to walk without assistance, Mom and Leverne hitched the horses to the corn planter for him and he planted the corn, changing the stakes at the end of the rows by crawling around on his hands and knees. But his corn rows were straight!

One year after planting 110 acres of corn, our hired man, who worked for $25.00 a month plus room and board, cultivated the fields of young corn three times with a single row cultivator, changing horses at intervals throughout the work day. Since my dad felt it was a disgrace to have weedy fields, when the corn was too big to cultivate with a team of horses, family members would walk through the fields, row by row, to cut out the cockleburs and sandspurs.

In August, we could pick corn to boil and eat "roastin' ears." It was horse corn, but we thought it was delicious. Mom cooked it for an hour, Mom cooked lots of things for an hour, it seemed to be the magic amount of time.

Depending on the weather, corn harvest usually began in late October and continued until the fields were stripped clean. During a South Dakota fall, everything turns a warm beige color; the corn ears hang downward, drying in the fall sun, waiting to be picked by a farmer wearing a husking hook. A leather appliance with a metal hook held snugly in place by two or three buckles, the husking hook was worn over the glove with the hook strapped to the palm of the right hand. The left hand grasped the ear of corn, the right hand brought the hook down the length of the ear, and with a coordinated movement of fingers and thumb, the ear was snapped free of the husk and flung up against the wagon bang board where it would hit and tumble into the wagon. The hand movements were quite fluid and no time was wasted in moving from one stalk to another. Ear by ear, the corn was picked and hauled to the slatted waiting bins. The corn fields, now a sea of stalks with drooping empty husks fluttering in the fall breezes were opened for the cattle to glean for remaining edible remnants of the crop.

Fleecy, orange-colored, cotton gloves called Husky Mitts were worn to protect the hands. Because of the bruising wear and tear and the onslaught of thorns and stickers, Cornhusker's Lotion was used generously to keep the skin on the hands from cracking.

Since it was picked by hand, ear-by-ear, the corn-picking season lasted a long time. Men prided themselves on being able to pick more than a hundred bushels in one day. My brother was able to do that. One young man in the neighborhood picked a record 220 bushels in one day and everyone in the county heard about it and admired his ability.

The horses that pulled the corn wagon had to be trustworthy and obedient, and it was important that they obey the verbal commands of the picker. The reins were knotted and hooked onto the left side of the wagon as near to the picker as possible. Every year it seemed someone in the neighborhood would experience a runaway; a team would spook and dash away in whatever direction struck their fancy. This could be dangerous, because in the days before contour farming practices, ditches and ravines could be deep and treacherous.

Obeying spoken commands, the team of horses pulled the wagon up and down the rows all day, for the corn husker's hands were occupied. Fritz and Fred were Dad's picking team. Leverne related that he would run a rope from the reins along the side of the wagon and allow about 20 feet of rope to drag behind, so that if the team spooked he could grab the rope and stop them before they had a good start. One time he said his team had developed the strangest habit of hunching up to piddle, poot or poop, (horses do that a lot) and they would scare each other, promptly bolt and try to run away! That was when he would use the trailing rope.

Being surrounded by Norwegian farmers, the usual attitude toward work prevailed and doing anything the easy way was not considered admirable. One of our many local Norwegian bachelor farmers prided himself on being the first in the field each morning. Days were short, and because of late sunrise he would hang a lantern on his wagon and hold a flashlight in his mouth so he could see the corn ears. Pickers received 2 cents a bushel for picking corn so if 100 bushels were picked in a day the picker earned the grand sum of $2.00.

Dad was a sheller of corn as well as a thresher of grain. Early on, the sheller (called an Advanced Rumley) would be loaded on one truck and the tractor on another and transported in that manner. Later Dad mounted his sheller on a Mac truck and the sheller was then self-propelled, albeit very top heavy. At one time during this period, Leverne drove this rig 28 miles to a farm north of Beresford and shelled 2500 bushels of corn. It was not only considered a big job it was done by a lone 15-year-old kid.

Using an oil lantern for light, Dad would work late in the evenings, fixing the sheller; oiling, greasing or repairing a chain, here again acting on his aversion for "breaking down" or stopping for repairs while on the job. These were the years when there was very little money. When there was no money in the family coffers, Dad would go out and try to collect from farmers who owed him for shelling their corn. Depending on the size of the job, he received 1-½ cents a bushel for shelling corn and sometimes the farmers couldn't pay him. Dad hated "collecting" because he knew money was scarce for everyone, but in all those years of shelling corn, he had only one bad debt.

Shelling was usually done in the wintertime. He would often be called to shell corn on cold winter days, drive 10 or 20 miles over frozen roads, set up, and shell as little as 50 bushels of corn for the

61

grand total of 75 cents. But 75 cents was better than no cents at all..

Driving home one evening after an ice storm, Dad drove his sheller rig up a very steep hill, but the road was so slick with ice he didn't make it over the top of the hill before losing his momentum, and he proceeded to slide backwards all the way to the bottom of the hill. How he guided that top heavy rig backwards down the hill remained a mystery.

Dad loved this part of his work and he bore the scars. As a young man he reached into a feeder (auger) to dislodge a pile-up of ear corn and the piece of wire causing the impaction, wrapped around the fingers of his right hand and pulled 3 of them off at the knuckles. He had just a thumb and a partial pinkie finger on his right hand but he did everything with it including write.

The corn and grain grown on our farm was fed to our animals: horses, cows, pigs, chickens and geese. The animals were the source of our food and were sold at market for money, and hopefully a profit. The horses provided the horsepower to operate the machinery necessary to grow the crops. It was an on-going almost self-propelling cycle of planting, growing, harvesting, feeding and selling.

A by-product of cornliness was the corncob, which was left behind when the corn was removed and sent to whatever giant maw awaited it. A fresh corncob is rosy, rough and shiny and was considered a valuable commodity. Corncobs could be burned in stoves and furnaces and produced a hot flame, but had the disadvantage of a short burn life. Wood and coal were preferred, but in the depression years when we couldn't afford coal, we burned cobs. During one cold winter we ran out of wood and coal, with no money to purchase more. All downstairs rooms were closed off and we lived in the kitchen and relied on corncobs in the iron cookstove to keep us warm, which it did. Some people made corncob jelly and even corncob wine, but we burned our cobs.

Carrying the corncobs to the house and into the kitchen "wood box" was a kids' job. We would fill big #2 washtubs and two of us would carry the tubs into the house and empty them into the "wood box" by the kitchen stove. Not an unpleasant task, however there was a side to this chore that I really hated.

Our pigs ate corn on the cob! With their front feet firmly planted to hold the corncob steady, a pig could gnaw the kernels off a cob, tickety-boo! When the time came that the clean cobs had been used up and fuel was still needed for the stoves, we had to glean our cobs from the hog yard which meant carrying our tub into the pens and picking up the full length cobs all covered with hog spit, mud and poop. This we did as the pigs wandered around grunting and sniffing at us as we filled our tubs. Then off we went up the hill with our vile load of cobs, which had to be placed dirty or not, into the "wood box" by the kitchen stove and burned.

Mom hated it when we had to burn cobs from the hog pens. I wonder how we survived the clouds of bacteria that must have been airborne during some of these maneuvers, yet we were a healthy lot and rarely sick. The regular challenges to our immune systems must have precipitated our resistance to illness and disease. In the lean years my folks were grateful for those corncobs, clean or not. They kept us warm and provided the fires to cook our food.

In this day and time, 2005, farm activities are totally mechanized and have become push button, hydraulic operations done by a single person on an air-conditioned tractor with an FM radio playing and a generation or two away from the need to find fuel for a cook stove in a hog pen.

THRESHING IN THE THIRTIES

The threshing of grain signified the rewards for a season's work, a gathering of harvest from the seeds sown earlier in the spring. After the preparation of the land, the planting and the concerns about weather and rain, the reality of life-giving grain was at hand. Threshing was a family tradition; my maternal and paternal grandfathers as well as my dad and his brother, (and my brother, as well) were threshers.

The threshing rig was made up of an enormous steam engine that furnished the power to the separator, which as its name implied, separated the grain from the straw. Grandpa Klemme's steam engine was his pride and joy and he maintained it accordingly. Water for the steam engine was hauled in a 500-gallon, horse-drawn water tank. For each full workday the engine required about 1000 gallons of water, which was hand-pumped from a nearby creek. The coal to heat the water was furnished by the farmer whose grain was being threshed and about two hours were required to get up a satisfactory head of steam.

Local farms in close proximity to each other made up a "run," and starting at one end of the run, the rig went from farm to farm leaving in its wake bins full of grain and stacks of golden straw in vast piles. The straw was valued as bedding during the winter months when the animals were housed inside barns and sheds. After use as bedding, the straw evolved into huge piles of manure, which in spring was distributed onto the fields as fertilizer.

The responsibilities of threshers were divided between the "engine man" and the "separator man," one responsible for the

65

engine that supplied the power and the other tending to the workings of the separator. My dad was the "separator man" responsible for its management and maintenance and I vividly remember him standing atop the thresher watching carefully to its operation. The "engine man" was my Uncle Elmer, who had inherited the position from his father and saw to the power source, making sure there was water, wood and oil for the engine.

This steam-powered behemoth traveled at two miles an hour and when it was our turn to have our grain threshed we listened for the shrill steam whistle that announced its slow progress over the hill near our farm. As the rig inched its way up our driveway into the farmyard, Grandpa always gave an anticipated three additional blasts.

Setting up was no simple matter. Machines had to be angled safely according to wind drift, leveled and placed where the farmer preferred his straw piles. Leveling occasionally required digging holes for rear, back or side wheels in order to achieve a level position. The steam engine was turned around to face the separator and an enormous leather drive-belt was unwound from its wooden storage box and attached to an engine pulley, which measured three feet in diameter. Once this leather, 20-inch wide, 90-foot long circle of leather was twisted and placed on the pulleys, the engine inched to a spot where the belt was taut enough not to slip and the traction was perfect.

While this was taking place the rest of the crew was not idle. Eight men in horse-drawn, wide-based bundle racks arrived and immediately entered the grain fields where countless tepee shaped grain shocks stood waiting. There were two "spike pitchers" assigned in the field to assist the men with loading their racks. Evenly distributing the bundles of grain in the racks was important, for off-center loads could capsize. By the time the rig was ready, the haulers had filled their racks and returned to the rig to wait their turn to unload.

Lined up two by two, on either side of the 36-inch wide separator feeder, the bundles were pitched methodically, tops first, into the separator, taking care not to overload and choke the machine. Once the rack was empty, it was returned to the field for another load in rotating orderly fashion.

A long metal auger tube spewed a steady stream of grain into a waiting grain wagon. Two grain haulers and their teams of horses were ready; as one wagon was filling, the other loaded wagon was hauled to the area where the grain was scooped and augured into the bins. (In earlier times it was sacked and carried up ladders and dumped into the bin from the top.) As grain poured from one auger, a blower spewed the straw into a nearby pile that could reach massive proportions.

This was an arena of intense activity, with horses, men, machinery, wagons and hayracks, in swirling dirt and chaff, all going their appointed ways, knowing the routine so well and accomplishing their tasks with ease. The coordinated movements and absence of wasted motion was an impressive sight. It was no wonder that I viewed this scene with such fascination.

A typical threshing season lasted ninety days. In the event "stack threshing" followed a regular run, the season could last longer. The farmers, who stacked their grain, built conical stacks in clusters, with grain heads facing inward. These stacks were allowed to dry for longer periods and were threshed later in the fall. This involved the separator being pulled between a cluster of stacks by a cable to enable two pitchers standing atop the stacks to feed the bundles into the thresher.

My dad never stacked his grain but preferred using a grain binder. After a binder had cut and tied the bundles, eight of them were placed together, grain heads up into a shock to dry in the sun. Both methods worked well; the method adopted was left to the personal preference of the farmer.

Accidents happened; unevenly loaded hayracks tipped over, driver-less horses obeying spoken commands occasionally spooked causing runaways and with the abundance of dry chaff and straw there was the ever-present danger of fire. There were careless mistakes such as the time a pitch fork was inadvertently tossed into the feeder, or a bundle pitcher accidentally heaving a horse collar into the machine, causing serious breakdown and delay to repair equipment.

The outdoor activity was high but it was matched by the activity that took place inside the family home during this time period. The farmer's wife was expected to serve a mid-morning lunch of sandwiches, cookies or cake with lots of steaming hot coffee, a mid afternoon lunch of sandwiches, cake/cookies and coffee and a hearty noon time dinner each day that the threshing crew was on the premises.

Before the scheduled day, my mom butchered the chickens and had them ready for frying the next day. If the crew was there on subsequent days the menu would change to roast beef or perhaps pork chops . Mom would extend our round dining room table to its greatest length so the entire crew of 14 or more men could sit at table together. She always covered the table with a white damask tablecloth, a common practice, which seemed strange since the crew was a dusty, sweaty, soiled bunch. I never remember her not using her best appointments for the table.

At exactly the same time each day, the steam whistle would blow and everything would grind to a halt for the dinner hour. The crew would make its way to a shady place near the house where there would be a wash bench, enamel wash bowl, soap, towels and water waiting for them. Everyone washed hands, arms and faces, then sat down on the grass to await the call to dinner. When Dad and Uncle Elmer arrived at the house, it was a signal for the men to file in to the dining room.

Large bowls and platters of food were brought in and served family style. The meal would include meat, potatoes, vegetables, side dishes of macaroni and corn, stacks of homemade bread, coleslaw, home made pickles, home made pie and lots of coffee. Looking so similar with their tanned lower faces and white foreheads, the men would talk and laugh finding the tasty meal a highlight of the day. A farmer's brow was always lighter than the rest of his face because he wore a straw hat.

After dinner the men filed out, thanking Mom as they departed; they would then stretch out on the sloping lawn on the south side of the house, place their straw hats over their faces and take a short nap before returning to the rig.

It was during the noon hour when the men were being fed, that the horses were also at rest and being fed and watered. I would slip away from the house to go to where the teams were tethered and take note of their condition. I would walk among them and compare the horses and harnesses with my dad's. He took excellent care of his horses, had good harness and in summer his horses wore "fly nets" to keep them free of flies. Not all farmers were good stewards when it came to their workhorses. I was particularly concerned with the horses that had developed galls and sores from ill-fitting harness or horse-collars. It made me sad and I would pray over them, praying that the horses not feel pain or discomfort from their wounds as they worked.

Activity remained high in the kitchen. High and hot! The table would be hurriedly cleared and the dishes washed, wiped and put away followed immediately by preparations for delivering the 4:00 p.m. lunch. Sandwiches by the dozen were prepared, all thoroughly buttered before the meat was added and placed in large enamel dishpans and covered with two dishcloths to keep them from drying out. The bread was homemade but the meat was usually what we called "minced ham" which in reality was bologna with a fancy name. In another container would be placed pieces of cake and cookies. Mom would make two gallons of open pot coffee in big speckled, enamel coffeepots. She made a mash of coffee grounds and beaten eggs, which she poured into the pot of boiling water. I must say, I remember the coffee was very tasty.

At exactly four p.m., the lunch arrived and was made available for distribution near the rig. After the haulers came in and had emptied their racks, they would squat down on their haunches, balancing sandwich or cookie on one knee while they drank their steaming hot cups of coffee. After that short repast, off they would go to continue their work. The work was hot and dirty and at day's end the men were covered in sweat, dust and fine chaff, as were their horses.

At 6 p.m. a blast from the steam engine signaled an end to the threshing day and the crew peeled off one by one and headed out for their nearby farms to tend to their teams and other evening chores. The same crew followed the rig until the end of the run, spending from one to three days at each farm, continuing the routine of the previous day until the entire run was finished and the grain was threshed and in the bin.

The farm wife received no respite from work if the threshing took more than one day for she would have to do a repeat of the previous day's activities until the job was finished and the rig moved to the next farmer in line on the run.

After the run was completed, Dad and Uncle Elmer would host an evening thresher's party and the men and their families would gather to celebrate the end of the fall threshing season. The men sat out doors on the lawn while the women stayed indoors and visited. The children ran about in the gathering evening darkness, catching fireflies or sitting in a circle telling ghost stories. Mom served coffee, sandwiches, Jell-O, cake and coffee to everyone at about 9:30 p.m.

Hard work was held in high esteem by the Norwegians, the harder the better. It wasn't until later that short cuts came to be accepted. The drought of the thirties caused the creeks to dry up; the resulting shortage of readily available water hastened the demise of the steam engine. An Altman/Taylor gasoline powered tractor replaced it. Also large and cumbersome, it was nowhere near the size of its predecessor. With the advent of the combine in the fifties, harvesting grain could be done in one operation, making the threshing machine obsolete.

In spite of the passing of an era, in his later years my dad bought a small threshing machine, already a relic of the past, and did some threshing for those who missed the time honored custom of threshing the grain. A proud family tradition had passed into history.

Addendum: One summer shortly after Dad had finished some "commemorative" threshing, the children and I were in South Dakota at the same time that the Kinsley children were visiting. To them, the tall, new straw pile south of the barnyard looked like a great place to play. All farm children were warned never to play on new straw piles because they could contain air pockets and were considered dangerous until the pile had "settled." We, in turn, had warned our children not to play on the new straw pile for that very reason.

Unfamiliar with the seriousness of farm dangers, the temptation was too great to resist and unbeknownst to their parents, the kids climbed up to play on the new straw pile. Sure enough, our son, Mark, plunged through an air pocket and disappeared from sight. His cousin Debbie led the effort to excavate him from the hole and after much feverish clawing and digging they reached him and pulled him free. They knew they had committed a spanking offense so the secret was maintained for forty years.

FOUL FOWL

I could not complete this manuscript without paying chickens their due. It is not because I failed so miserably at chicken craft, but rather the fact that when other farm activities provided little or no income during the depression years, our chickens continued to lay eggs like good little soldiers. The eggs were sold or bartered for the food staples needed for a family of six. Mom was our chicken expert.

Chickens are purchased by the box. When Mom enlarged her chicken operation, she no longer hatched her own, but chose to purchase the baby chicks from a local hatchery. Divided into four compartments, twenty-five in each section, there would be one hundred chicks in a box. One of the greatest joys of childhood was assisting Mom when she transferred several hundred newly hatched chickens into our brooder house.

The brooder house was cleaned thoroughly; the feeders and watering jars were scrubbed and filled with mash and drinking water and the little kerosene space heater, with its sheltering skirt, was lit to provide warmth for the little chicks. Sitting on the clean, straw-covered floor, we would remove the chicks from the box, one by one, dip their beaks into the mash and water so they would know where to find sustenance, then release them to run free.

Upon arrival the baby chicks were beautiful, fuzzy, sweet smelling and fragile. As soon as their feet hit the floor, the challenges began. A chicken's head is very small, for a reason; they have a miniscule brain and what little there is of it is seldom put to good use.

Our brooder house was round, for a reason; any area with corners provided the perfect place for chicks to pile into and smother each other. The term "pecking order" originated from the observation of chicken behavior. As the fluffy darlings begin to mature, they take up many bad habits; they mess in their food and drink, then start pecking on one of their own, and if let be, will peck the unfortunate chick to death. Any unusual sound strikes panic in a brain that dictates, "Okay, guys let's go smother each other!" If penned outdoors, young chickens will squat under a building's eaves in a rainstorm, allowing the water to pour over them, wetting their feathers and suffering hypothermia...within three feet of a sheltering overhang or entrance to a protected area. I remember Mom and Dad collecting boxes full of wet chickens under the eaves, bringing them into the house to warm up and dry off. Wet chickens smell bad.

We girls were expected to help with the gathering of eggs and it was a job I enjoyed. Sometimes there were hazards. A hen lays an egg, cheers about it, then goes on her merry way until a second hen enters the nesting box and makes her deposit in a similar manner. Some nests would contain six or seven eggs and how wonderful it was to find a nest full. But occasionally a hen would grow "clucky," which indicated some biological message in her pea-brain told her that the nest and the eggs were hers, and she must now sit and hatch them out. To someone in the egg business, a "clucky" hen is a crabby non-producer that will search until a nest of eggs is located, plop down, and sit there with fluffed-out feathers and beady eyes daring anyone to reach in and gather "her" eggs. Any gesture in her direction would earn you a good peck on the hand.

We had our methods of coping. I took a large tin can with me and put it over the hen's head and pinned her while I gathered her eggs. LuIda used a slat and held the hen's head against the side of the nest while she collected the eggs. Mom never let it bother her at all.

Being the good chicken steward that she was, Mom would segregate the "cluck" in an area with no nesting facilities in order to get her through this phase. Unfortunately, the hens in their frustration would then molt, shed their feathers and run around minus a good portion of their plumage. Ugly sight.

A chicken hatches from an egg in three weeks. During earlier times, Mom hatched chicks in an incubator, which was kept in our basement. Made of heavy, dark wood, sitting on sturdy legs, it resembled a baby grand piano, minus its keyboard. The interior of the incubator was kept at an even temperature by a kerosene-fueled heater and the eggs were rotated on a daily basis, marking them to indicate which had been turned and which had not. When the little peck holes began to appear, we watched in wonder as the chicks appeared, wet and feeble, struggling to shed their protective casings. Within a very short time, they fluffed themselves out and began to peep and explore their cramped quarters surrounded by a mess of cracked and abandoned shells. A hen will gladly do all this work herself when allowed.

When Mom chose to use a clucky hen to hatch baby chicks, she did a most inventive thing. To keep the hen in clucky mode until the proper number of fertilized eggs could be identified, she would place white porcelain doorknobs in the nest to fool the hen into thinking she was sitting on her own eggs. In the meantime to ensure that the nest of eggs would hatch out at approximately the same time, Mom would select and candle eggs from other laying hens to determine their fertility. She would then remove the doorknobs from the clucky hen and replace them with the appropriate number of fertilized eggs. The hen would resolutely keep the eggs warm and rotated, according to nature's dictates, until the chicks pecked their way out of their shells. A mother hen, proudly making a first appearance, trailed by a flock of newly hatched chicks, chirping and peeping at one another, was a thrilling sight.

Anyone dealing with chickens has my sympathy and my admiration. Keeping them fed, housed, free from mites, worms, drowning and smothering is a challenge. I would think it is the major reason most chickens are now raised in cages. I felt a desire to share this information, not because I love scrambled eggs and chicken casseroles, but because I want no one to take their chicken for granted.

TOILETS OF THE THIRTIES

(This chapter is not for the squeamish)

As I enjoy the luxury of three bathrooms in our home, I think back to the toilets of my childhood. They were called toilets, not bathrooms or restrooms. Certainly no one would be tempted to bathe or rest in them since they were usually some distance from the house; hot in summer and very cold and drafty in winter. Various terms identified a toilet: two-holer, three-holer, the biffie, the can, the john, the head, the crapper, the privy or the backhouse. At our church all of those terms were considered inappropriate so the outdoor privies were called "the men's walk" and "the women's walk." Our family called it the backhouse. We were rather proud of ours for it was spacious as toilets go, it was a three-holer with a large hole, a medium hole and off to the side a small hole for children. It also was decorated around the exterior with layered shingles with gingerbread trim around the eaves. Ours was indeed a fine backhouse, but I still hated it.

During these hard times my mother knew a million ways to save money. It wouldn't have occurred to her to expend any hard cold cash on toilet paper when there were so many useful, available pages in the Montgomery Ward and Sears Roebuck catalogs. Part of the catalogs contained hard slick paper, but in the back sections the paper was coarser and the slightest bit softer, especially the index pages. How I dreaded when the index pages were all gone, and we had to move to the furniture and clothing sections. We were prudent not to waste even that supply because catalogs were mailed out but twice

77

a year and supplies were expected to last. In the summer we felt blessed when we were allowed to use the soft paper that came with a lug of peaches. Each peach was nestled in its own wrapping of tissue paper and the paper was put to good use, but expended all too soon. For some young men in the area, a favorite Halloween prank was tipping over outdoor toilets. One young man known for his wild ways usually got the blame, and although he may have been guilty part of the time, I am quite sure others participated as well.

About the time I was in second grade at our rural school, the school board replaced the tiny little toilets with larger more sturdy ones that were set on a concrete foundation. The old ones had begun to show the effects of countless tippings. These sturdy ones were never tipped thereafter. And at our school what a joy it was to be supplied with store-bought toilet tissue. A real luxury!

There were hard and fast rules regarding toilet etiquette enforced by our teacher: 1) only one person in the facility at any given time, 2) no inappropriate lingering or dallying and 3) only three squares of toilet tissue could be used at one sitting. Woe unto any boy who even walked within close proximity of the girl's toilet. It didn't happen. Sad to say one of my little friends was caught putting a few extra squares in the top of her stocking for use at home and was punished. These were the days of few gray areas, wrong was wrong, theft was theft.

Our home finally had indoor plumbing by the mid-forties, before that time we used a chamber pot, which we called the p-pail. It was a white enamelware bucket made for that purpose and kept in an anteroom off Mom and Dad's bedroom. It was used only at night when the weather was very cold. My brother and my dad didn't use it; men are lucky that way, the outdoor world was readily available to them. One did appreciate the convenience of a chamber pot when the temperature was below zero, the snow was deep and the wind was howling, but in daytime, we were still expected to make use of the outdoor facility, snow or no snow, cold or no cold.

What gives me cold shivers is the memory of reading late into the night by the light of a kerosene lamp that gave dim illumination, at best, then to my dismay feeling the need to empty my bladder before going to sleep. Lamp in hand, I would go down the stairway, which had no handrail, trying not to awaken my parents. I would place the lamp on the kitchen table while I went to use the outdoor "facility" or if lucky, the "pail" inside. Then carrying the lamp, I would creep up the cold dark stairway to my room, blow out the light and crawl into my bed.

I would say our facilities were rather typical for the time and we made the best of the situation with minimal concern for any inconvenience we experienced.

A KIND WORD ABOUT MANURE

Thinking back, we lived surrounded by excrement: horse, hog, chicken, bird, goat, dog, cat and goose. I have accidentally stepped with bare feet in all of it at one time or another. But in spite of this, farm families seemed to ignore its existence and seldom considered its disadvantages. There were many names for excrement: manure, quawk, poop, pewie, dump, dung, #2, crap and road apples. Surprisingly no one ever called it the four-letter word that it was!

I would never have considered saying that bad word, and in fact rarely heard it spoken until I was in high school. My Dad was known to say the German versions of it when he was angry. I knew full well that if I spoke that evil word a bar of P & G laundry soap would be across my teeth faster than you could say "Jack Robinson." So who was he, anyway? I just knew he went with "faster than you could say!"

My favorite was horse manure. I enjoyed cleaning the horse stalls, except for Dolly's, for she had a habit of squeezing me against the wall when I entered her stall. Agnes would just give her a punch and she would move over, but I always knew, given the chance Dolly could pin me and crush me to death.

Goose was my least favorite and we had a lot of that. Mom raised about twenty-four geese each year and they preferred spending the night on the cement slab outside the gate in front of our house, so anyone walking to the car sometimes had to wade through it. Nothing we did would make those dumb geese sleep elsewhere.

Dad was particular about making sure there was ample straw bedding in the barns so the animals could stay dry during the winter months. Regular cleaning of the animal stalls resulted in vast accumulations of manure forked into piles outside of the barns. Manure in the spring was the final by-product of the fall harvest. It was distributed onto the fields as fertilizer in the spring and represented re-cycling at its best. Manure was the only fertilizer farmers used at that time and they would have discussions about which was the best, pig, cow, horse or chicken. For some weird reason, most gave the honors to "chicken."

Manure was forked by hand into a manure spreader which was a large wagon-like piece of equipment, with metal wheels and pulled by four horses. When arriving at the spot that was to receive this bounty, the big gear handle was pulled which activated a slatted wooden conveyor and an immense, rotating spike-covered wheel positioned along the entire width of the back end of the spreader. Once the manure was fed into the turning wheel, it was flung high and wide into a fan-like pattern behind the wagon. Little pieces flying everywhere!

As a child, I loved to ride with my dad on the manure spreader as he distributed a winter's collection of homemade fertilizer on his fields in the spring. I enjoyed it because it was almost comic watching all that poop and straw flying out through the air behind us. After distribution, back to the barnyard we would go for another load until the yards were totally scraped clean.

On their way to separate fields while hauling manure for a neighbor, two local young men met each other on the road with loaded spreaders. They both activated their rotary spreader gears as they passed, showering horses and each other with manure...They found this to be hilarious. Boys will be boys, and I am sure they were cautioned against the waste.

Manure piles fermented and generated enough heat in winter to send steam emanating into the cold winter air. It was a common sight to see livestock standing around on these piles seeking its warmth.

One cold winter day when I was about three years old, I strayed away from my mom. There are many places to hide on a farm and she must have feared for my safety. She found me in the barnyard, asleep on a large pile of manure, surrounded on all sides by four of Dad's immense draft horses.

In retrospect, it is easy to understand our forbearance where manure was concerned. It served to nurture and renew the land and in some instances provided warmth for the animals. If one was unfortunate enough to have encountered a skunk, the removal of the skunk smell from clothing was simply a matter of burying the offensive clothing in the manure pile, leaving the garments there for a time, then retrieving, washing and boiling them in hot, soapy water. Oila, no skunk odor!

For all the modern day concern with smells and odors, as a daughter of the soil my experience with manure did not serve to de-sensitize my olfactory senses, in fact it sharpened them. The odors of a farm can be pungent, no doubt about that, but the scent of lilacs, bridal wreath, roses, honeysuckle and plum blossoms are imbedded in my childhood memory, as well, and serve to overwhelm the memory of manure.

KONGSVIK, NORWAY

THRESHING MACHINE RIG

MY PARENTS ANNA AND EMIL KLEMME

GERMAN GRANDPARENTS, H.F. AND LENA KLEMME

THE NORWEGIANS: LARS LYKKEN FAMILY
(my mother, standing, second from left)

MY CHILDHOOD HOME IN WINTER

COUNTRY SCHOOL BODY AND RHYTHM BAND

AUTHOR AT 15 YEARS OF AGE

SECTION TWO

THE MIDDLE YEARS

1940 - 1944

Having spent my first eight grades in a one room rural school, the prospect of going to high school in town was a very exciting thought. Lu Ida and Leverne had preceded me and I would anxiously await their return home on Friday evenings so they could tell me everything that had happened during the week; Lu Ida would have to relate what everyone was wearing, who was dating whom and information about classes and teachers.

Leverne was a senior the year I was a freshman and because everyone knew him, I came into my class with an entrée, of sorts. It could be difficult for kids coming from the country schools to find a social niche within their high school class. Class relationships had been long-standing in town school for many years, sometimes from the first grade. I didn't expect it to be a problem and it wasn't. In fact, I was elected to a class office in my freshman year. I participated in choir, declamation, drama and began to play the trombone in the school band. We had a fine band director and our band was better than most for high schools of our size.

We lived fourteen miles from Elk Point; it was wartime and gasoline was scarce so it was necessary that we stay in town during the week from Monday until Friday. My folks rented a tiny apartment for us in the upstairs of a private home where four girls shared a kitchen, one bedroom and one small closet. Our mothers would send food with us on Monday that would last most of the week. My folks would send a 15-dozen crate of eggs to the Council Oak Grocery on Monday morning, which would provide a small credit at the store in the event we had to buy other foodstuffs during the week. There was no money to eat in restaurants; my spending allowance was 50 cents a week, which also had to pay for school supplies. We brought our clothes on hangers, our food in boxes and lived in our little apartment until 5:00 p.m. on Fridays when our fathers would pick us up and return us to our homes for the weekend.

The apartment bathroom was downstairs and it was necessary for us to walk through the living room, the dining room and the kitchen to get to it. Thinking back I wonder how we managed that without driving our landlords crazy. There was no bathtub. During the week, we used our little washbowl upstairs and took what we called "spit" baths or "cat" baths. Four girls in one washbowl! There was a kerosene stove on which we prepared our meals and heated our bath water.

We walked the short distance to school and it was very cold in winter, outdoors and in. There was no central heat or insulation in the house; the only heat finding its way to our upstairs apartment arrived through a hot air register in the floor of the bedroom. Thank heavens warm air rises. Interestingly, I do not remember being cold. A Midwest winter is always cold, and if we felt the effects of low temperatures, we expected it.

There was a young married couple who also rented a one-room apartment in the tiny upstairs and I don't know WHAT they did for a bathroom. When I carried the wastewater down those steep stairs in a five-gallon bucket I always hoped I wouldn't drop it. We seemed to bathe in about a quart of water, since we had to carry it up as well as down in a bucket. Our rent was $2.50 a week.

I lived with the Card family for 4 years and I marveled at their patience with our coming in from school functions and dates, oftentimes after they had retired for the night. They slept in a double bed in what at one time had been a dining room but was now the third bedroom. I think it was necessary for them to rent out rooms in order to support themselves. Mrs. Card was a pianist and had many piano students and from our upstairs rooms we heard them one after the other pounding out their piano lessons. I took piano lessons during my freshman year; I rarely practiced so I never became very accomplished at the keyboard.

My mom once said the years when we stayed in town and attended high school were her least favorite ones because each Friday we would arrive home with all our soiled laundry to wash and press. The house was always strewn with our books, clothes and suitcases and she would spend her weekends helping us get our clothes ready, cooking and baking so we would have food to take back with us on Monday morning. She had many years of this routine since I followed Lu Ida, Agnes followed me and we all three had the same living arrangement.

I loved every minute of my four years of high school. I made fast friends among both boys and girls and we had rollicking wonderful fun. A group of us would stay in the assembly hall after school to chitchat. One member of our group was the son of the superintendent, which may have been an advantage, but sooner or later his father would stick his head in the door and tell us to go home.

We would walk each other home, back and forth, until separating at the halfway point, making sure we arrived home in time to hear Fred Waring and his Pennsylvanians (choir) at 6 p.m. on the radio. We would yell to each other as we parted, things like: "Farewell, and treasure deep, That which I love most, I leave thee behind." Or we would call goodbye in many languages as we parted. Some times we would speak to each other at length, using the idiomatic speech of Klem Kadiddlehopper from the Red Skelton Show.

In the fall of my freshman year a group of us would meet once a week at a friend's home and play a tag game. There was an "IT," there was hiding, catching and home-free runs. On many crisp fall evenings we would run and holler, hide in pairs and knock each other down trying to get "home free!" On one occasion, a fellow pushed me to the ground, (For sure, he was over achieving.) and he pinned me down in a pile of fallen leaves, sat on me, holding my hands behind my head. We were near the sidewalk that ran in front of the house, and there was lots of thrashing about and noise during all this. Suddenly the boy leaped off of me as if he had received an electric shock. As I sat up brushing the fall leaves out of my hair I looked up into the face of the boy's father, a local attorney, who was walking home from his office. The sight of his son sitting on top of a struggling, young girl in a pile of leaves must have given him pause. I remember it well. He was wearing a homburg, a black overcoat, carrying a briefcase and I was on the ground covered with leaves.

Needless to say, I felt a bit foolish, the boy went home shortly after this incident and I remember he never joined us for tag games again. Thinking back, it was such innocent fun. Shoving and pushing, yes, but there was no kissing or groping when we were hiding, for had there been, the girls surely would have told each other about it. I remember laughing ourselves silly and rolling around like teddy bears, boys and girls alike. After our freshman year we no longer participated in these frolicsome games.

By the time I was a sophomore I had decided I wanted to be a majorette. I played trombone in the marching band as a freshman, and liked the fact that the trombones always marched in the front row so our horns wouldn't poke fellow marchers in the butt. We practiced our marching before school, not in itself unusual, however, when the temperature was 32 degrees or lower, a metal instrument is very cold, even colder when you hold it to wet lips. I was lucky because one can play a trombone wearing mittens, which I did. The poor trumpet players got cold fingers. I didn't like before-school practice because having blown on a trombone for 30 minutes, I would walk into assembly hall with a big, red circle around my mouth where the cold mouthpiece would have chapped my lips. Lipstick was out of the question for about two hours. I felt that was justification enough for becoming a majorette.

I learned to twirl a baton and to catch it most of the time. In October on Dakota Day at the State University town of Vermillion, we would march in a city parade along with many other bands. Compared with some of the marching bands from larger cities, we may not have looked too impressive, but we made a good sound. "Stars and Stripes Forever" was usually played when all the bands performed en masse on the football field, and the trombones have a very heavy part in that selection. My freshman year, I remember "faking" it on that piece, just pushing the slide back and forth as if I were playing, for I never mastered that song on the trombone. Our parade songs were relatively easy numbers and we played them each and every time we performed outdoors "on the march."

Our majorettes wore rather modest blue and white-skirted costumes and only the Drum Majorette wore white boots. The rest of us wore white tennis shoes. I would have loved having boots, but some of the majorettes could not afford them and the school took that into consideration.

I made fairly good grades in high school, I should have studied harder, but fun was my first priority. I had some wonderful teachers, and some poor ones, as well. By the time I was a senior in 1944, the War had depleted the work force to the point that it was necessary to hire teachers who were recent graduates from college, with no real experience, or in some cases, no great interest in teaching. But the good ones more than made up for the poor ones. I shall never forget a newly graduated teacher who taught English III. She was young and pretty much to the pleasure of a big, mouthy football player in the class who provided entertainment for us and frustration for the teacher.

We were studying a classic involving knights and castles and there was mention made of "explosions in the fortress magazines." When Mr. Touchdown asked what was meant by "explosions in the fortress magazines," this poor dear hesitated a moment and said, it was apparently an area where the "owners of the castle stored their publications." My friend, Nancy, and I almost passed out trying to suppress our laughter. Mr. Touchdown believed her, I am sure.

Discipline was no problem in our high school. The superintendent, Mr. Leyman, found scolding unnecessary. A man of few words, he merely walked the halls, and we knew the consequences for breaking the rules of behavior. I recall a couple instances of a football player being brash enough to talk back, something totally unacceptable, and Mr. Leyman handling matters in his own way. One fellow was given a good swat and he tumbled backward down the wide staircase, head over heels and landed at the bottom of the steps, a bit humbled by the process.

School dances were held in the gym twice a month and I attended them all. We danced to songs such as: String of Pearls, Tuxedo

Junction, I'll Get By, I've Had This Feeling Before and Green Eyes. We did the two-step and the jitterbug to the music of Sammy Kaye, Harry James, Tommy Dorsey and Glen Miller. Mr. Leyman would show up during the evening and walk among the dancers. If couples were dancing cheek-to-cheek or inappropriately close, he would tap the boy on the shoulder. That's all, just tap him on the shoulder and that ended that!

Some students came with dates, many did not, and it was customary for dancers to change partners. The girls sat on one side of the gym and the boys hovered near the opposite side; boys would walk over and ask the girls for a dance and when the dance ended, the fellow would escort his partner back to where she had been sitting. There were always a couple of "Ladies Choice" dances when the girls could ask the fellows to dance. I loved that. The girls would have many partners during the evening, some times dancing with the same fellow more than once. If attending with a date, the guy was expected to dance the first and last dance with her, other than that, he was free to dance with whomever he chose and so was she. In later years when our children were in high school, the school dance protocol was greatly changed; they danced with the same partner all evening. I always thought how boring it must be to attend a school dance and be expected to dance with the same fellow all night.

There was an operetta, a junior class and a senior class play presented each school year. I enjoyed declamation and competed every year; my sophomore year I progressed to regional competition with a declamatory monstrosity called "David Garrick." I acted in many school plays no matter how small or how big the part, this gave me great pleasure. We had a fine glee club and I sang in the soprano section.

To create greater opportunities for participation among the student body in editing the high school newspaper, The Pointer had two staffs, a Blue Staff and a White Staff. I was editor of the Blue Staff and would write editorials about how important it was to keep up school spirit and respect our mentors etc. One of the advantages of attending a small high school was the opportunity to participate in many extra-curricular activities if the student had the desire, talent and motivation to do so.

I was allowed to date with my parents' blessing when I reached the age of 16 and I thought that milestone was a long time in coming. My folks thought 16 was the magic time for dating to begin. They were right, but at the time I didn't think so. A typical date during my high school years cost about $.50 cents: two tickets to the movie (on 10 cent night, amounted to 20 cents total) and two malted milkshakes after the movie cost 15 cents each. OILA! A fifty-cent date of the forties!

During the early forties, some of my favorite movies were Stage Door Canteen, Men With Wings, Old Acquaintance, and This is The Army. The radio shows I enjoyed most were Wayne King (the Waltz King whose program was sponsored by Lady Esther Cosmetics), Pleasure Time, Lux Radio Theater and Hour of Charms. Bob Hope, Jack Benny, Red Skelton and Fibber McGee and Molly were big radio stars and the movie stars I liked best were Bette Davis, Katherine Hepburn, Fred Astaire, Ginger Rogers and Gene Kelly. My favorite books were Gone With the Wind, Disputed Passage and all of L.C. Douglas' books most of which were eventually made into movies. The movie, Magnificent Obsession, comes to mind.

The summer of my 17th year it was my turn to "work out" and learn the finer points of being employed. I answered an ad in the Sioux City Journal advertising for a live-in hired girl for "light housekeeping" and care of three school age children. I was hired, packed my meager belongings and moved into the home of a prosperous Jewish family in Sioux City, Iowa. The children were 7, 9 and 11 years old and I bonded immediately with the girl who was the youngest. The older boy spent most of the summer at camp and the other one was a quiet, well-behaved child. I had a big room to myself; my duties were mainly acting as a nanny to the children and I had Thursday afternoons and alternate Sundays off. A laundress whom I rarely saw worked in the basement, another woman came to do the heavy cleaning, and my duties consisted of caring for the children and doing the dishes after meal times.

What a learning experience this turned out to be. These parents were home only on those evenings that I had off. They went out every evening. The mother would order her groceries each morning, dialing the phone with a pencil so as not to ruin her polished nails and the groceries would be delivered to the back door within the hour for the meals of that day. She was a friendly woman, a good cook and very talkative. On Friday evening they observed the traditional Jewish Sabbath meal and I was asked to sit at table with them. I closely observed how she entertained and how she dressed. They were very kind to me.

One weekend when the parents were out of town, the children attended a special show at the Orpheum Theater in downtown Sioux City. About 4:00 p.m., the kids were delivered back home followed closely by a truck hauling a Shetland pony, which was unloaded and delivered to our back door. It seems my little 7 year old had won a horse at the theater that afternoon. This presented no problem for me. I tied the pony to a tree, provided it with a pail of water and he began to graze on the bluegrass in the back yard. This scenario attracted many neighborhood children. The reaction of the parents on their return on Sunday evening was one of shocked surprise. The mother's first comment was, "Thank Gawd, you are a country girl and knew what to do with that darn horse."

The oldest child was still at camp when the parents went on vacation, so they allowed me to take the two youngest children to my home while they were gone. The children greatly enjoyed their two weeks of country living. Since their parents had never met my folks, I am amazed at the trust this mother and father showed in me and my family.

One day when the parents were gone and the kids were playing at the neighbors, I tried on my employer's evening gowns and her satin evening shoes. They fit me quite well and I twirled and preened in front of her mirror. Looking back, that was quite presumptuous of me and until this writing, I have never told anyone that I did it. I knew my mom would have disapproved mightily. I was expected to save my salary of $8.00 a week, and I did save a little, but most of it went for clothes. I loved pretty clothes.

The impending visit of a conservative Jewish grandmother from the East made it necessary to set up a kosher kitchen, which proved to be a very interesting exercise. This family did not keep a kosher kitchen, but apparently the grandmother did. So three of us worked for several days getting the kitchen ready. This involved baking all the pots and pans in a hot oven for an hour, then scouring and scrubbing and sterilizing everything. After the cleaning and sterilizing was completed, the kitchen was separated into two separate sets of everything, including the dishtowels. One set was used for fleishidicker (meat) based meals and one for milkdicker (milk) based meals...and never the twain would meet. My time with this family came to an end with the approach of the new school year and I never had the opportunity to observe the kosher kitchen in operation.

As a result of my wonderful experience with this family, I developed an intense interest in Jewish culture and during one period of my life, read everything I could find on Jewish history. Years later in college, I wrote a paper on the "Myth of the Wandering Jew," for which I received an A+ .

In the fall of 1943, my senior year in high school, the war was causing many shortages: chocolate, silk stockings, gum, gasoline, rubber bands, film, fruit cocktail, and countless other products. These shortages impacted every level of society. Our school homecoming was held each year in October with the traditional parade and floats. Previously, floats were made by sticking paper napkins into a mesh chicken wire frame in a specified design, but in the fall of 1943 there were no floats. It would have been unpatriotic to use that much paper for so frivolous a reason.

That was the year the student body elected me homecoming queen, Miss Elk Point of 1944. In lieu of a float, I rode atop the back seat of a convertible, borrowed from a young, unmarried, alumnus who had enough gasoline to loan his car for the event. It was a wonderful feeling taking a turn around the football field at half time.

A professional photographer took the only picture that I have of the coronation: the queen and her court, me in a borrowed white evening dress, wearing a long white and blue train and a gold crown made by the Home Economics teacher. Before the evening of the scheduled coronation ceremony, the senior class sponsor explained to me that traditionally the student body president would present me with a gift from the school. In the past this gift was a gold chain with a pendant containing the Elk Point High School crest, similar to what was on the school class rings. Because of the wartime shortage of precious metals, she explained that the box would be empty and that the presentation would be merely ceremonial. She assured me that the chain and pendant would be sent to me at a later time when the war was over. So at the coronation ceremony, I was presented a beautifully wrapped white box that contained nothing.

I didn't vote for myself. That would have been tacky to my Norwegian way of thinking. I voted for my best friend and she voted for me. Early in my freshman year I sensed how discomforting it must feel to be excluded from the groups that set the pace for a class. Some kids were poor and had to wear clothes that were different than what was considered cool. My heart always went out to them and I made a serious effort to acknowledge them in some way. I would say "hi", or sometimes walk to and from class with someone who usually walked alone. I consciously did this all through school. It costs so little to be kind. I believe that was why I was elected homecoming queen; I may have received some votes from those whom I had taken the time to acknowledge or befriend, however briefly. Or maybe it was the result of my earlier membership in the Compliment Club.

Later amid the excitement of war's end, retiring staff members and numerous projects placed on hold for so many years, providing me with a gold Miss Elk Point pendant never rose to the top of anyone's list of priorities.

Some of the fads of the 1940-1944 era were cardigan sweaters worn backwards, wearing our dad's or brothers' dress shirts hanging out and loose, and white bobby socks, just coming into style, worn with white and brown, rubber soled, saddle oxfords. One pair of school shoes and one pair of Sunday shoes made up my shoe wardrobe.

Girls wore flowers in their hair and the side on which they were worn signified whether you were going steady or not. I always forgot which side meant what and probably sent out some wrong signals. Hair was worn long in pageboy style, we wore Tangee lipstick and Chen Yu nail polish. Evening in Paris was the ultimate in perfume and even high school girls wore hats to church.

Some of our guys had left school to enlist in the armed services before the time of their graduation. For the thirty-six seniors in our class, the graduation ceremony was an emotional experience. There was hugging and crying, joy at this milestone in our lives, sadness for those already in the war and concern for those facing induction into military service soon after graduation.

May of 1944 was a climactic time during the war; manpower was needed on the battlefields, on the home front and in the factories to produce the materials of war. Several families moved away to work in the war plants, mothers went to work, and some worked at rolling bandages or knitting wool sweaters for the soldiers. (Packed away in a trunk in our attic, is a heavy, black wool sweater knitted by a pair of caring hands from the State of Utah and sent to my husband while he was serving in the Aleutians during the War.) It was a time of all-out mobilization and there was great patriotic fervor. Everyone was affected in some way and felt concern for brothers, husbands or fathers serving their country in wartime.

Every family was issued a ration book and grocers would tear out the numbered stamps, which represented the points that each item of food required. Meat required more stamps than staples. In that respect we were lucky because our family raised our own meat. Everyone was encouraged to have a "Victory Garden" and grow as much food as possible. There were over 20,000,000 victory gardens in the nation and they produced 40% of the vegetables eaten during that time by the civilian population. There were wartime cookbooks containing recipes for cooking without sugar and there were substitutes for hard to acquire ingredients.

The O.P.A. (Office of Price Administration) ruled this segment of our lives. Gasoline was in very short supply, but it was not withheld from the farmers, which were producing the resources for feeding the nation and the armed forces. Pleasure drives were prohibited.

Each time we went to the movies, there was a Pathe News segment, which showed filmed battlefield footage of the war in the European and the Pacific Theater of Operations. Posters were everywhere, cautioning people not to speak inappropriately about war activities. "A SLIP OF THE LIP, MAY SINK A SHIP" was posted everywhere.

America showed its coping skills. Most women in the prewar era would not have considered working outside the home but before war's end, 36% of the adult women in America had gone to work; Rosie the Riveter, became a reality. Within a few short years, the nation moved from severe depression and high rates of unemployment to 0 % unemployment. Everyone worked at the consuming task of winning the war and there were more jobs than workers to fill them.

Automobile plants and steel plants turning out the machines of war universally adhered to three, 8-hour shifts, seven days a week. Many jobs were "frozen," meaning once someone was hired for a position, it was impossible to leave or transfer to another job. Only family emergencies were accepted as a suitable reason for release and I was caught in that wartime rule later on.

Most families had someone serving in the armed services. Mothers of soldiers were encouraged to hang the traditional small banner in their windows with a blue star representing each member of the family who was in the armed services. Many windows displayed 2, 3, and 4 blue stars. When the blue star was replaced with a gold one, it meant the soldier it represented had been killed in action. So many windows! So many stars! Far too many gold ones!

Private individuals, factories, organizations, all entities were encouraged to purchase War Bonds which, cost $17.50 and were worth $25.00 at maturity ten years later. War heroes and movie stars went coast-to-coast selling war bonds to the people of the nation. It was considered a patriotic duty to buy them and provided a way for the American people to loan their government the money needed to finance the war. This they did, for by 1945, 85,000,000 people owned war bonds.

By the time I had graduated from high school, full employment had put an end to the depression as we knew it. Farmers had prospered and the nation had rallied. The hard times of the thirties had faded into history. I was 18 years old and ready to face adulthood armed with little but the ego of youth.

CAREER LAUNCH

1944-1945

I had no desire to go to college after I graduated from high school. Wanting to take the quickest route possible to gainful employment, I chose to attend Nettleton Commercial College in Sioux Falls, South Dakota where I registered for a course in business machines. A student job busing dishes in a little tea room called The Treasure Cove paid very little but I earned my noon meal by working an hour and a half a day. Most of the waitresses were the wives of servicemen stationed at the Air Base near Sioux Falls and appeared to be experienced waitresses. The manager was a real barracuda. This was before the day of sharing tips, as is done in this day and time and if I so much as glanced at a tip, a waitress would let me know that I had no right to look at her money!

While in Sioux Falls, I met two girls who became my dear friends; both had great aptitude for business, which I did not. They were studying to be secretaries and were excellent typists. I was learning the Monroe calculator/comptometer, a weird machine that pre-dated the computer or digital calculator. After punching in the numbers, a little hand crank on the right end of the bar was twisted around and around until the calculation was completed. Within fifteen years, comptometers were hopelessly out of date and I would be essentially unemployable in the business machine sense, but an eighteen-year-old in a hurry to take a job and savor life doesn't worry about the future.

My friend, Virginia, and I rented a room from an elderly couple who was very nice to us. Their other renters were a Jewish couple who had escaped from Hitler's Germany. The young husband was in the Army, stationed at the local Air Base and his wife seemed unwilling to discuss anything about her life, so I learned very little about them.

I corresponded with everyone I knew who was in military service and wrote letters every evening. It was not unusual for me to receive eight to ten letters in a single day from friends and acquaintances in the service. I felt it my patriotic duty to write to everyone I knew and some I didn't.

Razor blades were one of the commodities in short supply during the war years. Our landlord had apparently saved up a few in advance of his need for them and he stored them in the medicine chest in the bathroom that we shared with him and his wife. My legs didn't know there was a war on and shaving them became a challenge during this time. And I did a very bad thing. I would carefully unwrap one of my landlord's razor blades, quickly shave my legs, replace the razor blade in its wrapper and return it to his little reserve pile. What a luxury it was for me to use a good razor blade! What a problem it must have been for him to get a good shave! I am sure he blamed the poor quality of his blades on the war. I have always felt bad about this naughty thing that I did.

There was a large army air base near Sioux Falls and the city was teeming with servicemen. During my time at Nettleton Commercial College, the opportunities to date were endless. I had enough excitement in my life, dancing in the ballrooms and the local USO, to make practicing my business skills difficult. One Saturday night at the big Arkota Ballroom, Gene Krupa, the famous drummer, was playing as a member of the orchestra. I remember one of the G.I.s saying he was out of his skull, zonked or something. I didn't know what he meant by that statement, but I do remember that Krupa looked "transported," for sure. Servicemen in uniform who had formerly been professional musicians would take turns playing with the band to the wild cheers of the G.I.s in attendance. The big dance bands would come through on a regular basis, but I do not recall whose band was playing that evening when Gene Krupa was playing the drums. He had his own band after the war.

I finished my courses in late September and returned home to decide what I would do and where I would go. With the ability to operate a Monroe calculator, I knew somewhere there was a real need for someone with my fine skill. I jest.

My training completed, I visited a classmate in Sioux City and went to a recruiting office where I was interviewed for a position at Badger Ordnance Works, a subsidiary of Dupont, in Baraboo, Wisconsin. It all sounded great to me and I agreed to sign on with the company. My parents didn't think much of the idea, but my mind was made up. My dad took me to the train station and I headed off to Madison and thence by bus to Baraboo, Wisconsin.

Many years later my dad told me that when he put me on the train and watched his eighteen-year-old daughter going off so far away by herself, it broke his heart. He said he cried all the way home and crying was out of character for my dad. The memory saddens me to this day.

Baraboo, Wisconsin was a well-known summer resort before the war and was the summer headquarters of the Barnum and Bailey Circus. But on my arrival, all I saw was a vast expanse of grim low buildings of temporary construction that seemed to stretch to the horizon. The plant manufactured explosives….gunpowder. Outside the entrance were countless barracks type buildings where many of the workers lived. I was assigned to the purchasing department, which was on the periphery of the main manufacturing area. The work force was made up of draft rejects, older men, spinsters and middle-aged men with too many domestic responsibilities to be eligible for the draft. So much for my romantic job out in the exciting world of commerce.

The atmosphere was rough and tumble, but I met a dear and wonderful girl, Darline, and we shared a room in the Women's Barracks at the site. She loved to dance and the two of us did a lot of it. The Barracks had typical communal bathing facilities and it was the first time I had ever experienced taking a shower with other women present. This was most uncomfortable for me, but I gradually became accustomed to it.

Leaning over my "business machine" one day, I overheard the man sitting at the desk next to mine answer his ringing telephone, then heard him say in a very matter of fact voice, "call the fire department." I asked him what that was all about, and without raising his head from his work, he answered, "Oh some guy called to say that the milling house was on fire." This struck me as funny, since a fire in a gunpowder factory should warrant more of a reaction than that.

By the time spring arrived I was homesick and wanted to go home and leave Wisconsin forever. Easier said than done. To keep a stable work force in place during the war, the government put a freeze on some jobs, most especially in the production of war materials. Once in the job, it was difficult to move to another. What better material for conducting a war than gunpowder? However, I was determined to leave that dead-end job and those dead-end people and go back to South Dakota. I do not remember how I finagled permission to leave my job, but I did. After eight months I was eager to leave Baraboo having never seen the beautiful nearby Wisconsin Dells in their summer glory. Still haven't. Maybe I will go there someday.

I had a wonderful visit at home, but grew fiddle-footed and began to think about leaving again. This time I decided to go visit a boyfriend who was stationed in Jacksonville, Florida. I am sure my parents disapproved, but my mom always said she hoped I had enough sense to take care of myself and be a good girl. What a foolish young girl I was. Mom and Dad drove me to Sioux City to the train and I remember looking out the window at them standing in the station waving to me as the train pulled away, and my heart ached. I asked myself, why am I doing this? How can I leave those wonderful people that I love so much. Oh, but I was determined to leave and live the exciting life. So far the excitement had eluded me.

The train that took me south and east was packed with servicemen and their wives, the windows were kept open, no air conditioning, the train burned coal or wood, so we were all covered with black cinders and soot before the train had gone very far. My boyfriend met me at the station and we celebrated my arrival with a big breakfast in a nice restaurant. I ordered bacon and eggs and my plate came back with what looked like rice piled beside my eggs and bacon. My thought: rice for breakfast, now that's a new one! It was my introduction to grits. Seeing my dismay, the waitress said if I would try butter, salt and pepper on the grits that I would learn to like them. I thought they tasted terrible, but I learned to love grits in due time, still do.

Jacksonville's climate was warm and humid, the food was fried and tasty and the people were black and white. The city had a large number of black residents, and having lived in the homogeneous Midwest, I had never seen many black people. Jim Crow rules were still the law of the land in the South and there were separate facilities for blacks and whites: separate drinking fountains, restrooms, eating areas, theater seats and public transportation. This seemed very strange to me.

After a few days, I decided the boyfriend was not very dear to me and any chance of a meaningful relationship was non-existent. I found the Florida climate very pleasing and decided to stay and look for gainful employment. The demand for comptometer operators was not great. I took an office job with an Auto Parts Company and received a wage of $1.25 an hour, the same as I had earned in Wisconsin. The owner sat in the office and tapped his pencil all day, the office manager was an older woman who hustled, bustled and rattled the papers on her desk and the other clerk and I worked as best we knew how.

The owner of the business had a policy of hiring ex-convicts in the shop area downstairs below the office. They were an assortment of tough looking men with a multitude of tattoos. They seemed to work hard and never gave us any trouble. Labor was scarce in 1945 and by hiring people who had prison records he assured himself of a good source of labor. Perhaps he was filled with the milk of human kindness. But on the other hand, if that were the case, why would he tap his pencil all day and drive me to distraction.

The other clerk in the office was my age and we became good friends. She invited me to have dinner with her family one Friday evening and it was a wonderful experience. Her father wore a white linen suit and served the food from the head of the table. The table appointments and linens were very attractive and I was fascinated

105

and impressed by the whole scene, which was so different from the way meals were served in our home.

It was the first time I had ever tasted avocado, didn't like them then, but love them now. When dinner was over, the father folded his damask napkin, placed it back into the napkin ring, leaned over, grabbed a corner of the white tablecloth and wiped his mouth on it. So much for gentility.

I didn't stay with this job very long. I applied for and was accepted for a position in the payroll department of National Airlines. A man named Baker owned the airline outright, and he ran a tight ship. I had originally thought I could do a lateral transfer and become a stewardess with National Airlines, but to my dismay I learned there was a company policy against that, so I stayed on in the payroll department. I had a wonderful little, bald-headed, cigar smoking boss named Harry Peck and I treasure his memory. In later years, National Airlines merged with larger carriers and eventually ceased to exist.

At this time in 1945, I was renting a room from a Jewish woman. She referred to her son as "my son, the dentist." He was in the Navy and away, so she rented out her extra bedroom. She was a nice, Jewish lady who asked me why I never turned my clothes inside out before hanging them in the closet. That was a new one for me to ponder. After a few months, she received word that her "son, the dentist" was being transferred to Jacksonville Naval Air Station and would be coming home, so I had to move to other lodgings. I know she didn't want her son dating a non-Jewish girl, but after his return we did go out a few times. He was a very nice man, and I don't think he ever told his mom, for he was very devoted to her.

I rented a room for a very short time from a couple that were about 30 years old, at 19 I thought they seemed quite mature. The husband was in the Navy and his wife was not a happy camper. She had a bookcase full of bestseller books lined up in their pristine book jackets. I wanted to read them all! But she told me I couldn't read her books because the book covers would get worn looking. Even at my tender age, I couldn't understand anyone who wouldn't share a book. Books are written to be shared.

Soon after that I rented a room from a wonderful woman, whose 14-year-old daughter was delightful company. I loved living with them. I continued my extensive correspondence with people whom I knew in the military, and spent most of my evenings writing letters and reading every book I could beg or borrow. The mail was delivered twice a day and stamps cost 3 cents.

Housing was scarce during those times, and because it was the patriotic thing to do during wartime, anyone who had an empty bedroom would rent it out to help fill the need. I was making $1.35 an hour and after paying rent, transportation and food, there was little left for the pretty clothes I yearned for. Charge cards had come into use, but I didn't own one. Some of my girl friends had credit cards and were so in debt they had nothing left over from their paychecks. One month when I had over spent, I remember living on raw carrots and donuts, the cheap kind that come in a box. It is a wonder I didn't develop a deficiency disease.

To save gasoline most people willingly shared a taxi, and one evening I caught a cab that already contained two people and the driver stopped to pick up a fourth rider. I was headed downtown to do some Christmas shopping. The man next to me kept shifting his weight and I remember wishing he would make up his mind how he wanted to sit. Alas, I was the last one out of the cab and when I went to pay the cab driver, my wallet was gone. The guy who couldn't get comfortable had snatched my wallet, which contained all the money I had in the world. He was also long since out of sight. The cab driver felt so sorry for me he made it a free ride. I walked all the way home, about two miles, and fell across my bed and cried my eyes out. My family did not approve of making long distance telephone calls unless there was an emergency, we kept in touch by writing long and frequent letters. But I decided this was emergency enough and I called home and told them my sad dilemma. Christmas was coming on and my Christmas money was gone! Mom asked how much I had lost, and she said she would send me that amount, which was $90.00. In the meantime I was penniless until payday and had to borrow $5.00 to keep body and soul together.

I discovered early on, that I couldn't date during the week. I needed a full eight hours sleep every night in order to do my work at the office, so dating was a weekend activity. I began to wonder if I would ever meet a really worthwhile guy that I would enjoy dating.

One fellow was a naval officer with movie star looks, a dead ringer for Robert Taylor, but after a couple dates I learned he was married. The cad! Then there was the nice army Lieutenant who was a college football player before the war and now wanted to study for the priesthood. Gad ! Then there was the fellow I met through a friend who was a delight to be around; he had a wacky sense of humor and made me laugh. I thought this is a gem. When he asked me out on a date, he was the most dour, sober-sided stick-in-the-mud I had ever met. Then of course there was the one with dandruff on his shoulders, and the pilot who wanted to sit and recite poetry all evening. I rejected them all. I felt that I would rather become a nun than keep company with any of these fellows.

There were soldiers, sailors and airmen by the thousands stationed in and around Jacksonville. It was acceptable during these war years for women's organizations to supervise the recruitment of young women, who could furnish suitable character references, to serve as hostesses at dances, USO and Officer's Clubs. I applied, was interviewed and accepted as a hostess for the Women's Club dances and also at the downtown Officer's Club. There was a rule that hostesses could not leave the club with anyone they had met on the premises, but that rule was broken on a regular basis. This sounds bizarre in light of present day customs, but was very acceptable during that period in time.

The war was winding down. Being insulated by two oceans we were spared disastrous bombings such as those that had flattened the major cities of Europe. The Battle of the Bulge, the last big gamble of the German army in December of 1944, had been the turning point of the war in Europe. With great loss of life on both sides, by May, 1945 the German army was defeated, Hitler was dead and the war in Europe was over. VE Day served as justification for national celebration.

Earlier in the war, in a pique of national sour-grapes over having so many American soldiers on their soil all of whom were young, virile and looking for dates, the British had coined the phrase: OVER PAID, OVER SEXED AND OVER HERE! Not to be outdone, the

American response to the British was: UNDER SEXED, UNDER PAID AND UNDER IKE! (General Eisenhower, popularly known as Ike, was Supreme Allied Commander of the European Theater of Operations.)

I am thankful that President Truman had the courage to make the awesome decision to drop the atomic bomb on Hiroshima and Nagasaki in August of 1945, for it brought an end to the war with the Japanese in the Pacific, ultimately saving many more lives than it cost. VJ Day on August 14, 1945 marked the surrender of Japan and the end of the war.

I was in downtown Jacksonville when the news hit and there was a celebration unparalleled by any other. The entire town turned out, the downtown streets were packed with towns-people and servicemen celebrating the news. People climbed the light poles, hung out of upper story windows and everyone was dancing, hugging and kissing each other. Throughout the land, the church bells tolled, sirens rang out in joyful celebration and people whispered prayers of thankfulness that the war was over and fathers, husbands, sons and daughters who had survived the war would be coming home.

Peace! How sweet it was to know we were at peace! The war had changed the basic social and economic structure of our country and those who lived through the World War II experience instinctively understood, that many ideas, habits, behaviors and customs common to prewar America would be forever changed, and in some cases, irretrievably lost amidst the turmoil and the challenges of the war years.

During the few short years of World War II, the national mobilization of millions of men and the machines to support them was a true phenomenon in the history of mankind. The young men who served, and the families who supported them truly earned their special niche in the history of this nation.

The one blot on an otherwise exemplary national effort was the United States Senate voting overwhelmingly and without any constitutional justification to send west coast Japanese-Americans to ten designated rather primitive internment camps until the end of the war with Japan.

COURTSHIP AND MARRIAGE

1945-1946

While attending a dance at the Jacksonville Women's Club in December of 1945, I noticed a tall young man from across the ballroom; to my Nordic eye he looked very Norwegian. Our paths did not cross that evening. The following week I was doing my hostess bit at the downtown Jacksonville Officer's Club and who should walk in the door, but "the Norwegian" I had seen the previous week. This club was small and he eventually asked me to dance. Later in the evening, he invited me out to dinner, couching the invitation in Navy terms he said, "Why don't we chow-down on Friday evening." I accepted the invitation.

This tall, blond, blue-eyed man impressed me and oddly, I took immediate notice of his hands which were strong, long-fingered with nicely shaped nails. It was strange that I should even notice his hands, except I had met men in the past whose hands were a real turn-off. I was tall, so was he and I liked the way we fit when we danced or stood close together. So much for the frivolous! In Navy terms, I guess one could say I liked the cut of his jib. He must have liked the cut of mine, as well, for we started to date several times a week from that night onward.

Norman's ship, the USS PC 782, had returned from duty in the Aleutians and was berthed at Green Cove Springs, a sizable estuary on the St. Johns River. His ship along with hundreds of other gray-toned ships-of-war were returning from their overseas duty stations still carrying their equipment of destruction, and their crews of battle trained young men now blessedly headed home. To the ships' crews, home meant resuming their interrupted lives, returning to college, to jobs and to families who had been left behind. Tied in multiples of three and four adjacent to their mother ships, the long lines of war ships and their tenders made an awesome sight.

The crews aboard were headed for renewal and repair of their interrupted lives, and the ships were headed for mothball fleets in the various coastal harbors of the country where they would continue to wait for disposal or dispersal. Many would be scrapped, some would become Reserve Training ships, but as vessels of war they had served their time, and for most, their days of glory and usefulness were over. Ours was now a nation at peace and World War II was history.

The men from these countless war ships were gradually, systematically discharged from service to find their niche within their home communities. With their wartime exposure to widened horizons, many would strike out on their own to seek their unique destinies. For countless thousands, the U.S. Government G. I. Bill provided an opportunity to attend college that didn't exist for them before the war. They jumped at the opportunity of an affordable education and fell easily into their role as one of the most productive generations in our nation's history.

All servicemen were mustered out of service on a point basis; longevity, war injuries or family responsibilities all counted toward an early discharge. Waiting for the day when their name would rise to the top of the list proved to be frustrating, and their days were spent aboard their assigned ship on make-work details, preparing the ship for its retirement from active service.

Norman's commanding officer had the required points to be discharged and Norman was designated Captain of the USS PC 782. During this time he had found a second-hand car (there were no other kind at that time) a Dodge sedan with "fluid drive," which was the forerunner of the automatic transmission. He enjoyed his car and he put it to good use taking me out each and every time he could get away from the ship.

In April of 1946 Norman received orders to take the ship to Charleston, South Carolina for engine repair. He then proceeded on to the Brooklyn Navy Yard for more repair on the blower engines, which had been a constant source of trouble. He felt the repair was inadequate, but received orders to get underway and head for Boston in spite of his stated concerns. He filed a "sailing under protest" document, but sail they did for Boston, where another navy yard stopover was required for the same reason as before.

From the Boston Naval Yard they headed for Nova Scotia; their destination was Duluth, Minnesota via the St. Lawrence Seaway and Chicago. It was very foggy near Martha's Vineyard and following behind the USS PC 782 was the second ship in the convoy, the sister-ship, USS PC 781, which was headed for decommissioning. Her Captain was the senior officer and by Navy policy should have led the convoy. However, their radar was out and they were experiencing mechanical failures with their blower engines, so it was Norman's ship that was designated to lead the convoy through the fog.

Along this foggy route up the northeastern coastline, the convoy regrettably hit countless lobster trap buoys, which were not visible in the fog. With the buoys severed from the lobster trap below, Norman knew there would be some unhappy lobster fishermen come daybreak and even unhappier lobsters. The convoy headed up the Gut of Canso, on to the entrance of the St. Lawrence Seaway by way of Quebec, Montreal, through the Welland Canal and on to Chicago.

During this time, I continued to work for National Airlines until we were notified that the company was moving its headquarters to Miami, Florida. Everyone was invited to make the move, and if agreed to, we would be housed for two weeks at the McFadden-Deauville Hotel on Miami Beach until permanent housing could be obtained.

Three of my working colleagues and I agreed to make the transfer to Miami and thoroughly enjoyed the two-week stint at the McFadden-Deauville, living the good life. But reality set in and the three of us found living quarters with a family in a residential area of Miami. It was a long bus ride to work but we were employed at the same place so it turned out all right. If we came home late at night the city bus driver would drive us home, which was a two-block detour from his scheduled route.

Before Norman left Jacksonville in early April, we had an understanding that we would be married. He was a persistent suitor and kept saying, "we make sense together." Later when we would have disagreements I would wonder what had happened to all that sense that we were supposed to be making together!

In June of 1946 he sent me a diamond ring that had belonged to his mother. It was a beautiful stone in a basket setting made of white gold and while he was in Boston, he found a wedding band that complimented the antique setting of the engagement ring. We planned to be married in mid-August.

My girl friends at work were helpful in planning our wedding. My mom sent my sister's wedding dress and veil, and my brother, who was stationed at MacDill Field at Tampa, Florida agreed to drive down and escort me down the aisle. I cannot recall the reason that my folks could not attend the wedding, but it saddened me that they weren't there. There had been a previous decision about the inadvisability of making the trek to South Dakota to be married in Brule Creek Church. Mom and Dad sent us money to help defray expenses of the wedding and Norman paid a generous amount of the expenses, as well.

When the USS PC 782 docked at the Navy Pier in Chicago, the pier no longer held the countless ships-of-war customarily tied up along the vast expanse of berths; oddly the only ship to dock at that time, was the 782. Norman had spent twenty-seven months aboard this ship, which included his time in the Aleutian Islands during the war. He had arrived on board as the most junior commissioned officer and with time and attrition had served in all positions from Commissary Officer to Executive Officer. During his last seven months aboard, he served as her Commanding Officer. As her Captain he had taken the ship up the East Coast for repairs at three Naval Yards, to Nova Scotia, through the St. Lawrence Seaway to Chicago and he was eager to pass command to a new skipper, request leave, head for Florida and get married.

He turned over command to a naval officer who had special reasons for wanting to stay in Chicago, Norman was then free to request new orders or discharge from the Navy. Deciding against discharge, Norman opted to accept a Regular Navy Commission.

This ensured us a decent living, which at the time seemed more appealing than going back to school and trying to live on the G.I. Bill.

We were married August 18, 1946 in the Opalocka Naval Air Station Chapel near Miami; Norman was 23 and I was 20 years of age. The Chaplain performed a traditional Presbyterian wedding service. Leverne escorted me down the aisle, LaVonne was a bridesmaid and my dear friend, Grace Haile, was my maid of honor. Norman's brother, Richard, newly discharged from the Marine Corps, hitchhiked from Texas to be his brother's best man. He bought a blue suit for which he paid $22.00 and dressed in civilian clothes, he looked very dapper and so very young to be a veteran of the Marine Corps.

Since Norman was staying at the Naval Air Station in the Bachelor Officers Quarters, on the day of our wedding Richard was given the use of the car. He was to collect my personal belongings and me and drive to the florist to pick up the flowers en route to the Naval Chapel. I was unaware, and he didn't admit, that he had no previous experience driving an automobile. My bags were packed, my wedding dress was spread out across the back seat of the car and we headed for downtown Miami to the florist shop.

Pulling away from the curb into traffic, Richard drove into the path of an on coming car. Crash! The elderly man driving the other car was in an angry state, spouting all manner of accusations, all of them quite true. It certainly was our fault. A policeman drove up, took out his little pad and began to take statements. The little old man was full of statements. Richard admitted he was newly released from the Marine Corps and taking his brother's fiancé to the Naval Chapel to be married. I looked crestfallen and pointed to the back seat strewn with my wedding finery. Our combined stories would have melted a heart of stone. The policeman did what few do, he showed real concern and compassion for the situation. He said if we would exchange addresses he would let us go, since I continued to say, I was going to be late for my wedding. So with the policeman's blessing we took off for the Naval Air Station, leaving the couple in the other car with nothing but an address. Our car had sustained some damage, things were knocked loose in the rear end and it rattled as we made our way to the chapel. I felt guilt about that play for sympathy, but it is gradually tapering off after 57 years.

As I walked into the chapel I saw Norman walking briskly down the street in the opposite direction, obviously in a hurry to get somewhere. That can be a disconcerting sight to a bride about to enter a chapel to be married. When the men were waiting for my arrival, Richard couldn't find the ring. He searched his pockets, said it was gone and Norman headed back to the B.O.Q. to see if it had been left there. Richard's new suit had a little watch pocket just below the belt, and he had placed the ring there and had forgotten that he had that civilian pocket. They found the ring in time for the ceremony to begin as scheduled.

Our wedding was simple but pretty. We had our reception at the Officer's Club and the guests were my friends from work, my boss and his family and my landlady and her daughter. The Commanding Officer of the base loaned his Navy sword for the ceremony of cutting the cake. After all the trouble of borrowing the sword, in the wedding pictures it is obscured and it appears as though we are cutting the wedding cake with a butcher knife.

Photographic film was hard to come by, but we convinced an Associated Press photographer we had met in a camera shop to come out and take our wedding pictures...for a price. The post war production of peacetime goods was not yet a reality and there were still many shortages. People were still using their food ration books on some items such as sugar.

As we drove away after the wedding and reception, the car was making a noticeable racket and Norman wondered what it could be. He thought someone had tied tin cans to our back bumper, but we didn't need any tin cans, we had rattles a-plenty. He took the news of the traffic incident rather well as I remember.

We drove to the Ritz Carlton on Miami Beach, where we were to begin our honeymoon. My going-away costume was a black dress, black pumps, a hat made entirely of blue feathers. And my gloves matched my hat. (awrg!) Norman wore his summer dress whites and I must say he looked very elegant in his uniform. At the age of 81, his uniform still fits; I might add that my dress doesn't !

On the beach the next day, we ran into Richard and a Marine buddy imbibing in spirits at a beach bar. Since we were headed up to Jacksonville the next day, we asked him to ride along with us. He was headed for Atlanta and enrollment at Georgia Tech University where he had taken three years of undergraduate study before being called to active duty in the Marine Corps.

We were still officially on leave and we headed for Jacksonville, where Norman had surgery at the U.S. Naval Air Station to repair a deviated septum in his nose. He couldn't breathe well through his nose and always ran out of breath when he kissed me.

It was about this time that we had our first spat. Norman raised his voice at me and we said unkind things to each other. Having never heard my parents quarrel, I thought, "Well, there goes the marriage! We have been married for three weeks and we're headed for the divorce court. This will be such an embarrassment to my family."

Up until that time, I didn't know that the Texas Fladoses were quite at home with spats and tended to say what came into their mind, keeping it all up front, then forgetting it ever happened. It was the forgetting that it ever happened that I found difficult to manage. As time went by, I gradually learned to make a real Flados out of myself and could spat with the best.

We rented a room from the same family I had lived with as a single girl before I left Jacksonville. They were lovely to us and we stayed there until Norman received orders to report to Cape May, New Jersey for duty on the USS PCCE (R) 852.

Norman had saved extra leave time so we took off for Texas in our car to visit his family in Nocona. His family was very gracious to me and immediately made to feel welcome. Norman's mother had died of cancer in May of 1945 while Norman was overseas and by the time the Red Cross was able to contact him, her funeral had been held. I never knew my mother-in-law but Norman's aunts told me many things about his mother. They described her as a wonderful, caring person whom everyone respected, and they regretted that I would never know her.

Norman's grandparents had emigrated from Norway but my immediate observation of the Flados family convinced me that they didn't know squat about how to act like Norwegians. I know how to act like a Norwegian, they didn't have a clue. They had been the only Norwegian family in a town made up of Irish and Italians and that is how they acted. I called them the laughing and crying Fladoses. They were hugging, kissing, stroking, crying, laughing or fussing all the time. Very non-Norsk. But they were all gifted with a sense of humor and a willingness to laugh so I found them very appealing. Plus they were marvelous cooks! In subsequent visits with his aunts and uncles I learned how to give a Southern spin to my cooking.

We stayed with his father in the family home; he was so kind and made me feel thoroughly welcomed into the family. After a week we headed back to Jacksonville and prepared for our move to Cape May, New Jersey. We could easily get all our worldly goods in our car, so the move was not very daunting.

WEDDING AT OPALOCKA NAVAL AIR STATION

118

THE NAVY YEARS

1946-1950

Norman received orders from the First Naval District to report for duty on the USS PCE(R) 852, a converted rescue vessel now a research ship berthed at Cape May, New Jersey. On the first week in October of 1946, we headed north from Jacksonville up through the Carolinas and traveled the Skyline Drive through the mountains of Virginia. It was a lovely time of year and the leaves were turning gloriously red and yellow. Motels were scarce, so we stayed in Tourist Homes, which were private residences turned into places for travelers to spend the night. Unable to find a suitable hotel room when we arrived in Philadelphia, we ended up in a spooky place called the York Hotel, which had no locks on the doors.

We headed down the eastern shore past Atlantic City to Cape May, New Jersey where we rented a little apartment from a kindly lady who allowed Norman to lay some badly needed new linoleum on the kitchen floor. We did a good job of it. Norman demonstrated that he was able to fix anything that was in disrepair. A marvelous quality in a husband, I thought.

The first time I mopped the floor I put down newspapers so there would be no tracking. Norman came home and asked why there were newspapers all over the floor. When I told him it was to keep the floor clean he made it very clear, he wasn't a cat and that I should disabuse myself of that practice. Where I got that idea, I will never know. I only did it once!

The ship was fitted out to test experimental Nancy gear (infra red) and operated at night in the Channel between New Jersey and Delaware. I had ample time to read and learn to like my own company, an important thing for a navy wife to learn.

It was at this time that I realized I was an uninformed person. So I subscribed to Time Magazine and read it cover to cover each and every week. I had read most of the national best sellers, but I knew very little about topical events. Fifty-seven years later I am still reading Time Magazine, trying to stay current with all aspects of the news.

Within six weeks of our arrival, the Naval Base was being converted into a Coast Guard Station and the Navy transferred the USS PCE(R) 852 and her sister ship, the USS Calao, to Fort Lewis near Rehoboth Beach, Delaware. We had to leave our pretty little apartment and move across the channel to Rehoboth Beach, which wasn't far as the sea birds fly but the land route involved traveling up the length of New Jersey and then returning down the opposite shoreline.

We rented a spacious cottage that was the summer home of people who lived inland. It was beautifully furnished, and I loved it. Norman spent much of his time at sea during weeknights so I was alone a great deal. The house had a basement furnace that required stoking with coal during the cold winter months. I would stay up late at night reading and listening to the radio; one of my favorite songs was Elmo Tanner whistling "Heartaches." Before I went to sleep on cold nights I would go to the basement to stoke and "bank" the furnace fires so it would produce heat all night. (To "bank" a furnace, the coal is arranged in a manner that makes it burn more slowly.) We made friends among the Army contingent that was stationed at Camp Miles/Fort Lewis and Navy personnel were welcome to use their Officers Club.

One of the naval officers stationed with us had been a prisoner of the Japanese for over 4 years after the USS Houston was sunk in the Pacific. He had been married before the war but as a Japanese POW he was unable to notify his wife that he was alive, and after a certain period of time he was designated as "lost at sea." After 2 years, she remarried and had a child. When Jerry arrived back from the

POW camps of Japan, he found his wife remarried and the mother of a child, which resulted in Jerry's marriage being annulled. At parties, he would be pleasant and behave quite normally until after the second drink, then he would become very quiet and turn aside as the tears ran, unchecked, down his cheeks. We felt bad for him and so inadequate for being unable to ease his hurt. The sight of him silently crying among our group of young, boisterous, happy people is a memory I will never forget.

Our home had become a gathering place and the Project Naval Engineer was a frequent guest. I had stayed in touch with a former roommate from my Miami days, who had returned to her home in New York City. Peggy loved to dance, in fact, on request she would do an Irish jig. Our bachelor engineer friend also liked to dance, so we invited Peggy for a weekend visit and we introduced them. After her second visit, we knew we had a match. They fell in love before our eyes and were married a year later. They had two fine sons and retired to the Boston area.

Before they were married, Peggy asked me if she should be concerned about her fiancé's drinking. He drank every evening, but we had never seen him intoxicated during the time we knew him. After 25 years of marriage they were divorced mainly because of his alcoholism and he died at too young an age as a result of his habit. Peg lived and worked in Germany and after retiring to Boston continued to dance. She was eighty years old when her dance club was asked to give an exhibition at a local mall. After the exhibition, Peggy sat down on a bench near the stage and died of a heart attack. Dear sweet, smiling Peggy O'Reilly who loved to dance, died dancing.

During our time in Rehoboth Beach, Delaware, we welcomed in the year of 1947 and enjoyed our lives to the fullest. Across the street from us lived an Army Major and his wife both of whom were alcoholics. What an eye opener that was. Shirley had been a nightclub entertainer and in her earlier career days had plugged songs for Irving Berlin, who at that time was an unknown songwriter in Chicago. She would regale me with tales of famous saloon singers she had met in the twenties and thirties. She had great respect for Al Capone, the gangster, who during the early thirties had financed soup kitchens in Chicago that fed the poor and unemployed. She always maintained she had seen his good side. When he was dying in Florida of the advanced stages of syphilis she wired him flowers, white roses as I remember.

Harp, her husband, was from Boston and still retained traces of an Irish accent. He was a rough and ready, up-from-the-ranks officer respected by his men, but not your typical career army man.

Shirley told me she had met Harp during the thirties in Kelly's Bar in Panama City, Panama. He and his army buddies would come into Kelly's to hear her sing. One night after a performance, he asked her to meet him at the Enlisted Men's Club at Fort Amador in the Canal Zone where he was stationed. She asked, "How will I find you?" He told her to go to the Entrance Gate of Fort Amador and notify the guard on duty that she was there to visit "the lowest damn private in the United States Army." He said the guard would know who to call, and that he would come to the gate and pick her up.

That is exactly what she did. She went to the Army Base Entrance of Fort Amador and told the guard she was there to "visit the lowest damn private in the United States Army." The guard's immediate response was, "Oh you must mean Harp Flaherty, wait here, I will call him!"

They were married, had no children, and by the time we knew them they were both alcoholics but never drank at the same time. She called it, "Up the Pole" (sober) or "Down the Pole" (drunk). When Harp was "Down the Pole," she stayed sober and took care of him. When he was totally "Down the Pole," she would feed him raw hamburger and coffee to sober him up; he would then begin a period of total abstinence. Now it was her turn; she would start drinking wine, and carried chocolates in her pocket to kill the taste after each drink. She would drink until she was stuporous, in bed, and in need of Harp's tender care until she sobered up. In a short while it was his turn again, and so it went.

These bouts took days before the stuporous phase took over. During the early stages of her binges, she did some interesting things. One day as I was standing by the front gate, she walked across the street, dragging her beautiful full-length fur coat behind her. She told me I was young and pretty and that I should have her beautiful coat, because she was no longer pretty and seldom wore it. I had seen pictures of Shirley taken during her time as an entertainer and she was very beautiful with green eyes and auburn hair. I told her I could not accept the coat, she insisted, and threw it on the ground at my feet, turned and walked back home.

I picked it up and ran my fingers through the beautiful fur, carried it into the house and hung it in my closet. About nine in the morning four days later, in a sober moment, she walked in, Shirley seldom knocked, and said, "Marge, did I leave my fur coat over here?" I said, "No, Shirley, you gave it to me, in fact you insisted I take it."

She said, "Now Marge, you know how I am when I'm 'Down the Pole'!" I laughed and went to my closet and returned the coat to her.

One night at about 2:30 A.M. when Norman and I were in bed asleep, we heard the front door slam, (this was before the days when people locked their doors) and then a tromp, tromp through the living room and into our bedroom. Shirley plopped down on our bed, and in her hands she had an enormous bowl filled to the brim with a picture book beautiful vegetable salad. It would have served 15 to 20 people. She said, "Here, I want you to have this!" We told her we would deal with it in the morning. She turned and left, slamming the door behind her, carrying the salad back to her house.

One Sunday afternoon when there were several Navy friends at our home, the Base Commanding Officer and his lady made a courtesy call on us. The tradition of courtesy calls in the military was still maintained by the regulars. The Colonel was Harp's Commanding Officer and knew of Harp and Shirley's shortcomings but this didn't make it any easier to deal with. During their visit, Shirley made an appearance, she was most definitely "Down the Pole" and true to form made a grand social blunder. The Commanding Officer of the USS PCE(R) 852, a bit of a rogue in his own right, was visiting with us that afternoon and Shirley walked in front of him, then swung around and accused him of "goosing" her "in the ass." What a mess! The Colonel's lady quickly began yanking on her gloves, which was obviously a wifely signal to her husband to get ready to depart, fast! They hurriedly said their goodbyes and left. I walked Shirley back home while the guys sat there and died laughing. I am not so sure the Skipper was guiltless. It was during this period of my life that I began to understand that my upbringing was NOT typical!

In March of 1947 the ship was ordered to Charleston Navy Yard for re- refitting in preparation for continuing research with infra red at the Under Water Lab in New London, Connecticut. We were on the move again. We had rented our cottage totally furnished, and our personal belongings were meager enough that I could pack a box and store it with Shirley and Harp during our absence.

The ship took off for Charleston, South Carolina and I headed, by train for South Dakota to visit my folks. During this visit I was given a bridal shower and received a collection of recipes from Mom's friends. I am still using many of them to this day.

About two weeks later, I met Norman back in Rehoboth Beach, collected what we had left with Shirley and Harp and we headed for Charleston, South Carolina. He had rented a one-room efficiency apartment on the Battery in the district where homes dated back to Revolutionary times. Our apartment was on the ground level of an old ante bellum mansion and we found it to be quite adequate for our five-week stay in Charleston.

Charleston was an interesting place and we did some touring but not as much as we should have, thinking back on it. Since the kitchen for the mansion was next door to our apartment, I would occasionally stop by and talk with the cook. She explained how after the food was cooked it was sent up on a dumbwaiter to the dining room, which was on the floor above our apartment. There was a row of buildings at a ninety-degree angle from the house that had once been stalls for horses, carriages and perhaps additional servants quarters; these were now car garages used by those who rented the apartments. Outside our door in a little courtyard to the rear of the house was a large circular fountain from where I could look up and see the massive chandelier in the dining room, the heavy drapes, the tall ceilings and wonder how it would be to live in surroundings like that.

The street venders walked up and down the alleys behind the mansion homes calling out what they had for sale that day. Black men pushed their carts along calling in their musical, high-pitched voices, "STRAWBERRIES, FRESH STRAWBERRIES," (or whatever else they had to sell) calling the words out in a long, sing-song-y wail. The cooks in their first floor kitchens would then go out and buy their produce. I wonder if that tradition is still in practice in Charleston.

Our landlord, a gruff man who wore white suits and a white Panama hat, made us aware that we were expected to keep our car in exactly the place assigned. He did not tolerate any deviation from his rules. The owners of the mansions on the Battery had created these living quarters during the War to help solve the desperate housing shortage experienced by service men and their families. As I write, I am sure they have long since been turned back into the very private residences they previously were. The old mansions along the Battery where we lived are now part of the Historic District of Charleston.

We did not spend one evening at home during the entire time we were in Charleston. Each evening we would drive out to the Naval Base, attend a 10-cent movie or eat dinner at the Officers Club. There was an elegant restaurant built out over the water on the Battery and one Sunday we splurged and had dinner there. A dignified, gray-haired, black waiter with a linen towel draped over his arm, offered us finger bowls after we finished eating, certainly a new experience for the both of us, but we used them, and tried to act as if we were quite accustomed to such elegance.

In May of 1947 both ships were sent to New London and continued to participate in research at the Under Water Sea Lab. We rented an apartment in a building owned by first generation Italians. They were good landlords and our apartment was attractive, however, they cooked with lots of garlic and the whole building reeked of Italian cooking.

It was necessary to test infra red equipment after dark and Norman would not arrive home until past midnight. In winter, he wore dress blues to work, including white shirt, tie and hat. The wool of his bridge coat and uniform always smelled of the sea and the ever-present ship's diesel oil, a navy scent I grew to love.

In the fall of 1947, Mom and Dad took an extensive motor trip to the eastern part of the country and visited us in New London;

they had, as yet, not met their new son-in-law. We toured them around and we enjoyed their visit. Before they left, they gave us a monetary gift of $200. Like impractical nitwits, we didn't buy anything useful with it, we purchased a big beautiful Zenith radio-phonograph console. The fact that we had no records and seldom enough money left over to buy any, was beside the point. We now had a big piece of furniture, but little else.

New London is an old town with narrow streets. The only chicken meat sold at the local grocery store, was undressed chicken; the kind that had to be butchered after you bought it, luckily I knew how to butcher a chicken. There were no super markets, as yet.

It was in the fall of 1947 that I decided I needed a sewing machine. My dear husband saw to it that I got one, post haste. For some strange reason, men gladly spend money they can ill-afford to buy their wives sewing machines; they would buy one even if they had to mortgage the family car. I think it is a throw back to the time when women would scrape the bear skins smooth, chewing on the hide to make it soft so she could use her little bone needle to sew fur clothing for him and the family. I know there is a primeval association there!

I had taken home economics but my sewing skills were minimal. After purchasing slate blue satin fabric and a dress pattern far too complicated for a beginner, I proceeded to sew myself a cocktail dress. It had drapes and folds, a low-cut square back and a "bustle," a forward fashion statement for that point in time. I didn't like the original look, so I ripped and adjusted and changed everything around and ended up with a garment that was quite smashing, if I must say so myself. I decided if a person could read, a person could sew, and sew I did. In later years I sewed most of what the children and I wore and some of the things Norman wore, as well. That portable Kenmore sewing machine was a good investment, and went wherever we went and I eventually gave it to my daughter who also learned to sew on it.

Norman applied for and was accepted for training at the Submarine School in Groton, Connecticut and classes were scheduled to begin in early January. We purchased a second-hand Chevrolet Club Coupe in good running order, and the purchase and financing of this car was our first experience with car payments and paying interest. How we hated those payments, which seemed to go on forever. We were usually "dead horse" with our navy wages and we hated that too. "Dead horse" is a Navy term used when one borrows against future salary. A portion of that advance is thereafter deducted from each month's paycheck until the "dead horse" debt is paid. In December, using some of Norman's remaining leave time, we drove home to South Dakota for Christmas and the rest of my family finally met my husband. It was wonderful being home for the holidays.

On the return trip we went by way of Olathe, Kansas to visit Norman's uncle Bill and family. We left from Olathe in a sleet storm and traveled from Kansas City to St. Louis on glare ice. Looking back, that seems pretty dumb. Our rush was that Norman had to report for duty in early January.

Driving through Pennsylvania in the middle of the night, we took a wrong turn and drove 120 miles out of our way up towards Bethlehem. More time lost. The Pennsylvania Turnpike was one of the first of its kind and we were glad to get on it and make up some lost time, although we found it weird to have to pay a toll for the privilege of driving on it. When we hit New York City we ran into the aftermath of a bad snowstorm and actually got stuck on the Merritt Parkway. A good Samaritan stopped and helped retrieve us from the snow banks and on we went, arriving in New London with little time to spare.

Norman reported at Submarine School in Groton, Connecticut in January of 1948, and began his training. We were issued base quarters and we packed up our belongings and moved across the Thames River to the Submarine Base, which would be our home for the next six months. The quarters were two story, two bedroom apartments and totally furnished except for dishes, pots and silverware.

All the submarine trainees lived on the Base and we made friends, some of whom we still have 55 years later. After completing six months of training, (graduating 7th in his class) and officially in the Submarine Service, Norman received orders to the Sea Owl (USS 405) berthed in the Panama Canal Zone. The Sea Owl was attached to a squadron of submarines that operated in the Caribbean.

The Navy packed us up in cruise boxes and shipped our personal effects, including our car, to Panama and, interestingly, we were assigned base quarters across the hallway from the same next-door neighbors we had at the Submarine Base in Connecticut.

After years of just-below-the-knee hemlines, Christian Dior made a radical fashion statement by lowering the hemlines to just above the ankle. It was hyped as "the New Look" and my clothes reflected the style of the day. Living a world away from the States, the Navy wives on the Submarine Base were curious to know to what extent the longer dresses had been accepted in the States since that style hadn't made it to their part of the world as yet.

Our Quarters on the Submarine Base were very spacious, nicely furnished, high off the ground and made of concrete blocks. Panama has a hot, tropical climate with two seasons, dry and wet. Our building had large, shuttered, screened windows without glass panes and they stayed open at all times. Heating equipment was never necessary except for the little heater in each closet that was supposed to prevent clothes and shoes from getting moldy, but it didn't. Mold was an on-going problem and anything black was particularly susceptible. We had the problem of a tiny insect, called a sand flea, getting in through the screens and biting us in the evenings. Many nights we sat on our legs to protect them from the sand fleas, but soon the screens collected just enough lint to keep them out.

I hired a local Panamanian girl to clean our house occasionally, and the first thing she did was brush the lint off the screens so we were back to sitting on our legs again. Our building was separated from pristine jungle, by a military fence and outside our windows, looking like miniature dinosaurs, we could see sizeable iguanas running about on their tall front legs. The locals ate them and would carry them dangling from a stick over one shoulder. One morning, I was washing some garments in the washtubs at ground level and sensed that I was not alone. To my chagrin, hanging upside down directly over my head was a two-toed sloth with his toes firmly wrapped around the water pipes. He must have weighed 40 pounds.

Norman's submarine operated at sea for 5 to 6 weeks at a time so I was alone for long periods. To pass the time during our husbands' absence, the wives would play bridge, visit, share mealtimes and spend time at the swimming pool. When we heard that the Boat was heading into port, we were all waiting on the dock for our husbands.

With a definite pecking order determined by the rank of one's spouse, social protocols were observed, including that of making a formal courtesy call on the Commandant and his lady and leaving one's calling cards on a silver tray in the foyer. These calls were never, but never, to last more than twenty minutes. Except for the separations, our Panama assignment was good duty.

We made a point to go to Kelly's Bar in Panama City a couple times. It was still a busy nightclub with singers and strippers who entertained the soldiers and sailors stationed in the Zone. I thought it probably hadn't changed much since the time that my friend, Shirley, had entertained there many years before the War.

The year of 1948 was coming to an end and I had sat at the pool on a regular basis getting a tan so I would look "bronzed" in my strapless evening dress at the New Year's Eve dance at the Officers Club. I found to my dismay, I do not "bronze," my Nordic skin just darkens a wee bit then lightens up almost immediately. What started out as a gala evening turned into a real tragedy. An officer on the USS Sea Robin was taken to the hospital in late afternoon diagnosed with bulbar polio and as news of his death spread throughout the Club, the party broke up. This officer had been a classmate of Norman's at Submarine School and those of us who knew him made our way to his living quarters to be with his wife. No one uttered the words "Happy New Year" that evening.

On New Year's Day Norman was on duty aboard the submarine. That afternoon the Squadron physician and his wife came to our quarters and told me that Norman had been taken off the ship and sent to Gorgas Hospital in the Zone, with a diagnosis of polio.

I remember my mind feeling blank and my reaction must have seemed unusual to my visitors. My old Norwegian upbringing clicked in big time, i.e. show no emotion, control your feelings and keep a calm exterior. This I did. They offered me a sedative and I wondered why, since I felt that I was totally in control of my emotions. The extent of his paralysis had not been fully determined,

129

but I was told his legs were affected and that he had very little feeling from the waist down. The stiff upper lip remained stiff.

He was in strict quarantine and the hospital was treating him in the customary fashion with hot wet packs to the lower body. The time soon came when I was told I could visit him from outside his window; that I could stand on a little, nearby knoll and they would roll him to the window so we could talk. This we did. I stood or sat on the grass and we visited. I could barely see him behind the thick screen.

Sensation in his left leg returned and his residual paralysis was in the hip and right leg. Since Norman was barely mobile, in preparation for his dismissal from the hospital, the Navy moved us to the Farfan quarters which were one-story dwellings. After all that time in the hospital my husband came home with six weeks of untrimmed hair, a thin body and a shaky pair of legs. We knew the Navy career was over. This seemed a crushing disappointment at the time, but there were no options other than returning to the States for rehabilitation and ultimately, discharge from the service.

After a few weeks, I took Norman to the Military Air Transport Terminal in the Zone and he boarded a military plane headed for Pensacola, Florida where his rehabilitations would begin. After the plane took off I went back into the terminal, found a quiet spot and for the first time, I cried my eyes out. I cried for my husband and his damaged leg, I cried for a lost Navy career and I cried for what might have been or should have been. I cried for the widow of the fellow officer who died and the other Navy wife from our squadron who had contracted polio in Philadelphia at the same time as those in Panama. I threw my Norwegian stoicism out the window and just bawled. Feeling better for having had the cry, I got up, drove home and set about preparing for my own return to the States.

About 2 weeks later and after arranging for our personal effects to be shipped, I followed him back to the States. I traveled by military air transport in a Globemaster C88, a very large plane with bucket seats along the sides. The plane was carrying military personnel and their dependents with a destination of Mobile, Alabama. It was a long trip; after droning on for hours we prepared for a landing in Mobile. Looking out the window, I saw very dark skies and rain.

130

The plane began to circle. I wondered why it was taking so long to reach the runway.

Our landing was rough and terrible, I felt the plane tipping or rolling, and I was hanging in my bucket seat. The lights had gone out and people were clinging to their seats and to each other. Strangely, there was no sound made by any of the passengers, even the infants and children aboard did not make a sound. I looked out at one point when we should have been on the ground but I could only see sky and wondered how that could be.

The plane had landed, skidded, slipped into deep mud at the side of the runway and did a ground loop of sorts before settling down, half on, half off the runway. The pilots came back and told us to be calm (we already were), that we would be removed from the plane as soon as possible, that the doors were not usable, and all passengers would exit the plane through the hatch behind the pilots' cabin.

In the meantime the crash trucks had arrived and covered us in foam. Someone opened the hatch door and the men in the plane began dropping the women and children, like sacks of potatoes, down the hatch opening. After the 3rd woman was dropped through the hole and caught from below, I thought, huh uh, that is not for me, no one is going to drop me down through that hole.

A tractor with a lift had driven up beside the plane and someone had pried the topside door open since the plane was still on a slant. An Army Major was making his way toward that door, to a little hydraulic lift waiting outside and I figured what was good enough for the Major was just fine with me so I quickly got behind him and we exited through the door and unto the lift which lowered us to the ground and took us back to the terminal. Norman was there waiting for me totally unaware that anything had been wrong with the landing until the first passengers began to file into the terminal. Oddly enough, another Globemaster (C-88) had the identical experience on landing in Lisbon, Portugal on the very same day. How is that for coincidence?

We made our way to Pensacola where Norman was assigned to a hospital for four weeks before receiving orders to report to the Naval Hospital in Corona, California. He was now wearing a brace on his leg and was able to drive a car although I am not sure he should have.

In April we headed out to California by way of Carlsbad Caverns. We wanted to see the Caverns and although we took the short version of the tour, it was still a rugged 1½-mile walk. The Caverns hadn't been slicked up like they are today but we walked the trails with a guide and Norman leaned one arm over my shoulder and away we went. I have, ever since, told people I carried my husband through Carlsbad Caverns in 1949, which is close to the truth.

Crossing a bleak stretch of west Texas headed toward Hobbs, New Mexico, a road sign stated it was 60 miles to the nearest gas station and warned travelers to have ample fuel. When we stopped for gas, I said to Norman, so help me this is true, "Maybe we ought to buy an extra fan belt, or something." Norman said he didn't think we would need it and we drove on with our full tank of gas.

It was late in the afternoon, midway through that desolate stretch of highway, when the car heated up. We stopped, Norman lifted the hood, our radiator was steaming and our fan belt was nonexistent. We were carrying a half case of 32 ounce size bottles of club soda, for what reason I cannot imagine. Norman promptly opened all the bottles and poured the club soda in our steaming radiator. Then he climbed up on the front bumper and urinated into the radiator. He invited me to do the same, I declined. I had never heard of anyone peeing into a radiator no matter how desperate for fluid. He cut the rope off of a box in the trunk and fashioned a fan belt, weaving and tying as he improvised. The challenged "Flados fingers" were in fine fettle! He placed the rope fan belt around the sprockets and eased them back as tightly as he dared. In the meantime, far down a ranch road to the west, silhouetted against a pink evening sky, we spied a windmill. We started the engine; the rope was noisy but doing a fair job of turning the fan as we left the highway and headed for the windmill. Upon arrival we found a livestock water tank and hanging on a nearby fence pole a worn, frayed tractor fan belt.

The Lord will provide! The famous "Flados fingers" took over once again. He installed the bleached out, frayed fan belt, filled the radiator to the brim, filled all the empty soda bottles with tank water and started the car. The radiator had cooled by this time, we made a U turn in the soft soil, and with the gentle flap, flap, flap of our raggedy fan belt, we started back toward the highway and proceeded on to the next little town 30 miles away. We stopped at a garage and bought a new fan belt for which we paid twice what it was worth. We installed it and I insisted we buy a second one just in case our car had developed a bad habit. If indeed, demand sets the price, apparently we weren't the only ones who had thrown a fan belt on that stretch of highway. I can't remember if I said, "I told you so" but I probably did. We had that second fan belt in our car toolbox for the next 30 years.

California was beginning to sprout motels along the roadways and the next night, we stayed in Yuma, Arizona in a nice motel for $5.00. We arrived in Corona, California, a small town, on the edge of the desert, which boasted a dry, pleasant climate. Nearby was a large Naval Hospital equipped to handle polio patients and servicemen with serious war-related injuries.   The occupational therapy department was well-equipped and Norman stayed busy making things. One project was using a loom (lots of foot work required) to weave a rug 30 inches wide and 30 feet long. He just kept weaving and weaving.   We had an apartment close by and he spent each day at the hospital.

At this time many wartime facilities were being closed down or consolidated and so it was, with this hospital. When August rolled around, the Navy packed us up and transferred Norman to the Naval Hospital in Long Beach, California. We didn't mind, moving frequently had become our lifestyle.

We found a nice second floor apartment near the hospital and Norman continued with his rehabilitation on a daily basis.   He was feeling and looking good. During this time the community of Bellflower, one of the largest, earliest, post-war suburban housing developments in the country, was being built nearby. There was row upon row of look-alike houses eagerly bought by returning vets of W W II, their purchase made possible by the Veteran's Administration which furnished housing loans at low interest rates. The area between Los Angeles and Long Beach was open pastureland with cows grazing on the hillsides and wooden oil derricks protruding from the soil like ugly sentinels in an otherwise bucolic environment.

It was January of 1950 and Norman wanted to go back to Texas. He was over the disappointment of having to leave the Navy and wanted to get on with his life. He requested and received orders to the Naval Hospital in Corpus Christi, Texas. Because he was headed for discharge from the Navy and had requested to be stationed near home, the Navy did not finance this move. We found a rickety old 2-wheeled trailer for $60.00, painted it red, packed our stuff and took off for Texas in our car with all our worldly goods in the little trailer we pulled behind us. We still had the Chevrolet Club Coupe that we had purchased in 1948 and we needed the trailer to haul that darn radio phonograph console, my sewing machine and the other stuff we had acquired along the way. I could have carried our record "collection" in my purse!

In Corpus Christi, we settled in an apartment overlooking the Gulf of Mexico and Norman continued with his daily therapy. The apartment was well located, but the interior was painted hot pink and chartreuse, this included the cupboards. Our stay there would be temporary, so we ignored the ghastly décor.

Because his Naval R.O.T.C. class had been commissioned and deployed to active duty before their graduation, Norman decided to return to the University of Texas to complete his degree. He was mustered out of the Navy on a tax-free medical retirement; he applied for the G.I Bill and admission to the University of Texas at Austin. We were starting a new life and we could see a light at the end of our tunnel.

SECTION THREE

BACK TO COLLEGE

1950 – 1957

Accepting the reality of a career change and setting his goals in another direction, Norman decided to finish work toward a degree. Except for some residual weakness and muscular atrophy in the right leg, he was feeling fit and ready to pursue a normal life. Before we left Corpus Christi we were delighted to learn I was pregnant and expecting a baby in January. We had been married for over four years and were ready for parenthood. We were eligible for student housing and waited six weeks for our application to rise to the top of the list. It was rather nice living in the student rooming house, for I was nauseated by the smell of food and as a boarder I could eat it, but didn't have to smell it or cook it.

We moved into the Deep Eddy Apartments in south Austin, which were two-story, converted, army barracks, very inexpensive and quite comfortable. We purchased some furniture and cut our thirty-foot hand-loomed rug runner into two pieces, sewed the two sections together and carpeted the living room floor. Norman was a University student once again and resumed work on his original major, secondary education.

I sewed baby clothes, read books on child rearing and we felt no insecurity about becoming parents. For several years we had the opportunity to observe how other people reared their children and we had firm convictions on what we weren't going to do when we had our own. We didn't have much money, but with our Navy retirement and the G.I. Bill we were more fortunate than most.

In spite of a bulging enrollment of returning veterans at the University, unlike today Austin was a rather smallish city with no serious traffic problems. There was open country between North Campus and the Main Campus and, the hills west of Austin offered a view of pristine woodlands unmarked by any signs of human habitation. Norman thought the hills above the lake would be a great place to build a house, and as time went by, so did countless other people as evidenced by the endless expanse of beautiful homes found there today.

We were nesting like two birds. Norman's dad generously contributed the money to buy a baby bed for his first grandchild. We purchased a Kiddie Coop, a full size, foldable, baby bed, enclosed in wire mesh screen with a screened lid that could be closed to prevent the child from climbing out or other children from climbing in. It also kept out mosquitoes, a common pest in Texas. After research, we chose a Baby Butler baby chair, which also had unique features. It could be moved to high or low position and could be a feeding table or in later years a chalkboard desk. We thought these items had it all, but apparently no one else did, for these particular brand items have totally disappeared from the marketplace.

Under our apartment building, we found an old rusted, collapsed baby buggy, the kind that rolls on big easy springs. We took it apart, refinished the frame and wheels and I sewed a new body for it out of soft blue plastic. It turned out great and we used it for all three of our children. We also located a rather primitive, but sturdy car seat from a junk heap somewhere, reupholstered it and our children were required to ride in it once they could sit and hold their head erect. At that time we were the only people I knew who placed their children in a car seat.

I ordered government publications on child care, and the one we adopted as our S.O.P, Infant Care–Birth to Six Months, made good sense in all areas and furnished the guidelines for the physical care of our babies. Dr. Spock had not, as yet, gained general acceptance as the guru he later became in the child-rearing arena. In spite of its unpopularity with young mothers and the medical profession of that time, with the full encouragement and support of my husband I decided to breast-feed our baby. Beyond comfort level or self-confidence in the concept, the decision to breast-feed had to come from within the mother's psyche, for the bottle fed infant was the vogue.

I did not want my husband in the delivery room or in fact in close proximity to me when I went into serious labor. I figured this was MY task to complete, I wanted to do it as neatly and efficiently as possible and if for some reason I was not in control or acted out badly, I did not want a witness to any lack of control on my part. I felt that the birth was my show. In light of what is customary in this day and time, my views seem a bit weird. It was probably the Norwegian thing.

We went to the hospital at 2 a.m. on the 7th of January, 1951 and our daughter was born shortly after 6 a.m. As it turned out, I did handle the whole process rather well. Ether was the anesthetic, the doctor charged $75.00 as his delivery fee and the hospital bill was $189.00 for a five-day stay in the hospital.

When our 6 pound 13 ounce daughter was brought in to me, she looked very tiny and she had gray hair. I felt no surge of mother love; I remember wondering if I was normal. She looked like something outside the realm of my conscious thought, a thing apart from us.

While reading The Big Fisherman, by Lloyd C. Douglas, we both liked the character of the Christian Arab princess in the book and decided that if our baby were a girl, we would call her Fara, after the princess in that wonderful story of St. Peter. This we did and tacked on the Ann because my mom's name was Anna.

After five days in the hospital, all meals in bed, on the day of departure, I dressed up in my best suit, hose and high heels and was wheeled out the door with my small daughter in my arms. I felt I had accomplished something SO GREAT and so wonderful, I doubted that anyone else had ever done it quite as well! It was a real high to produce this perfect little life.

Although she had never nursed properly during those five days in the hospital and I knew she was starving to death, on our arrival home, she suddenly got it right for the first time. It was then that I decided this little life was more precious than my own and that I

137

loved her with every fiber of my being. That night was the first time that Norman locked our doors before we retired for the night, an instinctive parental realization that we were responsible not only for ourselves, but for this new little person given into our care.

Breast-feeding was uncommon enough that we worried about many of the wrong things. Norman rented a baby scale so we could weigh Fara, before and after each feeding to determine if she was getting any milk. There was no one to counsel us, so we did what we could to reassure ourselves that she was receiving nourishment.

When Fara was two weeks old, my mom and dad came to Texas to meet their new grandchild. During their visit, we arranged to have her baptized in the Lutheran Church with my mom and dad as sponsors. After several weeks of increasing periods of fretfulness, we enacted our "program." We decided to reward our baby with lots of attention when she was happy and contented, whereas, unjustified fussiness or crying would be given the "big ignore." Norman was really a big fan of this theory and without his support, I could never have followed through. After a period of adjustment for the three of us, the results were quite wonderful. We had a baby who seldom cried unless there was a good reason for doing so. We used this system with all three of our children with similar success.

It was during this time that Leverne was called back into the Air Force, sent to Japan and flew 35 missions over North Korea. While he was overseas, LaVonne and their 2 children stayed in Austin and awaited his return. It was great having relatives close by.

Norman's father, Ole, and his brother, Richard, would come down from Fort Worth occasionally, and we enjoyed their visits. Ole wasn't too keen on being called Grandpa so we settled on Uncle Ole and we laughingly referred to Richard as Aunt Richard. They were Uncle Ole and Aunt Richard.

Grandfather A.G. Flournoy had purchased 468 acres of land in 1926 while on an excursion train visit to the Rio Grande Valley in South Texas. It was in 1951, that Norman became interested in this brushy, uncleared land that his mother and her brothers had inherited, and one weekend he rode the train to the Valley to look it over. The land was being used for grazing cattle, but Norman felt it had potential as an investment. His mother had been deceased since

1945, the three uncles who owned the remaining three-quarters had expressed no interest in the property, so Norman convinced Richard to join him in an effort to buy out all the heirs. This was made possible by using the services of the Texas Veterans' Land Board, a State board created to furnish low interest loans to veterans of World War II for the purchase of farmland. After about a year of negotiations with his uncles and the State of Texas, the land was theirs, and it became our first major acquisition of real estate.

Although the acreage was not within an irrigation district, the soil was rich and suitable for growing cotton and grain. We found someone willing to clear the land in exchange for the right to farm it for five years, after which we then contracted to receive yearly rent for its use.

Norman received his baccalaureate degree from the University of Texas and began work immediately on a master's degree, which he completed in 1952. As he neared completion of his master's degree, out of the blue he announced he wanted to go to Texas A&M and study agronomy. I thought he had taken leave of his senses. He would be entering Texas A&M as an upper-level sophomore and I found it hard to believe that at the age of 29 years of age he would be willing to do that.

I was pregnant again and in spite of not understanding his motives, I went along with this decision. We packed our belongings in our trusty, red trailer and moved to College Station, Texas, home of the Texas Aggies, where my husband with a master's degree, enrolled as a sophomore. We moved into the College View Apartments, a two-story converted army barracks, (déjà vu) which contained ten, 4-room student apartments. Our apartment provided adequate space for our family. We were on the ground floor, our rent was $25.52 a month and that not only paid for the apartment, but lawn care, electricity, water, garbage pick-up and the rental of two bedroom bureaus.

Norman launched into a course of study that included taking as many as seven courses in a semester. He was an eager student and after he received his degree in agronomy, he was hired as a teaching assistant and later as a research assistant. These jobs all paid a stipend and we managed very well financially.

During my pregnancy, I had become interested in a new theory regarding painless childbirth and decided I was a good candidate for this practice since I didn't want to sedate my body and jeopardize my baby in any way. For this delivery I had a Tulane Medical School trained obstetrician who charged $100.00 for girls and $125.00 for boys; the extra $25.00 was to pay for the circumcision of male babies. He proved to be no more enlightened than my former obstetrician. He had no interest in participating in a delivery without anesthesia and was dead set against my intention to breast-feed my baby.

On a Saturday in November Norman was committed to work at the Texas A&M Junior Varsity Football Game, friends from Austin had stopped by, and I served chili for lunch. They took off for the game in jolly spirits, but I stayed at home because our baby was due at any time. About 1:30 P.M. I began having labor pains and our neighbors took me to the hospital and dropped me off. During the game, a doctor was paged over the loudspeaker system and by the time Norman was able to determine that it was our baby that had required a doctor's presence, the doctor had already been to the hospital, delivered our son and returned to the stadium.

The doctor arrived just in time to officiate at the birth of Mark Richard, born November 22, 1952 then had promptly returned to the game having missed only the third quarter. When Norman brought our friends by the hospital after the game, they arrived to find me and little Mark looking bright eyed and bushy tailed. They couldn't believe their eyes, because Mark didn't have that red, squinchy, newborn look.

Giving birth is one of the most exhilarating experiences in the world. My second experience was as satisfying as the first, maybe even more so. The whole process is so miraculous it defies explanation. Once again I felt very proud of my efficiency, for I had popped that baby out like a pea from a pod and he was healthy and beautiful with a full head of hair. And best of all, I had my way about the delivery. Mark had arrived rather effortlessly and anesthesia was not required, which probably explained why he looked so bright-eyed one hour after he was born.

Since I had Rh Negative blood and Norman was A Positive, this poophead physician refused to allow me to breast-feed because it

140

could "put a second child at risk to react unfavorably to its mother's milk." The ill effects of breast-feeding for an Rh Negative mother had never been established and Norman and I could not understand why the doctor held this opinion but it is difficult to defy the so-called experts. We didn't, but we should have.

Mark was given into the care of a female pediatrician, and after a four-day stay in the hospital, we took our second-born home. He was a calm baby from the very beginning and he fit nicely into our family unit. Then the problem started.

He broke out with eczema on his head and scratched himself constantly. It was determined that he was allergic to cow's milk and/or processed formula and was placed on a soy milk formula (Mulsoy) that was the color of coffee. He drank it willingly but had periods of projectile vomiting. I would find him in his bassinet covered with his brown formula having vomited it all over himself, in his ears, eyes and nose, contentedly looking around as if nothing had happened. This child was on "the program" and rarely cried, even when he should have.

I was told to stop bathing him in water and that he could have no juice, cereal or the usual baby food. So he lived on soy milk and I cleaned him by pouring mineral oil in my hands and rubbing it over his body and then wiping the excess oil off. We had to apply a foul smelling concoction of coal tar ointment on his eczema. Water didn't touch his body until he was about 3 months old. Gradually his eczema disappeared and the coal tar applications were no longer necessary. He began to smell sweet like babies should; he was gaining weight and was a very happy, contented infant.

This was the child who would have benefited most from mother's milk and the one that was denied it. The pediatrician warned me that babies who have eczema usually have hay fever and allergies as children and asthma as adults. At about 3 ½ months, I wondered if some of this regimen was necessary. I decided to bathe Mark in water, feed him some cereal and a little watered down orange juice. If it worked, it worked, if it didn't we could return to the old regimen.

That day he received a triple whammy, a soap and water bath, rice cereal and orange juice. Then I waited for the symptoms.

Nothing happened so I repeated it the next day and the next....and nothing happened. I then decided I would treat and feed this child in a normal fashion. I would continue the Mulsoy formula but he would be fed what babies eat and we would face the symptoms, when they appeared.

Little Mark thrived and as far as we know never had an allergy in his life. He was an active little boy who crawled at 7 months and walked at 11 months. I wonder how long the doctor would have had me following a regimen like that, before suggesting an easing off. This may have been the origin of my on-going skepticism regarding dubious decisions foisted on us by the medical profession.

Norman continued to maintain graduate student assistantships in teaching or research. Since he had a master's degree in another discipline, the college allowed him to complete the course work, but skip the master's thesis and go directly into a doctoral program in Plant Pathology.

During this time at Texas A&M, there were 4500 students in the Corps of Cadets and no female students. We enjoyed watching the Aggie band practice and could hear them from our apartment. Our only recreation was an occasional ice cream party on the front steps, when student families in our building would donate ingredients, freeze hand-cranked ice cream and sit out side and eat it. On Saturday nights we would pop some popcorn, bundle the kids up in their pajamas and "keekee poos" and go to a drive-in movie, which cost $1.00 a car. The only time we ever hired a baby sitter was once a year in December when the faculty of the Plant Science Department held a Christmas party for the graduate students. Any other time we would take our children with us or exchange baby-sitting with other parents in the building, but that was rare.

After attending a church sponsored training course in teaching preschoolers, I began teaching Sunday School and Norman and I joined a class for married students at the Methodist Church. At one of our twice a month, Sunday night, potluck suppers, it so happened that everyone in the class brought cake to the potluck supper except for one dish of spaghetti and meatballs. So we all ate cake!

The student housing area where we lived had a unique smell. None of the apartments were air conditioned so the windows were usually open and the smell of cooking pinto beans permeated the atmosphere. The married students had very limited incomes and they ate lots of beans. On a visit to College Station twenty-five years later I drove through the College View student apartment area and it still smelled like pinto beans. So that aspect of student life had not changed. Those were wonderful years, and we still keep in touch with some of the people that shared our student days at Texas A&M University.

By the time Norman was finishing work on his Ph.D., Fara had begun first grade in the College Station Elementary School. He applied for and was accepted for a teaching position at Sam Houston State College at Huntsville, Texas a short 55 miles away.

It was rather typical for fellows receiving advanced degrees to leave college with big debts; we did not. During these seven years Norman had been in school, we saved every penny we could and our frugality had paid off. We had made the payments on the Valley farm, I sewed most of the clothes that the children and I wore and Norman had continued to work as a graduate or research assistant. When we left Texas A&M, we had enough money in the bank to pay cash ($2300.00) for a new Ford four-door sedan; plain vanilla, no chrome, but new, blue and ours. We dubbed it "the Blue Goose." We had achieved our goal. The little red trailer moved our worldly goods one last time. We made the move in January of 1957 and began a new life and gainful employment as a college faculty family in Huntsville, Texas.

THE ACADEMIC YEARS

1958 - 1965

After seven years of living in converted Army barracks, we were more than ready to leave student housing behind and occupy a real house. Norman was hired at mid-term as an Assistant Professor in the Biology Department at Sam Houston State College (now Sam Houston State University), in Huntsville, Texas. Fara was enrolled in school for the second half of her 1st grade year, Mark was four and I was pregnant again. In May of 1958 after being on the job for five months, Norman received his Ph.D. in Plant Pathology from Texas A&M, with various family members in attendance for the event.

Located in the piney woods of Texas, Huntsville was a beautiful city of 12,000 when we moved there in January of 1958. We rented a house on Possum Walk Road, rightly named, for on awakening in the early morning we occasionally saw possums peering in at us from the trees outside our windows. It was a big, old barn of a house with lots of space, a large yard and a rural atmosphere. No central heat or air conditioning, but it seemed wonderful to us.

The State Prison, a large complex of buildings surrounded on all sides by 15-foot high red, brick walls was located smack in the middle of the town. The walls were covered with English ivy, which gave the prison a rather benign look. Huntsville had always been known as a prison town, and it was a common sight to see trustees in prison garb working outside "the walls." We gave it little thought.

Huntsville's climate was warm and humid and the town had a very stratified social structure, as do most southern towns. Located in the eastern part of the state, the local accent, cultural habits and behaviors greatly resembled that of the Deep South. In descending social order, at the top of the pyramid were the landed, affluent, old families, next were the college faculty who would occasionally float up into the upper levels of society; they were followed by the prison professionals, the shop keepers, the hourly waged employees and the blacks who at that time made up about 28% of the population. It was still a segregated society. Deep-rooted attitudes were changing but much of the Old South mentality lingered in the long time residents and "Yankees" still had to earn the respect and trust of the locals.

Family was everything; if the family was old and distinguished, misbehavior was more readily tolerated. People judged others by the reputation of their ancestors and on the grace with which they deported themselves in social situations. As a Midwesterner, born and bred, this always struck me as absurd. I found it difficult to overlook a penchant for duplicity or inappropriate behavior merely because one's family had owned property in the area since before the Civil War.

Walker County was dry and the nearest liquor store was twenty-five miles away across the Trinity River in another county. Bootlegging was commonplace and the bootleggers were the biggest contributors toward keeping the County dry. The wife of the College president was an active member in the Women's Christian Temperance Union and the faculty kept their social drinking a very private matter. The President was heard to publicly declare, "There is not a drinking man on my faculty." Not true, as we knew some who did indeed drink to excess in spite of being residents of the "Bible Belt." A common joke at that time was, "What is the "Bible Belt?" Answer: "That's the "belt" you take before you go to church on Sunday!"

The woman from whom we rented our house was not social upper class, but she was definitely "Old Huntsville" and that imbued her with a status of sorts. Interestingly, the accents for each social group differed. I loved visiting with her for she was a wealth of information on the customs of the town. She would make interesting judgments regarding the local people, for instance, "they are in trade, you know," which meant they ran a business and were not quite upper crust. The city fathers prevented any major grocery chain from doing business in the town by refusing to sell land to "outsiders," but eventually Piggly Wiggly Grocery Stores broke the barrier with the help of a resident who felt no allegiance to such provincialism.

During an evening visit I witnessed a wonderful demonstration of skill and cooperation. My landlady and I were sitting in a porch swing, rocking gently to and fro, the smell of jasmine hanging heavily in the evening air. We heard a car approaching on her circular, pea-gravel covered driveway, most of which was obscured by shrubbery. Around the corner appeared a car of unknown vintage driven by an elderly man, also of unknown vintage. The car halted in front of the porch, the door opened and out stepped old Doc Smotherman, a local veterinarian. He approached the porch where we were seated and said, "Hidy," Mrs. Cline, I was checkin' my records and I noticed ol' T.C. was due for his shots again."

Mrs. Cline said, "Why, Doc Smotherman, that's right kindly of you to come out this way to vaccinate ol' T.C. I'll call him up."

She rose from the swing and walked to the edge of the porch and whistled for the cat. Now ol' T.C. must have stood for Terrible Cat, for he was big and he was terrible. He could cough up three times his weight and that didn't include the hairballs.

Mrs. Cline walked back to the swing, sat down and we resumed swinging as Doc Smotherman proceeded to fill a syringe from a vial removed from his little black valise. About that time ol' T.C. comes around the corner of the house, walking slowly, mincing along on his little cat feet, his tail straight up in the air, with just the end moving a wee bit. As he walked by he rubbed himself on Mrs. Cline's leg. She leaned over and grabbed him around the middle, stood up holding the cat in front of her, as if to hand the cat to Doc. Smotherman.

I thought, "I am about to see a cat fight and all my instincts tell me to bet on the cat." But she turned and pitched the cat up on the screen door and as he hung there with the claws of all four feet dug firmly into the screen, Doc Smotherman calmly walked over and injected T.C. in his hind leg.

147

It was a veritable ballet. I got the feeling this little scene had been enacted many times before. With a backward turn of his head and some switches of his tail, ol' T.C. released his hold on the screen and dropped unto the porch, giving us a dirty look as he passed by.

We joined the Methodist Church, I taught Sunday school, and we made many friends among the faculty and in some cases among members of the "old guard," as well. Forty-five years later, the city has grown tremendously and the tight hold on property has been broken and franchised businesses abound. The families, who had traditionally controlled the destiny of the town, gradually lost their firm grip on city real estate and local politics, allowing Huntsville to burst forth and grow into a bustling city. Although we lived there before this happened, I grew to appreciate the town's unique ambience.

For the first time, we were able to have pets and the kids had lots of space to play. We lived outside the city limits and two-tenths of a mile from the highway. Along both sides of this two-tenths mile stretch of road lived many black families. The school bus would stop at Parker's Store at the intersection of Possum Walk Road and the highway, where we would meet Fara as she got off the bus. Early on, I asked the Parkers if it was safe for my seven-year old daughter to walk that two-tenths mile to our house. I will never forget his answer.

He said, "Are you worried about the black people who live along Possum Walk Road?" I had to admit, that it was a concern. He said, "Mrs. Flados, these are our people and they have lived here forever. Your little girl is perfectly safe walking down that road to your house." He was right, and each afternoon thereafter she safely walked that distance. It was a gentler time in our history.

Agnes and Berdell came to visit us in June of 1958 and although they found the heat oppressive, we had a good time. We drove to the Rio Grande Valley in two cars, stayed in the Arroyo Motel where our group of nine was allowed to cook and eat our meals. Of course we all went shopping in Mexico I was seven months pregnant, having difficulty staying cool so I soaked my feet in ice water as we drove. There was no air conditioning in the Blue Goose.

Late at night at the motel Agnes and I went swimming. For a swimsuit, I wore a smock top over shorts, and the air would get under the smock and blow up like a balloon so I could barely peer over the top. Had I been tied to a sack of rocks, I couldn't have sunk with an air pocket like that. We laughed 'til we cried. We came into some disfavor the next day when Mark picked up the owner's cat and threw it into the swimming pool. He kept telling me, "But mom, cats can swim!" The innkeeper was not amused.

John was born on September 2, 1958 and he was a picture book, beautiful baby. Times they were-a-changing; I went home after three days in the hospital. I had no Rh blood problems with him and breast-fed him successfully. Mark was in kindergarten and Fara was in 2nd grade.

Shortly after John was born, my folks came to visit to meet the new baby. As they drove into our driveway, we all rushed out to greet them and while we were hugging each other, seven-year old Fara rushed back into the house, grabbed little John out of his crib and came running out, holding him out in front of her, hands firmly under his arms, his head flopping from side to side with his body swaying between her two little hands. We all rushed to save him, as Fara said, "Here's our new baby!"

In November of 1958 the Richard Flados family and Norman's father arrived for a visit. Their family included Jeanie Sue 4, David 2, and Paul 1, then there were our three aged 7, 5 and 3 months. All those kids! How did we manage? When we changed one diaper, we lined them up and changed all three. We fed them and bathed them the same way, like birds on a limb.

David who was supposed to be taking a nap took a jar of Ponds face cream and spread it liberally all over our dog. He stood there looking innocent with a sizeable glop of cold cream resting on his little nose and some in his hair, as well. Six children kept Dolores and me busy, looking back I wonder when we ever had time to visit. But we did!

Four-year-old Jeanie Sue had been diagnosed with carcinoma cancer two years previously and although she did not appear to be in pain, she had the look of an impending angel. She was eating very little, and would sit in our big rocker and rock by the hour. During

149

their visit Ole stayed near her side all night as she rocked. His devoted attention to this beautiful child was a dear, wonderful thing and later we determined he was quite aware that his days were numbered, as well. Within six weeks, Ole died suddenly of a heart attack followed soon after by Jeanie Sue's death in January of 1959.

When John was three months old I discovered I was pregnant again, but I was so busy with my young ones and my baby, the pregnancy went very quickly. I hadn't been overjoyed to discover we were to have two babies twelve months apart. We were busy with building a new home on a lot covered with young pine trees.

Our new house was 1720 square feet with 3 bedrooms and two baths. It had hard wood floors, indirect lighting, ceramic tile in the bathrooms, custom cupboards and we paid $15,750.00 for it. We built what we could afford, it was a lovely house and adequate for our family. The neighborhood was made up of young families, and our kids liked the number of available playmates and our proximity to the piney woods.

Throughout the pregnancy I had a nagging suspicion that this fetus was not normal. After having 3 babies, one has a way of knowing what feels right and what feels wrong. Of course I couldn't convince the doctor of this. During the eighth month, I went into labor and gave birth to a stillborn son. He was beautiful and looked perfect. I wanted an autopsy done, my husband thought otherwise, saying it wouldn't ease the hurt to know why it happened. He was probably right.

Our tiny son, whom we would never know, was buried in a little white coffin the following morning in the Huntsville cemetery with only our pastor and Norman present. Listening to the other babies crying in the nearby nursery was not a sound I wanted to hear. I had an 11-month old baby that needed me at home, and all I could think about was getting home to my children. Though it was thought unwise to leave so soon after giving birth, I went home the following day.

My grieving period was short and I put the loss of this child in the far back closed-off area of my mind. During the years of rearing our other children I seldom dwelled on the memory of our stillborn son, but now that I am at an age where I am facing my own mortality, I think of him often and can remember every detail of his beautiful face. I regret that I didn't mourn his loss for a longer period of time. So strange, isn't it?

Our children were thriving and happy and so were we. Fara was a pretty child with long, blond hair and during the week, the kids at school would run their hands down her long pony tail, which quickly became quite stiff from their peanut butter and jelly coated fingers. She made friends easily and was at ease when she was in social situations. She began ballet lessons at eight years of age and continued with them until she was fourteen. She and Mark were invited to participate in the college productions of South Pacific and The King and I, playing the roles of Polynesian children in the former and Siamese children of the king, in the latter.

Mark was an active little boy who made friends readily and found little boy activities the center of his life. He was an excellent student and his teachers praised him as well behaved, albeit, he could be a challenge at home. He was a good ball player and pitched for his team. There were 12 little boys near Mark's age in the neighborhood and they played together on a daily basis. They would play in a yard until the grass was gone and they were playing on dirt, then they would migrate to another yard and repeat the process.

They played certain games in designated yards. Our yard was where they played Ante-Over (the house), Kick the Can and Broad Jump over bamboo poles set up in the back yard. We sustained eleven broken windowpanes in the eight years we lived there. It was nice to have them play nearby, but I was glad to see them move on to the next yard when our season passed.

There were woods nearby and they built forts and were able to swing on grape vines like Tarzan. There were copperheads, coral and rattlesnakes in the area and I should have worried more about the danger they presented, but our kids were taught to keep a watchful eye.

One day when 12-year-old Mark was mowing the yard, I noticed that he had stopped the mower. I watched as he walked to the garage, picked up a hoe, walked back and calmly killed a copperhead that he had discovered in the lawn.

I was weeding my iris bed one day and a copperhead slithered out a few inches from my hand. I ran for a hoe, came back, swung wildly at the snake, and hacked off the end of his tail, swung again and missed completely. Someone came and finished him off for me before I herniated myself. All parents had their snake stories to tell. Some of them were pretty hair-raising.

With the other children in school, John, our caboose, was home alone with me and he was a model child. Always obedient, with a good mind and the ability to amuse himself near me as I worked at my various mother crafting activities. He had a great vocabulary and I never ceased to be amazed at how he conversed and reacted to adults. He was a handsome child, reclusive in many ways and I never tired of his company. He went to his first birthday party at the age of four and came home furious. He told me he never wanted to go to another birthday party because the kids acted crazy the whole time.

He had a very literal way of interpreting the speech of others. At the age of four our neighbor made the comment, "John, I see that your mama cat is going to have babies." Very patiently, John replied, "Mrs. Reidel, cats can't have babies, they have kittens." She looked at me and said, sotto voce, "Marge, I may choke that kid someday, he makes me feel stupid."

While we stood in line at a pancake supper, one of the local Kiwanians approached, looked down at little John, held up his fists, rotated them about, and said, "Hi, there young fella, put up your dukes!" Four-year-old John looked at him, hesitated, then said very softly, "I think it would be much better if you picked on someone your own size."

He was an obedient child, to a fault, as it were. At a lakeside cookout we were sitting around visiting with friends when to my chagrin I noticed that John had climbed into a rowboat with Mark and they were out on the lake 20 or more feet from the dock, against orders, for the water was deep and John could not swim. I should have known better than to yell, "John, get out of that boat, immediately!", for he did. John jumped out of the boat immediately! Eleven-year old Mark executed a remarkably quick and effective rescue and dragged him ashore to where I was standing, and commented, "This is a real dumb kid!" John's only comment was, "Mom, you told me to get out of the boat!"

It was during this period in my life that I realized how much I enjoyed performing. I had written and performed in a Faculty Wives Club skit and felt the excitement of being on stage and in control of an audience's reactions. I played the role of a lady of ill-repute in a melodrama produced by a local drama group and had the pleasure of slinking about the stage in a too-tight, red dress. The dress was my creation and it served in various forms as a costume for many other occasions. I had always enjoyed making costumes for our kids and liked making them for myself, as well.

I sewed a great pink bunny suit with magnificent ears and wore it at Easter egg parties and once was asked to play the role of Easter Bunny and distribute goodies to the residents of a local nursing home. Most of the residents had a smile for me as I went about, but I entered one room and an elderly woman yelled for help saying, "a crazy rabbit is in here!" Then she looked at me and sternly told me to "Get out, right now!" That was the last time I did a nursing home gig in my bunny suit.

Our neighbor had an elderly gardener who reported to her that he saw a big rabbit driving a car on the road near their house. She told him "Now Jake, you know rabbits don't drive cars!" And his answer was, "You say that, but I knows what I seen." She told me this story and asked if I was the guilty rabbit, and I had to admit that I was.

That rabbit suit had a life of its own. It made several moves with us. It was loaned out countless times and in later years, it was mailed to our kids when they were in college, until it was literally worn out. One of its last appearances was when Mark was attending the University of Texas and wore it to the traditional Halloween Party on 6th Street in Austin. He reported that everyone he met wanted to buy the "bunny" a drink.

These were the years when I was active with the Cub Scouts, Girl Scouts, room-mothering, PTA, Study Club, Bridge Club, local politics and teaching 5th Grade Sunday School. I cooked, gardened, sewed, read and taught myself to play the guitar. Young moms must be blessed with a special gift to be able to do so many things and still care for their families.

There were twelve identified Republicans in Walker County at that time; the Democrats were in full control. Within the Democratic Party, there was a strong conservative element, but there was no Republican organization, per se. Norman and I were politically conservative and voted our convictions. In that locale and at that time, it was customary to vote in the Democratic Primary where there were usually both conservative and liberal factions contesting for office. Many would vote for the conservative candidate in the Democratic Primary election and cross over and vote for the Republican, if there was a candidate, in the General election. This type of crossover voting made it possible for Eisenhower to carry Texas in the elections of 1952.

I became actively involved in politics at the county, state and national level. At times I worked with the conservative Democrats, sometimes with the tiny growing Republican Party. I learned polling procedures, attended training sessions on how to help the Republican Party grow and worked for Republican candidates when and if one ran for office.

One of the first things the small contingent of Republicans did, was to address the deplorable voting practices in the County. There was no such thing as a voting booth, or any privacy in voting. As a poll-watcher, I observed people waiting at a table until someone would step up, pick up a ballot and instruct everyone on how to vote. I was horrified. One time I observed an election judge open a ballot box and dump the ballots out on a table in the back room, stuff the pile of ballots into a sack and then return the emptied ballot box to the area where people were voting.

That tiny band of Republicans, with the support of conservative Democrats, requested poll watchers and privacy for voters, which eventually came to pass, albeit the changes came very slowly. I liked the organizational work and felt I had some talent for it. On the local level with the Democrats firmly entrenched, I admit to growing weary of losing election after election, year after year.

In 1963 we were excited about Barry Goldwater running for president and we both worked at the local level for his campaign. Norman was a State delegate and a delegate to the National Convention in July. We sent the children to my parents in South Dakota; we flew to San Francisco and attended that historic convention.

It was on the following November 22nd, that John F. Kennedy was assassinated and the buoyancy went out of the Goldwater campaign as a result of the tragic events that ensued. Lyndon Johnson was elected in a landslide victory and his administration embroiled our nation ever more deeply in the Viet Nam War.

In June of 1965, Norman and Richard purchased a 200-acre tract of irrigated land near Bayview, Texas. It was prime land with Resaca frontage capable of producing good cotton and grain and was subsequently leveled for more efficient irrigation.

During the time we lived in Huntsville we continued to share holidays with the Richard Flados family of Fort Worth. They had welcomed a wonderful little daughter to their family unit and our visits on Easter, Thanksgiving and Christmas were highlighted by some great and some harrowing experiences, but they were always fun. We usually had Thanksgiving at our house and we would prepare for the holiday by raking all of our pine needles into an immense pile in the vacant lot across the road, in preparation for the great "bonfire." The kids played around and poked at the fire until only embers remained. More than once the boys came in with smoking soles and hot feet.

On Easter in Fort Worth there was the egg hunt in their big, backyard and nearby Lake Benbrook provided a place for picnics, wading and for Norman and Richard to sail. With four little boys, we had our share of splits, splinters, stickers, stings, bruises, cuts and falls, but what wonderful times we had.

Through the years I had gone back to South Dakota at least once a year to visit with my folks and my siblings and they, in turn, visited us when they could. Norman had never begrudged my yearly trips home to be with my family. Sometimes we all went, sometimes just the kids and I would go and spend several weeks with my mom and dad. These were precious, memory making visits, but somewhat wrenching to me because I knew the time with my parents was all too brief, and my children had such short periods to be close to their grandparents. Bonding with grandparents comes in incremental parcels of time and exposure, and our increments were separated by too much time and distance.

In the fall of 1959, after successful surgical repair of an aneurysm in the brain, my mother suffered a stroke, which left her paralyzed on the left side of her body. She never wavered in her desire to be as self-sufficient as possible. She learned to walk with a full leg brace and was able to function quite well. Such irony, that this active woman had to curtail and adapt her zeal for work and activity to accommodate the fact that she had but one arm and one leg to do her bidding.

One summer after Mom and Dad had retired and moved to their small home in Spink, the children and I, Agnes and her three kids visited at the same time. Dad arranged to rent the vacant house next door, bought some old beds and cots for sleeping and we stayed there for over a week. My mom had eleven people for every meal, which we ate outdoors at a big picnic table. The kids were grade school age and it was a lively time for everyone.

The grandchildren of the Twedt family, who lived across the road from my parents, were also visiting at this same time. Lincoln Twedt would pile our six and their five or six into his old World War II jeep and drive the four miles to his turkey farm. Lincoln never did anything slowly and he didn't drive the jeep slowly either.

He tore down the road, kids sitting and hanging on at all angles and when he turned the corner at one intersection, a few kids flew off the jeep, but they picked themselves up, climbed back in and away they went. The kids enjoyed the wild ride.

There were eight of us in the little rent house, making it a bit crowded but it was comfortable, nevertheless. I was awakened from sleep one night, to the sight of Agnes doing battle with a bat that had entered our domain. Her weapon was a fly swatter and she was leaping over bodies from bed to bed, flailing her weapon at the intruder. My first inclination was to vacate, but of course, that would have been totally out of character for Agnes. So she battled the bat unto death, picked the nasty thing up with some paper and flung it out into the yard. We all felt a little safer, knowing we had such a fine gladiator to protect us from the wild life.

In 1966 when Norman decided to leave Sam Houston State College and accept a position as Chairman of the Biology Department at Midwestern College in Denison, Iowa, I felt very reluctant to leave. I had moved many times in the past, but this was the first time I cried about it. I loved living in Huntsville, and during our eight years as residents of this provincial, East Texas town, I had developed a comfort level living in an atmosphere where the social niceties were generally observed and supported. The children were none too happy about moving either, for they had made firm friends and hated to leave them behind.

Looming like a dark cloud over the nation was the ever more deepening conflict of the war in Viet Nam. The possibility of resolution seemed remote and our nation seemed on the verge of great social upheaval. An unspoken, implicit feeling of foreboding niggled at the back of my conscious thought; there are big changes ahead, and our growing family was in the pathway of this impending transformation of social and political behavior.

FIVE GREAT YEARS IN DENISON, IOWA

1966 - 1971

To prepare for our move to Denison, I flew up in April and bought a home on Fairway Heights, which bordered the city golf course atop a hill on the south side of town. This well built, spacious home on one of the best streets in town came with a beautiful view, a world of space, a full basement (a new experience for us) and cost $28,200. I arranged for purchase, selected paint, flooring and carpet within three short days, then leaving a local carpet consultant in charge of overseeing application and installation of my selections, I returned to Texas with my fingers crossed. I was amazed that it turned out as well as it did. Luckily, there was no problem with selling our home in Huntsville for more than we had paid for it.

Moving, at best, is a frustrating business and the move from Texas to Iowa was not without its trials, troubles and comedy. Norman and Mark departed for Iowa, and the two other children and I followed later, after overseeing the final items loaded into the moving van. We rendezvoused temporarily in Fort Worth, then Norman and Mark continued on ahead while the rest of us stayed on with Dolores and Richard, allowing our furniture time to arrive in Denison. At almost the last minute it was decided that Dolores and Vickie, aged 2 ½, would accompany us on the trip north. So on the Tuesday after Memorial Day, Fara, John, Vickie, Dolores, poodle puppy and I began our journey.

Of course we had car trouble, but we learned that the sight of two women, three children and a puppy all peering anxiously under the hood of a stalled car not only attracts attention, but stops traffic. One would-be good Samaritan had us puzzled, however. He stopped, asked if he could help, then proceeded to get a rubber mallet from his car and walked around our car stopping every few seconds to beat on the tires and the bumpers. When he had made the entire circuit, he peered under the hood and started beating up on my car motor. He beat the battery, the radiator and anything he could reach with his rubber mallet. He then assured us someone would be along to help at any moment, got into his car and drove off. Soon someone stopped who knew what to do to get us going again, and we were on our way. I always wondered if "Mr. Mallet" was an escapee from a lock-up, he was a car-beater, I knew that!

When Norman and Mark arrived, they barely made it into town ahead of the moving van. Our carpets were not yet installed, but the driver of the van who was supposed to have taken the holiday off, had driven straight through and insisted on depositing six rooms of furniture in the garage. What a mess. Dolores spent a week with us, working from dawn till dusk, unpacking and arranging furniture, keeping our lagging spirits high. She deserves some kind of medal for being such a nice sister-in-law.

Midwestern College was one of four Liberal Arts Colleges built to serve a special need during that time. The concept was to attract a distinguished faculty and provide a good four-year college education for those young people in the East, as well as surrounding areas, who could not gain entrance into State four-year colleges. It was a great idea. A large percent of the students were from eastern states; some were seeking an education, some were determined to stay enrolled in college with the hope of avoiding being drafted into the Armed Services.

The credentials of the faculty were excellent. Denison, home to three successful meat packing enterprises, was a prosperous community that eagerly supported the small, new liberal arts college in their midst. We spent a busy summer putting in a lawn, planting trees and settling into a midwestern environment. Our first impressions of this largely German community were that the people played hard, drank hard, ate well and partied often. We made friends among the townspeople, our kids adapted readily to the changes in their location and we settled into a very pleasant lifestyle. We were members of the Country Club and began playing golf on a regular basis.

Within a year, we had grown to love our new home in Denison; there were hills for sledding in winter and the snow provided a new experience for the children. We appreciated the distinction of four seasons and were quite the snow bunnies in winter, shoveling snow when necessary and driving on icy, treacherous roads. I was the only one on our street who could back a car out of the garage, spin completely around on the steep driveway and head down to the street, front first.

Norman remodeled the basement into usable family living areas, which gave us a whopping 4100 square feet of living space. We settled in to becoming Midwesterners and our kids were beginning to lose their southern accents.

The following summer Norman accepted a temporary position with a cotton research project at Oklahoma State College at Stillwater, and after renting an apartment near the campus, the children and I followed a few weeks later. They made friends and had a good time. Upon our arrival home, we were greeted by a yard with a problem, an absentee landlord. We had contracted for yard care but the weeds had grown in the flowerbeds and along the fence lines, unmolested for 8 weeks. No one can in their wildest imagination conjure up the sight of Iowa-grown weeds; as high as an elephant's eye, they were, and it required an elephant to pull them, so I did it!

My interest in antiques had continued to grow; I joined Questers, the local antique club, and continued to collect them. Sunday afternoons were often spent at estate sales and turn-of-the-century golden oak, which I liked, was readily available and quite inexpensive. My woodworking expertise continued to improve and I began refinishing the antique pieces I acquired at the sales. We purchased a fine, old player piano and I undertook the job of refinishing it. I took it apart, carried the parts into the basement and worked on it for about 2 months before completing the task. It had a nice tone and we had good times singing to the accompaniment of the old piano rolls in our collection. At our parties there was singing and harmonizing around the player piano, singing oldies such as "Shine on Harvest Moon," "My Gal Sal" or "My Wild Irish Rose." We added kazoos, a slip-stick, maracas and occasionally a "gut bucket" for added rhythm.

I resumed teaching 5th grade Sunday School at the Methodist Church; 5th graders were my favorite age group because of their curious minds and love of facts. Aside from the usual obligations concerned with mother craft, I moderated style shows at the Country Club, acted as judge in the regional "Make it With Wool" competition, chaired the Women's Organization at the Country Club and one year I was the gypsy fortune teller at the local Art Festival. That woman-of-ill-repute-red-dress was put to good use again. We began playing golf on a regular basis and we were members of two couples' bridge clubs.

For reasons I never understood, I was invited to join a local bridge club, known to be the oldest club in town. The women showed up in fur coats, sometimes hats, as well, played for money and a local caterer came with membership in the club. The meetings began with a luncheon, served by Angie. Then we would play bridge and during the last round, cocktails were served. These women were skilled players and affluent, I was neither. I do not remember a time when they were critical of my occasional wrong plays. Looking back on it, they were all old enough to be my mother, and I guess they kept me around for laughs, for I was out of their league in every way.

I dabbled in Iowa politics as a delegate to the County and State Republican conventions. My political activities were beginning to wane as I developed interests in other things. Denison was a partying town, and we did a good deal of it. Theme parties were commonplace and everyone seemed to enjoy dancing.

Mark had earned the Order of the Arrow before leaving Huntsville and continued on in scouting, earning his Eagle Scout Award at the age of fourteen while with his Denison Troop. Our kids were growing up fast; the two oldest were active in school activities, making good friends and receiving recognition, both scholastic and honorary. John, an avid reader, still in grade school, had a little paper route that earned him some money for his pockets and both older children worked at part time jobs after school from the time they were 16 years of age.

162

After obvious symptoms of anemia in the fall of 1968, Norman was diagnosed with cancer of the colon and underwent surgery for its removal at a hospital in Omaha. His recovery from cancer surgery appeared complete and he began to enjoy good health. Later, he also had the misfortune of catching the mumps, which laid him low for eleven days. He told me that if he died, I was to place him in an open casket naked from the waist down, for the "viewing" would establish his reputation in the town forever!

A neighbor related that she had called our home to inquire how Norman was doing after his surgery for colon cancer. Little John reported, "My Dad is doing fine, he just had some bleeding into his sawdust." Norman had in the past referred to his innards as his sawdust, a throwback expression to the day when dolls were stuffed with sawdust.

My family lived just two short hours away and I loved being able to visit them frequently. The children and I were contented to be Iowans, however, Norman never quite adapted to the winter cold, the ice and the snow. He presented a façade of Viking vigor, but that southern boy's lips turned blue just listening to a forecast of "possible snowfall tomorrow." He tried his best to like the colder climate, but he spent five years shivering in his clothes.

The Head of the Drama Department asked me to play the role of the mother in the play, Barefoot in the Park. The Department Head was a professional actor who invited professionals from the theatrical world to participate in college productions with Actor-in-Residence status. This made for a very dynamic drama department. The play was presented on seven consecutive nights, it broke all house records and I loved every minute of it. I was not familiar with the play and the director let me interpret the role as I saw it.

On the third night, I began receiving a little ovation when I left the stage after my biggest scene. Oh, what heady moments they were! After the final performance, I was high as a kite for about a week. I began to understand why people sought out the performing arts, there is nothing as intoxicating as an appreciative audience showing they like your performance.

The Viet Nam war was in progress and there was turmoil, rioting and disquieting behavior rampant in the country. Drugs were a problem among the young in the large cities and on both coasts, but Denison seemed insulated from all the unpleasantness.

Norman attended a post-doctoral six-week course in radiation biology at the University of California starting in late June of 1969. The course was given under the auspices of the Atomic Energy Commission and there were eighteen teachers participating from various parts of the country. We all traveled to Berkeley, rented a furnished apartment four blocks from the campus, three blocks from People's Park, and we had the eye-opening experience of our lives.

We lived in a sea of hippies and/or street people and because of our proximity to the action, which never seemed to cease, we witnessed anti-war rallies where we heard wannabee revolutionaries calling for revolution in the streets and the pulling down of the business establishment. We saw the sights and heard the sounds of what seemed like another world from the one we had so recently left. It was a panorama of dope-eyed, young people with long, uncombed, hair wearing bizarre clothing, begging for nickels and dimes on the street. Young women in long loose garments or tattered jeans stood on street corners with babies strapped to their backs selling underground newspapers that abounded in four letter words. It was prowling through bookstores and seeing children's books and pornography side by side on the shelves. It was seeing a boarded up, world famous campus in the grip of parading, rioting students and street people bathing their dogs in the beautiful campus fountains until the college found it necessary to drain them. It was breathing air filled with the scent of marijuana and the occasional extra joggle of inhaling the lingering tear gas that clung to the low lying streets after a rally.

There was a plus side to our stay in Berkeley; we took many tours of San Francisco and visited the city's wonderful museums. So what if we caught a glimpse of someone, who except for the garnish of a pair of military boots, was walking down the street stark naked. Fara, 18, and Mark, 16, found it all very exciting and would go out to watch the action on a regular basis. My husband, on the other hand, found it so disgusting, the veins in his neck stood out visibly for the entire time we were in Berkeley.

Our apartment house was gated and considered secure, but one day Norman entered the sauna and found two longhaired hippie types enjoying a good session in our private sauna. His sensibilities stayed in a continuous state of indignation. We had never seen young people who acted like that, dressed like that or played music like that and after eight weeks there was the pleasure of returning to Denison, which seemed to us, a haven in the storm.

Fara, who had graduated from high school in May, enrolled at the University of Iowa. We packed her "schtuff" drove her to Iowa City, deposited her in the freshmen dorm and said our goodbyes.

As we drove off, I looked back and I shall never forget the sight of her standing on the walkway in front of the dorm; our beautiful daughter with the long blond hair, short dress, half socks and the voguish, clunky shoes, looking like a little girl, far too young to survive as a freshman in a large University. I am not a weeper, but that was very wrenching to me, such a milestone in a child's life and in a parent's life, as well.

Within one year of our California experience, the long hair, drugs and bizarre behavior we had witnessed in Berkeley had made its insidious way across the nation and into the American heartland. Targeting the nation's campuses, the anti-war, anti-establishment, hippie mentality was on the march. Protests against the war in Viet Nam were common at the University of Iowa and the entire nation seemed to be losing its sense of decency and purpose.

By April, anti-war marchers were causing mischief, boycotting classes and students were crossing picket lines to get to their classrooms. Norman notified Fara that he was going to bring her home from the University. Because of the turmoil, the College allowed the students leaving the campus to receive the grades they had earned up to that date. Fara wasn't too happy about the whole situation, but home she came. She had sniffed the heady atmosphere of revolution and asked her dad why he hadn't told her the other side of the political story.

There were many long and sometimes bitter discussions on the political situation of the time. Some evenings we would sit down to dinner at 6 p.m. and Norman and Fara would still be discussing, arguing one might say, two or three hours later. We had always

165

been a verbal family and Norman had taught our children to justify their ideas and weigh things in the balance of rational thought; we didn't hesitate to discuss topics that many families might have found inappropriate or worse, boring.

We still do this at family gatherings and those who have married into our family have been known to feel uncomfortable with the head-to-head discussions that have taken place at our dinner table. Our kids will be enjoying a rip-roaring discussion only to discover that their spouses have departed the premises to avoid listening to them. In later years, I have had to make some topics verboten, only because, all the ground has been covered and there are irreconcilable differences. I feel I can declare any topic out of order, if I so ordain, 'cause I'm the cook and I'm the mother!

I had begun taking courses at Midwestern College, starting out slowly, thinking I would have a hard time keeping up with the young college students of the day. Well surprise, surprise, the courses I took were easy for me and I didn't find any of the young students much competition. I enjoyed my college courses and began to take two each semester instead of one. In fact, as I matriculated my way along I can truthfully say I never took a course that I didn't enjoy. My college age children thought that statement was ludicrous, since they disliked many of their required courses.

Our home was new when we moved into it and I felt compelled to plant trees and shrubs to beautify our environment. I know I have dug more holes than the average cat. While in Denison I had ordered twenty-five hedge plants to border one side of our yard. After their first year of growth, it was determined they certainly were not the hedge plants I had ordered, but locust trees. They grew like crazy and we ended up with a row of twenty-five locust trees planted 2 ½ feet apart.

During our five years in Denison, the Fort Worth Fladoses spent several Christmas vacations with us. It was their children's rare opportunity to play in the snow or coast on a sled or toboggan. More great times and precious memories.

As a result of being unable to compete with the tax-endowed State colleges and the on-going proliferation of Community Colleges throughout the country, the grand design of the small, private liberal

166

arts college, such as Midwestern College, faced financial challenges they were unable to meet. We hoped our college could survive, but in spite of admirable efforts made by the people of Denison, we faced the inevitable; the college would close. Once again, in spite of my utter contentment with our life in this small midwestern town, a move was in the offing.

Norman wanted to go back to Texas and he accepted a consulting job in McAllen with the Rio Grand Valley Development Council. We moved back to Texas in March of 1971, Mark stayed on with a local family so he could graduate with his high school class. He had done very well in school and was made a member of the Iowa National Honor Society. Once again, we packed up our household, bid dear friends goodbye and headed for Texas.

BACK TO TEXAS

1971 – 1972

I had misgivings about moving back to Texas, for the children and I had loved living in Denison. Norman had preceded us to McAllen and by the time we arrived he had purchased a house for us on Redbud Street. Leaving Mark behind to complete his remaining two months of high school, Fara, John, our poodle and I left Denison in mid-March and headed for Texas. We left Iowa driving in slush and snow-covered roads; we arrived in McAllen to a tropical scene of beautiful blooming trees, shrubs and flowers. Our introduction to the Rio Grande Valley was one of delight at its beauty and surprise at its hot and humid climate.

Fara found a job at the local hospital and made preparations for admission to Pan American University in the fall. After graduation from Denison High School in May, Mark joined us in McAllen and accepted summer employment at the hospital. I enrolled at Pan American University in Edinburg and continued on my academic way. As the fall semester approached, Fara opted for gainful employment and Mark enrolled at South West Texas State University at San Marcos, Texas.

A colleague had arranged a blind date for Fara, which resulted in Joe Jones showing up on our doorstep one evening to take our daughter out to dinner. Fara had not, as yet, made her appearance so Joe, Norman and I sat in our living room making small talk. Given an opportunity, parents always scrutinize their children's dates; what we saw before us was a very handsome young man, who appeared ill at ease and very nervous. One knee never stopped jiggling, one eye noticeably twitched and I sensed his great relief at the prospect of imminent departure, when Fara, dressed for their date, entered the room. Later when we learned that he had been recently discharged from the Marine Corps after a tour of duty in Viet Nam, had been injured 3 times, the last wound a near fatal one, we began to understand his edginess.

After that first meeting, they dated on a regular basis, and Norman and I wondered in amazement at the obvious growing relationship. They laughed and cavorted like cartoon teddy bears; falling out of the car unto the grass, he carrying her, or she dragging him. This was a total departure for Fara who had always dated the preppie type; Joe was not preppie. He was a sportsman who loved hunting, fishing, the more vigorous the activity the better, whereas Fara had always been the femme fatale.

Obviously having a rollicking good time falling in love before our eyes, we worried about Joe's pacing restlessness. One night I said to Norman, "we have seen them come and go, but this is the one she will marry, mark my word." And she did.

To accommodate Joe's plans for attending Texas A&M University in January, we began planning a wedding for January 8, 1972, one day after Fara's 21st birthday. She was estranged from the church and finding a place to hold the wedding became a challenge. Dad put a credit card on the coffee table and offered them the options of being married by a Justice of the Peace followed by the honeymoon of their choice OR a formal wedding in McAllen with members of our families in attendance. It would be their call. The card lay on the table for several days before they opted for a small, formal wedding and they emphasized the small. We rented a nearby church and began to plan the wedding.

Fara said, "no veil, no lace, no beads, no flowing tulle, no ruffles, no frills." So what else is there? She found a picture of her idea of the perfect wedding ensemble; it was lovely and it had none of the above-mentioned fripperies. The dress was simple with a swallowtail train complimented by a head covering, bordered in satin, reminiscent of a nun's headdress. The dressmaker reproduced the dress in the picture and Fara looked lovely in it.

I made the bridesmaids' dresses of pink and wine colored matte flowered jersey with babushka type headdresses of the same material. Unusual, but they complimented Fara's dress very well. About 50 people were in attendance at the wedding, including my folks and other members of the Jones and Flados families. We had asked a friend and former Presbyterian minister, to come from Dallas to perform the marriage. He was willing to marry them in a non-religious ceremony, which they had selected and adapted to their liking.

We were in the back of the church, doing last minute preparations for entry when the hired singer began strumming her guitar and singing, "The First Time Ever I Saw Your Face." As she began to sing, Joe came running into the church from the outside entrance, saying he wanted to hear the song when she sang it. He stood and listened, then ran back out the door and around to the front of the church where his groomsmen were waiting. Such a Joe-like thing to do!

The ceremony was lovely, except the groom and I had the flu. One of my symptoms was a hard cough and during the ceremony, as luck would have it, I had an uncontrollable fit of coughing, so I concentrated on making no coughing sounds, but my shoulders shook with the effort. At the reception, someone was heard to say, "Marge took it really hard, didn't she?" It seems all that was visible from the back pews were my shaking shoulders, which made it appear that I was sobbing my heart out during the ceremony.

My folks were not altogether comfortable with non-religious, originally worded, wedding ceremonies, and privately wondered, "are they really married?" They were and are. Many years later when they became professing Christians, they renewed their wedding vows in a religious ceremony.

The following week when I went back to the florist and others to whom I owed payment for wedding services, they were all sick with the flu. I had infected a portion of the McAllen business community in my going from place to place preparing for the wedding.

The morning of the wedding, Joe and his wedding attendants had arrived back from a fishing trip with a large amount of fish. Joe paid the minister and the organist with coolers containing freshly caught, filleted red fish. The following Monday, Fara and Joe hitched his boat to his car, filled it with their wedding presents and worldly belongings and headed for College Station where Joe would study at Texas A&M University, ultimately receiving a degree in wildlife management, with a specialty in fish science.

We have grown very fond of Joe through the years and treasure him as a son-in-law and father of our grandsons. He has become a respected civic leader and successful businessman. He has lost the nervous habits of the former combat Marine, mellowed out and although he is still very energetic, he has learned the art of relaxation. For short periods.

Mark had been enrolled at South West Texas State University in San Marcos since September, Fara had married and moved to College Station with her husband, and our nest was two short of a full count. During his first semester at college, Mark was drafted into the United States Army by the Draft Board in Denison, Iowa.

He had a very low selective service number and we were surprised to learn that the draft call numbers had fallen that low. Thinking back on it, since he had registered in Denison, Iowa and we had subsequently moved away, the Draft Board may have found it easier to draft him, low number or not. If in the process of serving his country, he was injured or killed they would not have to look into our eyes when they met us on the streets of Denison. Just a thought.

During our time in McAllen we celebrated our 25th wedding anniversary. B.O. Plenty and Gravel Gertie from the Dick Tracy comic strip were married on August 18th, 1946, as were we. On the day we celebrated our 25th wedding anniversary, the comic strip had B.O. Plenty and Gravel Gertie doing the same!

Our wonderful poodle, Poochie Remus, had been a great pet and was appreciated for his clownish ways. At six o'clock one day I discovered he was not in the house; he had followed me indoors and out as I carried in groceries, but it was not typical for him to stay outdoors for he disliked the heat. I feared that he had been dog-knapped. I was right. I advertised and posted signs all over town, in English and Spanish to no avail. Interestingly, people called to offer condolences or share their own experiences in the loss of a pet. One dear lady called to sympathize with this memorable quote, "I feel very sad for you, for I could never have made it through the menopause without my Chihuahua." Sadly, we never found our Poochie.

When following an academic path toward a baccalaureate degree, sooner or later one must declare a major. I would have loved a major in modern dance, theater arts or even international politics but those doors were not open to me. In fact they were shut tight!! But a major must be declared. So in spite of an inability to remove a sticker from a child's finger without feeling squeamish, I thought there might be a blood-free, pain-free, death-free nursing position somewhere out there. I decided to fulfill my mother's unrealized dream of becoming a nurse so I declared a nursing major.

During this time, Norman had been working as a consultant for the Rio Grande Valley Development Council, but felt the position would be short-lived. He applied for the position of Department Head in the Health Science Department at California State College in Bakersfield, California. We scattered. John and I went to South Dakota on a visit; Norman went to Bakersfield for an interview and to buy a home if he was hired for the position. The position was offered and Norman accepted.

In preparation for our move, we held the traditional "moving sale," and had our household effects shipped to our new address in the Park Stockdale community in Bakersfield, California. Leaving our daughter in Texas and our older son in the Army, Norman, John and I made our move to California. I had not had time to put down an extended taproot in McAllen so it was a bit easier to yank it up and move on.

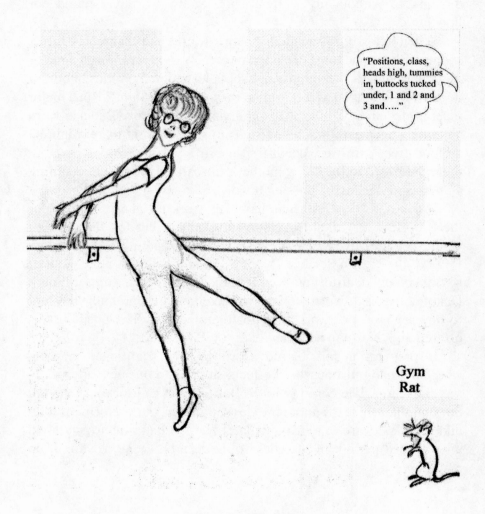

Gym
Rat

Modern Dance Class
Pan American University
10:05 A.M.

10:20 A.M.

10:40 A.M.

10:50 A.M.

THE CALIFORNIA EXPERIENCE

1972-1975

Upon arrival in Bakersfield in early June, we immediately visited the house my husband had purchased for us. It was in a very desirable location, but I deemed it too small, totally unacceptable and informed Norman I would not move into it. This might have posed a real dilemma for some people, but when Norman understood that I was deadly serious, he said, "then we will buy another house." And we did. We found a lovely 4-bedroom, 3- bath, beautifully landscaped house in the same neighborhood and we immediately rented the other house to a local minister who was willing to pay us a generous rental. Although Norman entered the college community as the poor devil who had to buy two houses before he got one that pleased his wife, we didn't let it bother us.

I liked Bakersfield; the climate was hot, there was little rain, the humidity was low and everything appeared green and beautiful. Many of the flowering shrubs and trees were the same as those we had in the Rio Grande Valley with the exception of camellias, gardenias and roses, which thrived in that locale due to the acidic nature of the soil. The area was totally irrigated, making the San Joaquin Valley a fertile region of grapes, cotton, orchards, nuts and vegetable crops.

It was while we lived in Bakersfield that I met Ruth who had been born and raised in Sweden. She was a delightful friend and we enjoyed the same things, one of which was attending a Kola dance club where we learned and performed the folk dances of Eastern

Europe and the Mediterranean countries. The commentary entitled For Ruth, which follows this chapter, was inspired by experiences we shared while residing in the Park Stockdale suburb of Bakersfield.

I had previously taken courses at two colleges; I had the bit in my mouth and was filled with an over abundance of ambition and desire to continue my education. It was too late for me to be accepted into the fall nursing classes at the local community college so after settling into our new home, I used the intervening school year to meet requirements for entry into the Nursing School at Bakersfield College the following fall. I also enrolled in two courses at Cal State Bakersfield where Norman was teaching, one was very interesting, the other a disaster which I dropped to save my sanity.

I found my inorganic chemistry course at Cal State Bakersfield to be very frustrating, so much so, that every time I looked at my red chemistry book, I felt the urge to cry. Mark was home on leave after completing Army Boot Camp at Monterrey, California. and observed my obvious discomfiture. He graciously offered to help me. After a brief tutorial period, he asked, "Mom, do you know about exponentials?"

I said, "What is an exponential?"

He said, "Do yourself a favor, drop the course!"

I did. I then enrolled in a remedial algebra program for the mathematically challenged. I didn't repeat the course at Cal State, but took chemistry during my interim year at Bakersfield Community College. I had a masterful teacher and I truly enjoyed the course although it required a minimum of 17 hours of my time each week. The professor told us it would, and it did. It was a prerequisite for entry into the Nursing School and 50% of the class flunked the course.

Mark was transferred to Fort Sam Houston in San Antonio where he was trained as an army medic. After completing his training, he received orders to a remote base in Turkey whose purpose it was to eavesdrop on the activities of the Soviet Union. As he said, it was intended to be a secret base but everyone in the country knew where they were and what they were doing. He wisely used his furloughs to travel and visited Austria, Germany and Italy during his two years in the Army.

Nurses were in short supply in California and competition was stiff for the limited number of class openings. Once accepted into a nursing class, however, the training was free to the student. My only school expenses during my two years of nurses training were for a student activities card and a campus-parking permit. It was a free ride.

I had never aspired to be a nurse. As a young woman my mom had wanted to be a nurse and she would have been a superb one. She never realized this goal because of her obligations to work on the family farm during the same portion of every school year. I chose nursing, not convinced that I had a talent for it, but because it was a profession that didn't discriminate against candidates who were in their late forties.

Before being accepted into the School of Nursing, prospective candidates were given psychiatric and achievement tests to determine if they could stay the course. I knew I could stay the course, since my grades were excellent. I also quickly concluded that the interviewing psychologist was a bit coo-coo. He told me that aside from having a problem with authority I would probably be a capable nurse candidate. Regarding the "authority thing," it was accepting it, not using it. But then I had already begun to suspect that might be true. The achievement tests indicated I was off the charts in some subjects, but really a dumb doo-doo in math. As if I didn't know that!

A psychologist once told me that a personality crystallizes at about 19 years of age and that after that point in a person's life whatever changes take place are minimal. I don't think that was true with me. I had assumed the role of wife and mother willingly and had taken satisfaction in the knowledge that my husband would always smooth my path and take care of me. He was my buffer between my comfortable little environment and the hard tough world around me; he was my cushion against whatever hard knocks might come my way. But as I settled in to my academic pursuits, I felt empowered in a way that was new to me. I had the desire to study and do something commendable with my newly discovered proclivities and aptitudes. I had developed an "I-am-woman-hear-me-roar" mind set.

A wellspring of self-confidence and power was surging within me; I felt I could accomplish anything set before me. That feeling had begun to grow in me at about the age of 40, at least that was when I became aware that I had untapped talents somewhere in the depths of my being. Of course this normally should have happened twenty years earlier, but I had always shown symptoms of being a late bloomer.

I entered the nursing program in full sail. Our class was an interesting mix of very young and the not so young, several Licensed Vocational Nurses going for their Associate Nursing Degrees and five male students. Men were beginning to enter the nursing profession; most had been medics in the military services. I enjoyed knowing my classmates, especially the young ones. School was a pleasure and I was determined to get the best grades possible.

Classes have personalities and our nursing class certainly had one. The class before us had been a tribulation to every member of the faculty. They had held protests over the course work, protested the pharmacy professor and signed petitions to have him fired, in truth, they were a class of disgruntled people who made trouble throughout the entire period of their training.

Our class was just the opposite. We were a very congenial group who laughed a lot, and grew closer as we studied and trained together. Our introductory classes with the pharmacy professor were an eye opener. Although he was young, attractive and held a Ph.D. in his subject, he looked miserable, indecisive and his hands shook noticeably. We held an impromptu meeting and decided it was our duty to turn his life around after his bad experience with the previous class of barracudas. So we treated him with respect and invited him to join us for lunch a few times, and even invited him to one of our parties. He gradually relaxed, realized we weren't going to petition to get him fired from his job and by the end of the semester he was acting positively mellow and contented in his work. We took full credit for his rehabilitation.

My best friend at school was a young girl named Carla. We were in competition in every class and every test. We became good friends, we laughed a lot and I found her delightful to know. The nursing faculty couldn't believe how they had lucked out with our class. We were compatible, easy to teach, competitive, we partied and enjoyed what we were doing. I was deliciously close to enjoying a second childhood during this time and luckily my husband didn't resent my obvious new interests and acquaintances.

A faculty member threw a poolside Christmas party during our second-class year. Long skirts were in, and I went to the party dressed for the occasion in a long party dress and gold sandals. We were having a wonderful time when suddenly to everyone's shocked surprise a very strange thing happened. Three of the guys calmly walked up to another fellow and threw him into the swimming pool. We thought it was hilarious as he climbed from the pool looking cold and bedraggled. A short time later while sitting in a deck chair at poolside, I looked up into the faces of our five guys hovering over me, saw their evil intent, and cautioned, "You will NOT throw me in the pool. I am a mature mother of grown children." Without a word, they lifted me out of my chair and tossed me in a high arc into the center of the pool...long dress, hose, sandals, wristwatch and all. This crazy exhibition of foolishness was greeted with cheers and laughter. They assured me it was their way of paying me homage!

Upon my arrival home from the party, I walked into the family room where Norman was sitting and without a change of expression, he asked, "Did you enjoy the party?" There I stood in my wet clothes, wet hair stringing down, my toes poking out through my nylon hose, wet shoes and a wristwatch that would stop dead by morning. Bless him, he accepted my explanation with good humor.

Our bearded, male Nursing Psychology professor had mentioned that he had been a gang member during his youthful days in Baltimore. It was his practice to hand out a test, go to the blackboard and write how long it should take us to finish it. He had other little habits that were a bit odd, but we tolerated them. Late in the evening on the night before the final exam, before graduation, we hatched a plot to play a trick on him the next morning during test time. Every member of the class was called and all agreed to participate, even the little "goody-two-shoes."

The plan was to go like this: After the test was distributed, and he turned his back to write his silly little messages on the black board, I would "cough" two times and that was a signal for everyone to assume a position or action that we had studied in Abnormal Psychology.

And so it went. He distributed the test, turned to the blackboard, picked up some chalk and began to write. I coughed two times and the entire classroom became bedlam. Some crawled under their desks, some howled, some tore off their upper garments, banged their heads, some assumed a catatonic posture, or swayed and pulled their hair. We were to hold the pose for thirty seconds. A half-minute of that behavior is a long time.

His reaction was most interesting. He swung around in a crouching position with his arms out as if ready to fight, which we thought must be a flashback from his gang member days. Then he slowly straightened, the expression on his face never changed, but he had turned an ashen white, except for his nose, which was red as a cherry. He never cracked a smile, although we were all whooping it up. He calmly turned and wrote on the board, "you now have 43 minutes to finish this test." His color slowly returned to normal and we busied ourselves with our final exam. It made our day.

In May of 1975 I graduated from Bakersfield College with an Associate Degree in Nursing. Our nursing class pinning/graduation ceremony was held in the college auditorium; I was mistress of ceremonies. In our new white uniforms and caps, I felt very proud of our class. I was allowed to plan the entertainment for the event and before we proceeded on to the serious part of the ceremony, there was fun and laughter. We presented gifts to the faculty and when the spoofing was over, the faculty, in turn, did their thing and presented the scholarship awards, our diplomas and pins. With a G.P.A. of 3.84, I was valedictorian of my nursing class and was presented with a nursing reference book inscribed by the Director of the Nursing Department. I had made this my goal and it felt great to have achieved it.

We planned a graduation banquet with professors in attendance and our class presented a program of humorous poetry and an original skit that we entitled, "A Mid-Summer Night Sweat." We arranged for two "streakers," members of our class dressed in flesh-colored tights and leotards, to run through the assembly during the evening; they looked, for all the world, buck naked. We had a jolly good time.

I insisted Norman and John attend the evening outdoor College graduation exercises. (groan, groan) The Goodyear Blimp flew overhead during the ceremony flashing congratulatory messages along its beam. The ceremony was over-long and a bit tiring for my guys sitting on concrete risers as a couple hundred graduates walked to the edge of a parapet, stopped for a moment in the circle of a spotlight, before proceeding to their seats. (groan, some more.)

We heard a local judge tell us how glad he was to be at Bakersfield College addressing so many "engineers." This was a Junior College and there were no engineers! The poor dear had used an old script and hadn't changed it. It was a real bummer, but I wouldn't have missed it for the world. I was enjoying my retrogression in the maturing process, so what the heck!

We had advertised our player piano for sale, and the judge, who had presented the boring address to the "engineers" the evening before, rang our doorbell early the next morning, purchased our player piano and hauled it out the door and loaded it into a truck.

We had acquired a silver poodle while we were in California but he was not a pleasant pet and we chose not to move him back to Texas. A man, his wife and teen-age son arrived on our doorstep in answer to an ad I had placed in the local paper; they were interested in our poodle. The woman was carrying an album under her arm. We invited them in and Pitou came into the room and promptly jumped up on the young boy's lap, the only action he had ever taken that I totally approved of. I thought that might be a good sign. Then the woman opened the album and showed us her pictures.

It seemed they had a poodle that was old and not long for this world; she was depressed because she knew her dog wouldn't live much longer, so her husband thought she should be getting acquainted with another dog. The album was filled with pictures of their dog: dressed in Christmas clothes, dressed for Easter, having a birthday party, and in every possible doggie position. I knew I had the right home for our dog and sure enough, Pitou was acting decent for the first time in his doggie life. I gladly surrendered him to this family.

Several weeks later the lady called to tell me that when they brought Pitou home their other dog went into a funk, crawled under the couch and wouldn't come out except to urinate and defecate. They thought he would die under there. Then one day he crawled out and they put him in the back yard with Pitou who was a bouncy, jumpy dog. She said their old dog was so inspired by Pitou that he began to run, play and act like a young dog again. She said she thought it was a miracle!

John was in seventh grade when we arrived in Bakersfield; he liked his school and resumed his membership in a Boy Scout troop. He found the mountains to his liking and had the experience of camping up at snow level occasionally. He earned the Order of the Arrow and became an Eagle Scout in 1975, becoming the 3rd Eagle Scout in the family following in the footsteps of his brother and father.

Norman had become very disenchanted with the College and it was a source of constant irritation that he was not allowed to teach in a manner he considered essential in the sciences. He grew more and more dissatisfied and we decided to return to the Rio Grande Valley as soon as I graduated from nursing school. Fara and Joe were living in Harlingen, our farms were located nearby and the city had a sizeable hospital where I could work. Harlingen seemed a logical place for us to live.

I applied for a job as a staff nurse at Valley Baptist Medical Center and was accepted for employment, sight unseen. We held the usual "moving sale" and had our personal belongings moved back to Harlingen. Both of our houses sold immediately for a good deal more than we paid for them and off we went, hoping to get to Harlingen before our furniture arrived.

We bought a new home, selected carpeting and it was barely installed before the moving van arrived. The mover, drove straight through from California, arrived at 1 a.m. on the 3rd of July and informed us that he had to unload and be gone before morning. We called Joe out of bed to help us unload; our furniture was deposited, kerplunk, and the trucker took off for Oklahoma at 4 A.M.

We were back in Texas, at last. We had a new home two blocks from the high school, an easy walking distance for John. I was embarking on a nursing career with great anticipation and some apprehension. Being near our daughter and her husband pleased us and we were convinced our decision to return to Texas had been a wise one.

M.L. FLADOS R.N

FOR RUTH

Note: My dear friend, Ruth, and I had a mutual friend who was smart, pretty, witty and Chinese. Ruth and I came to wonder why, all too often, we found ourselves doing something that benefited only our friend, Mae, such as going places we didn't want to go or offering a service that inconvenienced us, simply because that was what she, not we, wanted to do. Looking back, we would say to each other, " How did we fall for this ploy again?" No one was immune to Mae's charismatic, manipulative nature. This commentary was written in Bakersfield, California in 1973.

Last week I had a horrifying experience. While we were working in our little communal garden, Mae, my Chinese friend, asked if it would be a convenient time for her to remove some of the meat that we were storing for her in our freezer. Then she said and I quote, "I would like to go with you when we take my ham and bacon to be smoked at a locker on the Edison Highway."

I acquiesced. I realized that if I lived in China, I would have a language problem, too. She said, "How about Wednesday, we can stop at an antique shop on the way home." That was agreeable with me, and she then said, "I will pick you up at 10 o'clock." At 10 o'clock on Wednesday morning, Grace, Mae's 10 year old daughter and young manipulator-in-training, called and said, "My mama is working in the yard this morning and wants me to tell you we will be a little late."

189

At about 11 o'clock they arrived. In the meantime, I had lost my enthusiasm for the trip, but I assisted in the loading of the meat and we took off. That's when it began.

Driving down Brundage Road, I was enjoying the sights and sounds of business-busy Bakersfield; it was a very pleasant morning. I glanced over at Mae and to my surprise, she had opened a bottle of liquid make-up and had applied little patty dabs of it all over her face and forehead.

I said nothing. Then she began rubbing the make-up into one side of her face only, peering into the rear view mirror, constantly weaving in and out of traffic as she drove. She turned to me and asked, "Is there an improvement, that you see, Madtzie?" That was as close as she ever came to Margie.

"Yes," I said, "it looks very nice."

Then she proceeded to finish the remainder of her face and forehead in the manner she had previously followed. Holding her face an inch or so away from the mirror, she then slowly began to apply her lipstick. Meanwhile the traffic was heavy and unrelenting and it seemed to me that Mae was changing lanes more often than was necessary. But she wasn't finished! I had in the meantime decided to tighten my seat belt, which I did. Tight!

Grace, during this time was riding in a most relaxed manner, with her little face hanging over the front seat, her little black eyes, expressionless and inscrutable. Mae then took her comb from her purse and began to backcomb her hair. Now you know, Ruth, if you have ever done it, that backcombing takes two hands and Mae was using two! We were at this moment, tearing down a busy city thoroughfare at 45 miles an hour. I can't in all honesty say she was "driving", for NO ONE was driving. I knew I was riding with a crazy lady and I began to make deals with the Lord: "If You let me out of this one, to safely see all my babes to adulthood, I will agree to be a nicer person from this time forward. I will think only benign and saintly thoughts, I will never cuss again, I will quit biting my cuticles, I will not stuff my body with too much food and drink, I will not condemn all liberals to hell as evil and foolish, I will in thought, word and deed be a better human being."

I opened my eyes a slit to discover we were turning into the parking lot of the locker plant. Nothing more exciting transpired while we were there, other than learning one could buy a side of choice beef for 88 cents per pound.

Driving from the parking lot after completing our business, Mae asked, "How best do I get out of here, Madtzie?" I ventured, "Why not drive over to the other exit and out onto the highway." She proceeded to do this when I noticed a seriously eroded area between our car and the street and I added, "I guess we can't go that way, Mae, there seems to be a few potholes there."

Resignedly she says, "It is best not to ask advice when one is driving, but do what one feels is right. Do you not agree, Madtzie?"

I wanted to go home. Oh how I wanted to be back in my safe little nest. We then drive to a Fruit Farm where Mae said she always buys fruit when she is on the east end of town. We bought some wilted grapefruit, no bargains there. The young Chinese man that helped us was very friendly, and as we were leaving, Mae told him she was sorry to learn recently of the death of his father, and was his mother planning to sell any of his Chinese belongings. The young man said no, that his mother was still very sad and he didn't anticipate that she would be selling his father's things at this time. (What unspeakable bad taste, I thought..)

We stopped at an antique shop nearby and we began to "seek joyfully and find with pleasure," or rather Mae did, my spirit had long since been broken. I was fading fast and I found myself thinking of nothing but HOME SWEET HOME. Mae looked and peered into every nook and cranny. She placed six items on the counter and began to haggle with the proprietor over the price of the items. The total amounted to just over $15.00, but she told the woman that she was "only prepared to spend $10.00 today." The poor lady tried to withstand it, but in the end she capitulated and agreed to sell all six articles for $10.00. As we departed, the woman looked very unhappy with the sale she had just made. We know the feeling, don't we Ruth? She had been Mae-oed as we have been many times.

About this time we had the added diversion of observing a man, obviously desperate for his next bottle of rot gut wine, enter the shop and try to sell the owner, then us, two steam irons. They looked to be in perfect condition, and he wanted just 50 cents apiece. He found no buyers and was headed for the next second-hand store down the street, as we drove out. I am sure his poor wife will miss her irons and I was surprised Mae didn't try to buy them for 30 cents!

The trip home was mercifully quick and I found myself relaxing and wondering how I was going to keep all those agreements I had made with the Almighty. I was sustained by the thought that I had bought nothing. I was amused by the thought that Mae had bought a lot of junk, was convinced she had a bargain, when she didn't.

I consider it my duty as your friend, and a mother of young children, to caution you to take all necessary steps to prevent this ever happening to you.

I am grateful to be alive, the sun seems brighter, the sky bluer and I haven't bitten my cuticles since yesterday!

A SELF DESCRIPTION

Note: The following self description was written in 1974 in response to a nursing class assignment in Psychology.

I grew up in a religiously oriented middle-class family where leadership, hard work and honesty were indigenous to the clan. All of my siblings dutifully accepted their mantles, but I did not. A carefree and frivolous life was my considered choice, and I pursued it with unfailing vigor.

As far as leadership was concerned, I observed at an early age that the Indians had far more fun than the Chiefs; I elected for the Indians! Hard work was fine when relegated to its proper place, somewhere beyond fun and relaxation.

Honesty, however, was mine to bear almost to a fault. I tried stealing at the age of eight. I stole three table grapes from a basket on the counter of the local grocery store, and spent an average of fifteen minutes a day for the following five years praying to the Lord for forgiveness. Since atonement proved to be so time consuming, I had to be realistic and forego a life of crime.

I knew that lying caused pimples on my tongue, so I didn't do that either. However, when I entered nurse's training, I began to suspect the validity of that belief. I may have missed the opportunity of many years of fruitful lying because of that old saw foisted on me by my mother.

I have always preferred the company of men to that of women because they are infinitely more interesting. I gain no intellectual stimulation from discussing diets, menstrual cramps (ovaries are such a bore), childbirth or the price of groceries. I have always maintained a few close friendships with women who have a healthy disregard for the above-mentioned subjects.

My personality crystallized at about forty years of age. It was at that time that I realized that I had seen about all the bridge hands, began to suspect the P.T.A. was subversive, and commenced to regard all Girl Scouts as monsters except when they were singing.

I progressed from mother craft to politics, from politics to theatricals and finally in my sunset years, I took off like a rocket into the halls of academia. If I were to take an aptitude test, I am convinced it would show a natural talent for the performing arts: belly dancing, acrobatics, mimicry, or perhaps ballet, for I love to perform and make people laugh.

I am and have always been a prodigious reader, I relate to people rather well and my antenna is well developed. Conversation stimulates me; I love the English language and spending time alone. And I know how to listen.

Acquaintances have said to me, "Why did you choose to become a nurse, I just can't picture it!" I keep a wise and knowing expression at the ready for just such moments so I can assume it effortlessly and say, "And why ever not? Who wants a nurse who can't sing, dance and stand on her head?"

I must confess to some traits that tarnish my psychological breastplate, however. I admit to a problem with authority, accepting it not using it. I am opinionated and in certain situations, indecisive. I feel no guilt about disliking some people. I think discrimination is a good word and altruism is a suspicious one. I think self-discipline is gorgeous, I think laughter is the best part of living and regret is the saddest. I think old people are beautiful, marriage is comfortable and I like the kind of adults my children have turned out to be.

I anticipate no academic challenges or professional hurdles with which I cannot cope. In summary, I am a nice kid and a peachy dancer!

ZOOLOGY

(A non-tribute to one of my professors of Zoology. 1970)

The world at best, can be called diverse,
Divided twixt wild and tames,
But one stands apart at his obnoxious worst,
And his name is Dr. Haimes. *

Equate this diversity with "haves" and "have nots,"
Albeit L. Haimes would still give me the botts. **
He's boorish and mean and gall he's got lots
He tries to teach Zoo, but he gave me the botts.

Dirty black slacks, red hair all in knots,
Wearing a crown, he'd still give me the botts.
His attitude stinks, his teaching's a farce,
Saddest of all, there's flies up my arse.

* Name has been changed to protect the guilty.

**"The Botts" was an expression used by my dad, to describe his
disgust with someone. Bott flies are parasites that live in the
lower bowel of a horse.

LAB A

(Written on completion of Anatomy and Physiology.
Pan American University. 1971)

Lab A doesn't cheat, and we're there on the dot,
But we lie, and we steal and we cry a whole lot!
We consider our bodies God's finest creation
How creative He was is some revelation

What action required for organs to work
They pump, they pull, they jump, they jerk.
Inside there's bones, blood, muscles and nerves
Outside there's skin, hair, teeth and curves.

We stuff it with food, that is hard to digest,
We make it do work without proper rest.
We drown it in coffee, we drink things we shouldn't
Then expect it to do things, Superman couldn't.

When we know we've abused it, we're sorry,
well SORTA.
So let's all drink a toast to our darling AORTA!

THE LAST LAB REPORT

(Written as a tribute to the professor who taught our chemistry
class at Bakersfield College and read to him at our graduation
banquet. 1975.)

Just thought you should know, a tribute is due,
Not to us, heaven knows, I am speaking of you.

We learned about minerals, pH and that other,
We looked on our Prof, as our wise little father.

We considered the earth God's finest creation
How creative He was, was some revelation.

We analyzed liquids, we checked for co-valence,
We tested for ions, we weighed on the balance.

We spilled it, we splashed it, we cracked it, we shattered,
We melted it, burned it, we singed it and splattered.

You guided, where we were reluctant to go,
You crammed our hard heads with the facts, blow by blow.

You were patient, forbearing, unfailingly kind,
A masterful teacher with a disciplined mind.

The course is now ended and I'm sorry it's over,
But THANKS for the romp through the Chemistry clover!

BACTERIA

Our knowledge was widened, we were made quite aware,
Of the problems we face when we give nursing care.

We are crawling with critters, we can't wash away,
They grow and proliferate, dig in to stay.

When we cough it's disaster, they fly all around,
They roost on your teacups, and nest in the ground.

Bacteria, viruses, molds, how they grow,
It's a heck of a shape we are in, once we know.

We learned a great deal, we'll not be the same,
Since we once thought...E.coli was somebody's name.

(This was written as a tribute to Dr. Allsman, my pharmacology
professor at Bakersfield College. When read at our nurses'
graduation banquet, there was a last verse that read:)

Dr. Allsman so kindly just sent me word...
That this is the very best poem he's heard...
He states, "there's no Final." He's found other ways
To keep us all happy, by giving us A s.

MEANWHILE BACK IN CALIFORNIA

(Note: This was written in 1972 after a pre-admission physical examination which was required by California colleges. In retrospect, it seems a bit flippant.)

After our move to California, land of progress, enlightenment and ten lanes of traffic, I decided to continue my college education at California Community College at Bakersfield. I was required by law to have a physical examination before I entered college. This was inconvenient, but to someone new in town with no doctor to call her own, it was bothersome indeed.

We were aware of the severe shortage of doctors in the area and that one could not randomly select a physician. Most physicians were restricting their practice to their regular patients and accepting referrals; they were not particularly concerned with acquiring new patients. This became a personal challenge because I fit into the category of new patient. "Rain on all of them," I thought, I would be wildly efficient, consult the yellow pages, let my fingers do the walking, pick my doctor willy-nilly and hope for the best.

Upon reading the lengthy list of physicians and surgeons, I noted with dismay that most had offices on the opposite side of town from where we lived. Being unfamiliar with the city, I reluctantly faced the prospect of driving across town through the hectic California traffic which can be daunting. Ah, but there was an exception, a Dr. William Bullworth. (Name has been changed to protect the guilty.)   I promptly called for an appointment and a voice asked many questions of me, one was, "Who recommended Dr. Bullworth to you?"

"No one," I replied, "I found him in the yellow pages." There was no sound, just breathing from the other end of the line, so I lamely added, "I figured someone with a name like Bullworth, wouldn't be all bad." Another pause, then she said since it was to be a routine college entrance physical, to come in at three and they would try to squeeze me in.

When I located the office, no easy matter in itself, I approached the front door of what had obviously once been a family residence. The door was a shock. It was the dirtiest door I had ever seen, with the exception of one I remember that led to the ladies' room at a gas station in Tarkio, Missouri. I surveyed the office door, decided not to touch it, elbowed it open and sidled in.

Behind a desk was a nurse in white uniform who must have long since passed her eightieth birthday. I signed in, filled out a card, and turned toward the waiting room which was teeming with people. There were two varieties, mature women with menopause-blue hair and young women with babies in tow. At least he knows about menopause and sore throats, I thought.

There was no seat for me, all the babies were sitting in them, so I stood for a time until a toddler slid out of a chair, feet first, belly side down, to retrieve his pacifier, and I slipped into his seat while his back was turned. When he returned to the chair and discovered that I had filled it, he smiled and toddled over to his mother. I smiled at the dear child, and avoided the mother's glare.

I looked about for a magazine and spied a copy of Mother Goose Stories For Children, a Saturday Evening Post, a Colliers, and 2 frayed Liberty Magazines. I was a teenager the last time I had seen any of those magazines in print. Oh well, I thought, I shall use the time for quiet meditation. I calmly observed the waiting patients and speculated as to their ailments. I looked at the walls which were festooned with calendars and posters. One said, "PARK IN THE REAR," another said, "HAVE ALL YOUR FORMS FILLED OUT AND READY." There was a large picture of an angel with immense feathered wings, touching the brow of a bedridden patient. It was quaint, somewhat appealing and it held my attention for a time. Another big poster announced a revival and the services of a visiting faith healer, Wednesday at eight. I couldn't help but wonder if I was visiting a faith healer, when all I needed was a college physical.

During this interval the ancient nurse continued calling names, and people would rise from their seats and disappear behind a grimy door leading to who knows where. Intermittently the old girl would pipe up with little queries such as "Emma Lou, did you bring your medicare card today? Doctor can't see you without it, you know," and Emma Lou would dutifully produce it from her purse.

Finally at 5:45 P.M., my name was called. I go through the door and follow nurse person to a waiting room. She closes the door, hands me a sheet and says, "Take off your pants."

"What do you mean 'take off my pants', I'm not going to take off my pants, I am here for a college entrance physical, and no one takes off their pants for them! Nope, I'm not taking off my pants."

She gives a withering look, "Doctor has to examine your abdomen," she says.

"Let doctor do it the best he can, the pants stay on!"

She sighs and says, "Well, first go to the bathroom across the hall and give us a urine specimen."

"In what?" I ask.

"There are Dixie cups over the sink."

"You want me to wee in a Dixie cup?"

"Yes," she said, "that is what we always use."

"Then what?" I asked.

"You carry it to the lab."

"Where is the lab?" I asked.

"Around the corner and down the hall." (I was all braced to hear, A-round the corner and BE-hind the bush!)

I disappeared into the pot....no lock on the door. That figures, the doctor will probably walk in to take a leak just about the time I am....Holy Cow, I was peeing on my hand,. and not one crummy drop went into the little 'ol Dixie cup! I tried hard for just one drop, but nothing. I threw the cup in the trash. I considered putting it back in the dispenser, heaven knows it hadn't been used! I washed my hands, rearranged my garments and left the scene of my failure. I entered the examining room and she said, " Where is it?"

"Where is what?"

"Your specimen," she states firmly.

"I missed the cup and couldn't make any more."

"You will have to come back tomorrow, then, for that".

"I will not come back tomorrow then, for that," I say firmly, "I will pee for you before I leave, if it takes me all night."

There is a busy moment or two of getting my blouse unbuttoned, the sheet placed around me and I hear shuffling sounds behind the door. It opens and in walks "doctor." He had traversed the route so many times throughout the years, he had literally worn a path through the rug in a direct line between the foot of the examining table and his desk that I could glimpse through the doorway. From what I could see of his office, all that was missing were the jug of leeches and the cupping apparatus.

He peered at me through his spectacles, reached for a tongue depressor and asked that I say "Ah," which I did, wondering all the while, how many other tongues that stick had depressed. He took a pointy flashlight from his jacket pocket and held it close to my eyes and looked into them.

"Why are you looking into my eyes?"

"I am checking for blood," he stated.

"Why would I have bloody eyes?" I ask. "Not blood, but hemorrhages," he explained. I was relieved but fighting back belligerence.

The remainder of the examination was fairly routine; he looked and probed into the various places, he started to leave, turned back at the door, placed two spread out hands over his chest and said, "Any lumps here?" I smiled and said, "Only two, one on each side." Doctor was not amused. Without further word he turned back to his office. I ventured, "Oh, Doctor, since I am here, I need a prescription for birth control pills, written in-state, would you write one for Ovulen-21?" He nodded agreeably and said he would be glad to do that and he shuffled out and the office door closed.

"Can you do it now?"

"Can I do what now?" I asked.

"Give us a urine specimen," said nurse person, she apparently had my specimen on her mind the entire time. "I can but try," I said, as I slid from the table, buttoned my blouse, and turned to leave. Then I noticed a brownish smudge on the lower edge of the paper-covered examining table.

"Would you look at that!" I said, "Why don't you pull that off and throw it away. I am sorry about that...really sorry." I felt embarrassed.

"Oh that's all right," she chirps, "happens all the time." And she good-naturedly rips off the offensive evidence, pulls a new section of paper down and tucks it neatly under the pad between the foot stirrups.

I am successful in the bathroom. I carry my Dixie cup, still warm, down the hall to the lab. I am thinking that the lab is probably a real sheep-dip operation. I was pleasantly surprised; it wasn't so bad. I saw a nimble-fingered elderly nurse typing on charts, and a technologist, who had seen better days, but had some mileage in him yet, bending over his test tubes.

I handed him my Dixie cup. He seemed grateful. "Sit down," he said, "and I will prick you."

I must have jumped a little, for he asked, "what's the matter, 'fraid of blood?"

"No, it's that word," I replied.

"What word?"

"Prick" I said, "I don't like that expression, 'prick'."

"Well, let me, ah, stick you then," he said. This he did, and rather expertly at that, providing an ample supply of blood for the little vials he had to fill.

As I headed back to the front office, I am shaking my head in disbelief, with only one satisfying thought, at least it will be cheap!

"I would like to pay my bill. How much is it?" I asked of nurse person as I prepared to write a check. I thought, "I may never recover from this crazy experience."

"That will be $35.50." (This was considered a big charge for services in 1972.)

I was in shock, "I see, and what might the fifty cents be for, pray tell?"

"That is for the prescription that 'doctor' wrote," she said.

The check written, I turned, threaded my way through an almost empty waiting room, pushed the entrance door open with my elbow, slid through it, and headed down the outside steps. Then it slowly dawned. "THE BROWN SMUDGE! THAT WAS NOT MY BROWN SMUDGE, IT COULDN'T HAVE BEEN. MY PANTS DIDN'T LEAVE MY BODY....IMPOSSIBLE! I HAD BEEN LYING ON SOMEONE ELSE'S BROWN SMUDGE!"

As I walked toward the car, I looked back at the shingle dangling from two slightly uneven, rusty chains: WILLIAM BULLWORTH, M.D.

Unbidden, the word came into my mind, "PRICK!"

CHEMISTRY 101 CLASS – BAKERSFIELD COLLEGE 1972

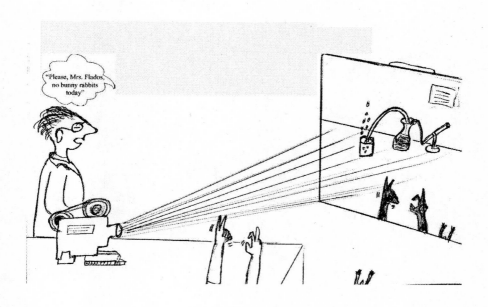

207

208

CAREER YEARS

1975-1991

I was a brand-spanking-new 49-year-old Registered Nurse facing gainful employment after 29 years of being a stay-at-home mom. In 1975, I began my career as a staff nurse on a 50-bed medical-surgical unit at Valley Baptist Medical Center in Harlingen, Texas. Having been hired in mid-July, I had missed the customary orientation for new nurses presented in June. I was assigned to the day shift and was placed with an experienced Licensed Vocational Nurse for orientation to the unit.

During my interview with the Director of Nurses I clearly remember her saying, "We have a limited number of R.N.s on your unit and most are new to nursing, I suggest that you allow the experienced Licensed Vocational Nurses (L.V.N.) on your floor to teach you how to nurse." With the changes that have taken place in the nursing profession in the past twenty-five years, this would never happen in this day and time, but at that time, the L.V.N.s were the backbone of the nursing staff and Valley Baptist Hospital had a cadre of exceptionally skilled ones. Her advice was prudent and well taken.

There was a total of five Registered Nurses assigned to our unit to cover three shifts, the Head Nurse and two R.N.s, (including me) on 7 to 3, one R.N. on 3 to 11 and one on 11 to 7. All other nursing staff members were either L.V.N.s or Nurses Aides. In addition to the Head Nurse, our unit had a total of forty staff members; the day shift was divided into two teams, each headed by a Charge Nurse, to cover a 50-bed floor.

In a very short time, I realized how little I knew about nursing and how experienced and knowledgeable the L.V.N.s and Aides were in contrast to my ignorance. Except for the Head Nurse, I was the only Anglo on our shift. I was suffering culture shock for I had not lived or worked with a largely Hispanic population and I was not made to feel particularly welcome by those on my unit.

Because I felt insecure, I asked many questions. The staff referred to every illness, procedure, department or entity in typical hospital terminology, a language of abbreviated terms, most of which I did not recognize. I struggled with trying to figure out what they were saying. The doctors spoke a language of their own, too, and I asked a million questions. Within a few short weeks I was placed in charge of a 25-bed area. Luckily I didn't kill anyone.

I felt disliked and unappreciated, and truth be known, probably was. One day as our very efficient unit secretary was standing by her desk, my arm accidentally brushed hers in passing. She drew away from me as if she had been scalded. I was surprised at this reaction. I was tense, scared and didn't sleep well at night.

Our Head Nurse was a Cajun from Louisiana and as wild and bizarre a person as I had ever known. She was tiny, profane, a gifted nurse and given to multiple romantic liaisons. She had brown eyes that turned red when she was angry, which could be frequently.

After a frustrating five weeks on the job, I asked for a consultation with the Head Nurse. The only nurse's lounge we had at the time was a room containing a table, chairs and lockers outside the tiny women's restroom. She called it "my private office, the toilet." I headed into the nurse's lounge and after a few minutes she followed. By this time I was teary-eyed. She sauntered in, sat down, crossed an ankle over one knee, lit up a cigarette and said, "So what's your problem, Flados?"

I said, " I hate to admit this, but I don't think I can do this job. There is too much I don't know, I am always behind in finishing my work and I feel that I'm not making the cut and should resign." By the time I confessed this psyche bruising reality, my tears were streaming down my face.

She looked at me with those little black ferret-like eyes, took a puff on her cigarette, and said, "Flados, if I didn't think you were worth a s--t, I wouldn't have put up with you for this long. Now get up off your butt and get with it. I will give you six weeks to get your act together." She ground out her cigarette and sauntered out of the room. She had a great saunter.

Was that a counseling, or what? I did get my act together within that six-week period and began to feel that I could survive as a nurse on our very busy unit. Looking back, she told me what I needed to hear; she had confidence in me and that is all it took for me to find a little confidence in my own ability.

The next hurdle was the staff. I felt quite sure that the L.V.N.s and sometimes the Aides were setting me up now and then. Someone who wanted an answer would say, "Why don't you ask the 'new' R.N.?" knowing full well I probably wouldn't know the answer. I began my campaign to win them over.

I showed my appreciation to the Aides, who were very good at what they did. I would ask their opinion sometimes, compliment them on work well done, and even asked them about some things they knew more about than I. I also made them aware that I would hold them to a standard of patient care that I considered right and appropriate. Then one day when three of them were standing in the back hallway, on some strange impulse, I began doing a silly little dance. I danced with abandon all the way down to end of the hall, and as I disappeared into a patient's room, looked back over my shoulder, kicked up a heel in a final flippant salute and gave them an exaggerated wink. They laughed and something magic happened.

Shortly after that, there was a general change in the attitude of the staff. An L.V.N. defied me one day and found to her surprise that I didn't accept defiance from anyone who worked as a member of my team. This was not lost on other members of the staff. As my nursing skills improved, so did my self-confidence and I began to assume the inherent role of Charge Nurse and gradually took total charge of my team. I was fair but indicated that I expected them to do their best. I continued to glean from their extensive knowledge and showed my appreciation for their abilities.

Many months later, I was standing at my spot where I signed off orders, intent on my task, when I felt someone leaning comfortably against me, the length of her arm touching mine. I looked up to see the unit secretary, the same one I had "scalded" previously, leaning gently against me, comfortably speaking to someone in the nurses' station. That gentle, leaning touch spoke volumes. It said, I was okay; I was one of them, that I was accepted.

After being on the job a short while, one event stands out in my mind as an example of my nursing inexperience. Upon entering a patient's room, I was shocked to see a pale, elderly man on the bed, with his mouth open, his eyes rolled back in his head; he looked very dead to me. Forgetting the ABCs of determining a patient's condition in this situation, I immediately thought he was in respiratory arrest. So I called out into the hall to bring the crash cart and call a Dr. 10, (Emergency Crew). Then I went to the bed and gave him a whacking precordial thump on the chest. He flung his arms up, his eyes flew open, and he yelled, "What the hell is going on, can't a man get a decent nap around here?" About that time the crash cart comes flying around the corner and the Dr. 10 team is on the way. I apologized and hurriedly removed the crash cart and told the secretary to call off the Dr. 10. Was I embarrassed, oh yes...(The precordial thump has since been discontinued as a procedure in respiratory or cardiac arrest.)

My skills improved to a point where I could tell the time of day by the relative elevation of a nurse's support hose. Marvelous garment, support hose, nurses won't leave home without them, but they inevitably seek that part of the anatomy that is the smallest in circumference and if you're lucky, that is your ankles. What hasn't gone south hovers in the shape of an arch right above the knees. That is why most nurses walk funny. I call it "low-crotch syndrome!" And I know from experience it makes you crabby.

Two years after my indecisive, unsure initiation into the profession of nursing, our Head Nurse resigned and I was appointed Head Nurse of our 50-bed unit. Now I could build an already good unit into a super unit. This I did.

My management style was quite different from my predecessor's. Nursing was changing, we were hiring more registered nurses, and the hospital was providing great in-house training programs for newly hired staff. Policies and procedures were being revised and rewritten and I took an active part as a member of committees responsible for these tasks. For many years I assisted with teaching orientation classes for the incoming new nurses mainly because my own orientation had been so inadequate. Among other things, I told them to have uniform pockets ample enough to carry a pen, paper, tape, scissors, safety pin, paper clip, anti-acid tablet (for themselves) and a stethoscope at all times. It was a unit joke, but they soon learned that it was good advice. This advice resulted from an incident I had observed on patient rounds. A physician asked a nurse for a stethoscope, she turned and hurried to the nurses' station to find one. He turned to me and asked, "Why do nurses always scurry?" I told him, "Mice scurry, Doctor, nurses ambulate." But ever after my nurses' pockets contained the necessary items that precluded ever having to "scurry."

I knew that leadership was getting work done through other people, that authority is bestowed from above but power comes below, from those you lead; a lesson that some head nurses never learned. I had the authority but I knew full well that my nurses must empower me in order to accomplish my leadership goals.

There was an on-going shortage of nurses, so I began encouraging anyone who aspired to become a Registered Nurse to do so. Whether secretary, orderly or L.V.N., anyone who wanted to go to school had my support. I agreed to schedule around their classes and part-time status. I gladly assisted in proof reading their written college assignments. Valley Baptist Hospital generously and I might add, wisely, paid tuition for anyone seeking a degree within the medical field. During the years I was Head Nurse no fewer than fourteen members of my staff became Registered Nurses. I rarely worked short staffed. I was as proud of them as I would have been of my own children. I fully understood how difficult it was to attend school, continue to work and care for their families too.

Representing our hospital as a nurse recruiter, I made many trips to various parts of the country and recruited nurses for our institution. I enjoyed doing this and felt I was good at it.

Our staff had great parties for which I would plan skits and entertainment. At a baby shower for one of our expectant mothers, we all came with pillows under our clothes so we all looked as pregnant as the guest of honor. One year, before the scheduled all-hospital volleyball tournament, I asked if there were any volleyball players on the staff. To my chagrin, there were several who admitted they had played intramural volleyball in high school. No nursing unit had ever fielded a team in the all-hospital volleyball tournaments, but we did. I was the coach and I had never played volleyball in my life, but I darn sure knew how to borrow a net, a ball and organize the practices. We had some very tough, competitive players and we took the trophy our first and second years in competition. What a thrill it was to receive the trophy for two consecutive years. The Physical Therapy and Pharmacy departments, which had won in the past, were quite surprised. During one game I held a player's baby so she could play in the finals. A coach does what a coach has to do!

When asked how many on the staff could swim, it was a surprise to learn that none of them could. I arranged for 23 staff members to take swimming lessons after work at the Elks Club pool. Some had never worn a bathing suit before, and one nurse asked if she could sew extensions on her suit, because it seemed so immodest. Oh this was a gentler time, for sure. They did remarkably well and the event was unusual enough to make the local newspaper, which included a picture of the class.

I encouraged learning and scrupulous professional honesty. I drew cartoons and wrote limericks and posted them on our bulletin board. Our slogan was, "We Have The Best on Second West." The staff behaved professionally and the doctors made no bones about wanting their patients on our unit.

My staff seemed to be always giving gifts to someone, so before having surgery in 1978, I told them they should not spend their hard earned money on flowers or a gift for me. On my return home from the hospital, a group of staff members showed up at my door with a dead potted plant, a beautifully wrapped gift that contained a worn out hospital gown signed by the staff and many of the physicians who regularly had patients on our unit. There were other hilarious items of half eaten refreshments etc. They reminded me that I had told them not to spend their hard earned money for flowers or a gift. We had a good laugh. It was quite a production and was the kind of gesture that warmed my heart, as they knew it would.

I was finding my way in a new culture and sometimes the learning experiences were interesting. At the first staff Christmas party, which was held at our home, everyone brought delicious Mexican food. I was ready to start serving the supper, buffet style, and announced they should begin serving themselves. I had in the meantime gone into the kitchen for something and a staff member came in and quietly said to me, "Flados, your husband is waiting to be served." I said something like, "he's a big boy and usually serves himself." I went into the dining room and to my utter surprise observed that they had filled plates with food and served their husbands who had all remained seated. Every wife had served her husband before they filled their own plate. I made a few comments about how my husband would indeed like this custom and we laughed about it.

The following year, at our Christmas staff party, Norman and I decided to show them how adaptable we were; when dinner was announced, I dutifully filled a plate and carried it over to my husband and served him. What I didn't know was that they had decided to do it the Anglo way and their husbands all served themselves, and I unknowingly was the only one who had done it the traditional Mexican way, serving my husband before serving myself. They thought this was hilarious. I asked them to please make up their minds and not confuse me in that way.

Because there were so many similar first names, we used only last names on our unit. We were the only unit in the hospital that did this and the staff took pride in it. It was part of our uniqueness as a staff. I told them to make a habit of learning something each and every day and when they learned something worthwhile they had the obligation to share it with someone who didn't know.

The 60th birthday party they gave me at work was another hoot with gifts and illustrations of the things we had found laughable through the years. I had always been accused of a willingness to eat anything regardless of its taste or condition, (not true, of course) so before they brought in the real food, they invited me to a half-eaten, very tired menu indeed. Even the cake was messed up and lopsided. After they all had their jollies, they brought in the really good Mexican food they customarily brought to our little celebrations.

I celebrated births, weddings and quincineras with them and I attended their family funerals, as well. I was there for them, they were there for me. Most of the staff were 1st and 2nd generation Mexican-Americans; they were comfortable in their skin, and their ethnicity did not intrude on our relationship. Nor should it. One of my nurses once said, "Flados, you've become a pretty good Mexican." She meant it as a compliment, and I took it as such.

Since we were a large unit with neurological, surgical and medical patients, many doctors visited our unit each day. I enjoyed the doctor-nurse game and learned to play it well. Early on I began keeping a notebook that contained every doctor's preferences and special needs for his specific discipline or procedure. I wrote their glove size, their likes and dislikes in brands and equipment. My little black book became a valuable reference for everyone on the unit. Best of all it made us seem so-o-o-o smart.

Let me illustrate how the doctor-nurse game is played. Scenario: The nurse finds her patient is having severe diarrhea. She checks the chart and discovers the patient has been on antibiotics for eight days. The first impulse would be to say to the doctor, "This patient has been receiving antibiotics for eight days, she is afebrile and I think the antibiotic should be discontinued because it is causing her to have severe diarrhea." No nurse alive would say that, think that, yes but never say it. She would say instead, "This patient no longer has an elevated temperature and has been having severe diarrhea, do you wish to continue the antibiotic?" The doctor would check the chart, and say, "Let's discontinue the antibiotic." A nurse can secure any order considered appropriate for the occasion if couched in the right language.

A head trauma patient had been admitted to the floor during the night shift; the neuro surgeon had seen her on admission to the Emergency room regarding her head injuries. That morning I was called to her room by one of the nurses who told me she thought the patient had some broken ribs, for when she turned her she thought she had heard a crackling sound. We looked on the chart and saw no notation regarding fractured ribs. Then I forgot the rules of the game!

The doctor arrived on the floor on his way to surgery, he asked about the patient and I said very matter-of-factly, "She's got some broken ribs." Then came "the look," then the inevitable, "Mrs. Flados, are you practicing medicine now?" He left the floor without mentioning it again, but walked back 5 minutes later and ordered chest X-rays. I had momentarily forgotten "the rules." I should have said, "Dr., your trauma patient who came in last night, is experiencing sharp pains in the chest area when we turn her." Then the doctor would have calmly replied, "She probably has some fractured ribs, let's get an X-ray." That is how the game works. I loved playing it.

Some doctors can be verbally abusive to nurses. This was not allowed on our unit. We acted professionally and the doctors were expected to do likewise and with a few exceptions they did. If a mistake was made on the unit, I phoned the attending physician immediately or I met the doctor on his arrival on the unit and informed him of the error. I then made sure that an incident report was filed. Invariably doctors responded well to the up-front approach.

If a doctor was rude or abusive, I had no qualms about discussing it with him. Our unit still wore white uniforms and many still wore caps, and if I had to deal with a physician I would always make sure I had on my cap which was a tall one as nurse caps go. I found my cap could intimidate most out-of-control patients or visitors and it certainly helped when dealing with the physicians.

A nurse came to my office one morning and said, "Dr. (Name Withheld) is sitting on the counter in the nurses station." No one sat on my counters. I walked into the station, close enough to the young physician that I might have been invading his space a bit and I said very pleasantly, "Good morning, Dr. (Name Withheld), we don't allow rumpies on our counters in this unit." He jumped off the countertop as if he had been given an electric shock.

The new, young doctors with their recently acquired attitude of self-importance would throw their weight around for a while but we learned they respected professional behavior and usually reacted accordingly. And if they were really young, they seemed to avoid getting crossways with a white haired nurse in a tall cap.

I loved my job, and I saw our hospital grow from 200 plus beds to 400 beds, and I saw great changes in nursing with the advent of computerization in all departments. There were big changes in every facet of the nursing profession, some of them good, some of them bad. With the advent of new nursing administrators, many of the traditional behaviors were changed. Caps were the first to go, then the white uniforms, and as a traditionalist, I saw an erosion, slow but insidious taking place before my eyes.

I served as Assistant Director of Nurses for Medical-Surgical Nursing for three years. It was a great learning experience for me to have four units to manage which included a total of 184 employees, including the hospital orderlies. Drastic changes and reorganization were taking place and there was turmoil, dissatisfaction and disagreement. After yet another reorganization, it was a relief to resume my role as Unit Supervisor and return to my former medical-surgical unit where I felt I could control my environment to a greater degree.

I made plans to retire on my 65th birthday and I did. I wanted to leave while my staff still wished that I wouldn't. I wanted to retire while I was still active and able to do the things I hadn't had time to do while I worked. Nursing Administration hosted a beautiful reception for me and presented a humorous skit that poked good fun at my known foibles. The hospital presented me with an exercise treadmill as a going away gift.

My staff held a supper in my honor, presented me with a silver tray engraved with the words, "We Have the Best on 2nd West" and surprised me with the appearance of a professional entertainer who serenaded us. I treasured my nurses and I feel they gave me the greatest compliment of all by doing their best for our unit. I don't see them often, but when I do, it is huggy-huggy time.

Upon my retirement, I was interviewed and asked about my leadership style. My comments were quoted in the hospital news publication as follows:

"I loved the day-to-day challenges of nursing. The disease processes may be similar, but each patient's ability to cope with them varies. Therein lies the challenge to the nurse.

As for my approach to nursing, I would be considered a traditionalist. The nursing profession has been seeking solutions to major problems inherent in the new health care structure as we see it today. Problems due to recent legislation, hospital reimbursement policies and nursing shortages are testing our profession as never before; we are struggling to meet those challenges.

As for my management style, my leadership philosophy was quite simple. I respected my nursing staff, and encouraged them to respect each other so they, in turn, could respect me. I recognized work well done, so they could take satisfaction in doing their work well.

I found joy in my work, so they could take joy in theirs. I encouraged innovation, delegation, and creativity so resolution of problems could result. I expected the staff to convey a professional image in manner and dress, so those with whom they interacted would feel inclined to do likewise.

I laughed so they could laugh with me. Laughter heals the healer and aids in healing the sick. Laughter makes it possible for nurses to deal with the sickness, and sometimes death and despair of those patients for whom they care.

In developing an effective leadership style, I respected the importance of fair schedules, consistency, and up-front dealing with differences and infractions of rules and regulations.

Those skilled devoted, wonderful nurses on 2nd West made my sixteen years at Valley Baptist Medical Center the best of my life, to date. They have been my inspiration and a great source of pride and satisfaction and I owe them my everlasting gratitude." End of quote.

I missed my wonderful staff, however I never looked back or regretted retiring from the job that had given me such pleasure for sixteen years. Walking into the back entrance of the hospital each morning at 6:30 A.M., I would take a deep breath, appreciating how our hospital smelled (clean) and looking forward to another day on the job. Taking pleasure in one's occupation is a true blessing, but I was ready to let go and turn toward other pursuits.

In the intervening years since my retirement in 1991, I have noted the changes in the nursing profession with dismay. I have been saddened by the dissatisfaction expressed to me by those still in the acute care setting. I am shocked at the number of skilled nurses leaving the profession entirely behind them. I am convinced that many of the solutions offered are not solutions but enhancements of the problems. I wrote my thoughts on the subject and submitted the item to the local newspaper, which printed it on the editorial page. I received many phone calls expressing an appreciation for my viewpoints.

I submitted a longer, more detailed version of the article to a professional nursing journal and was officially notified that the editorial committee had agreed to publish it. After four weeks, I received notification from the publisher telling me my manuscript had been withdrawn and that it would not be published. The article had enumerated many of the problems in nursing today and my opinion as to how and why the problems exist.

Those in positions of editorial authority apparently could not readily accept these opinions being published in a professional nursing journal. The guilt is hard to bear. Someone at the top over-rode the five junior editors who had agreed to accept and publish my piece. Change for the worse is insidious in nature and correction of the decline will come at an equally slow pace.

I remain grateful that I had worked in nursing during what I call "the glory years." I had enjoyed the best of all worlds. I was grateful for being able to stay at home to raise our children during their formative years and as they matured and left the nest, so then could I. With a free and easy heart, it was possible for me to enjoy a gratifying sixteen years in a profession that I loved.

(Note: At the close of this chapter I have included a short version of my manuscript, "Where Have All the Nurses Gone?")

WHERE HAVE ALL THE NURSES GONE?

Much has been written regarding the shortage of trained nurses. Politicians and hospital administrators have demonstrated a long-term reluctance to identify the root causes of the problem and an astonishing inability to provide solutions. There is no shortage of nurses. There is a shortage of trained nurses willing to work in an acute care hospital setting.

Hospital and nursing administrators who give the financial bottom line top priority tend to turn a blind eye to the needs of the front-line troops, the nurses, who provide the institution with its reputation, good or bad. Ironically, nurses are the first to feel the downsizing effects of economy moves.

The nursing profession has been the handmaiden of its own recession. Highly educated nurses who can't, won't or didn't nurse make the rules for those who can , will and are nursing.

Stumbling blocks are placed in the path of the returning nurse. On the surface the detailed requirements for returning to the profession may seem quite appropriate, however after so little as a four-year absence, the requirements for reinstatement can be extensive and expensive.

Depersonalization has permeated all levels of nursing. Nurse to patient ratios are determined by a computer, not in itself a problem, except once the magic staffing number is generated and in effect, it has not accounted for dismissals, transfers, admissions, oftentimes in double digit numbers, within a rather short period of time. Surviving that situation with all the required documentation becomes an awesome challenge and no computer, or nurse is equipped to deal satisfactorily with it.

Twelve hour shifts play havoc with a nurse's family life. Pile on short staffing, excessive paper work, and nurses understandably leap at the chance to leave patient care behind to do administrative work, with a 9 to 5 schedule and weekends off.

Those in authority demonstrate a staggering inability to understand nurses' attitudes and needs. The first inclination is to throw money at the problem. However generous the compensation, it will not diminish the concern of the nurse who completes an assigned shift feeling his/her patients did not receive the care they deserved or paid for, because that shift was working three nurses short that day.

It would be folly to blame computer technology for the recent depersonalization in health care delivery. Nurse to nurse shift report, always the consolidating thread of information and interaction that welded the shifts into one cohesive unit is now accomplished by dictating individual end of shift reports into a tape recorder, to be picked up by the incoming nurses. If there is a question pertaining to a patient's care, how can it be asked? Or answered?

The solution to the shortage of hospital nurses is most certainly complex. The erosion was slow and insidious. There will be no quick fixes. Some positive effort in the direction of resolution would be appropriate compensation, but that alone will solve very little. The problem is bigger and deeper than higher wages. Nurses willing to be pulled to work outside their areas of expertise to satisfy staffing needs should be compensated accordingly. The pay scale for patient care nurses should be considerably higher than that of an administrative nurse with the same academic credentials. In a small way this would affirm the value of the patient care nurse.

There are legitimate reasons why shift preferences may differ and should be a consideration in staffing practices. A dress code should be in effect that imparts a semblance of professionalism and provides a way for the patient to tell the difference between a nurse and a custodian. Exit interviews with nurses leaving the hospital setting would serve to identify problems before they become monumental. As of today administrators are clueless.

Advanced degrees in nursing should require, in addition to the standard academic subjects, a solid background and several years of experience in a patient care hospital setting.

This is not a suggestion to return to the so called good old days, this is an appeal to move forward into an era of professionalism that will provide job satisfaction to those planning to enter, to those who are presently in, and to those who wish to return to the field of nursing.

The young continue to aspire to become nurses, many experienced professionals are still out in the wings of the work force, wishing that working in their chosen profession was more gratifying, disappointed in the obvious diminished esteem within their ranks and disturbed at being a powerless spectator to the erosion of a grand calling.

(Note: This piece was published in the Another Opinion column in the local newspaper, The Valley Morning Star. Response from members in the health care field was surprisingly positive.)

LIMERICKS

THERE ONCE WAS A GUY NAMED PETE
WHO SMOKED A LONG CIGAREET,
HE LIT UP AT SEVEN, STUBBED IT OUT UP IN HEAVEN
'CAUSE IT'S LENGTH WAS 23 FEET.

THERE ONCE WAS A GIRL NAMED MARGE,
WHO GREW WEARY OF SERVING AS "CHARGE."
SHE TOOK FOUR DAYS OFF, WHICH SHE SPENT AT THE
TROUGH,
SHE ARRIVED BACK AT WORK LOOKING LARGE.

THERE ONCE WAS A NURSE NAMED MARCEL
WHO NEEDED A GOOD DOSE OF QWELL,
SHE SAID "NITS NEVER MATTERED," BUT OH HOW THEY
SCATTERED,
'TIL THE STAFF NEEDED QWELLING, AS WELL.

THERE ONCE WAS A NURSE NAMED MAGGIE,
THE STAFF SAID HER CLOTHES ALL LOOKED BAGGY,
SHE REMOVED HER CLOTHES ALL,
AND WALKED DOWN THE HALL,
AND SAID, "YOUR CHOICE IS TWIXT BAGGY OR SAGGY!"

There once was a doctor named Bounds,
Who misbehaved badly on Rounds,
Nurses said, "We all opt, on his head, he be dropped
From the 4th Floor to see if he'll bounce."

Nurse TRUE BLUE objected , she said,
"You fiends, you would all see him dead!"
So she fled through the door, ran up to 4th Floor,
And she jumped out the window instead.

THERE ONCE WAS A SMART GROUP OF SIX,
WHO SAID CLIQUES IS PRONOUNCED LIKE "CLICKS,"
"OH YES", I SAID, "IT'S NOW CLEAR IN MY HEAD,
IT'S LIKE MYSTICKS (MYSTIQUES), BOUTICKS
(BOUTIQUES) AND ANTICKS (ANTIQUES)!"

THERE ONCE WAS A NURSE NAMED KAY,
WHO FRITTERED HER MONEY AWAY,
SHE FAILED TO REMEMBER, CHRISTMAS CAME IN
DECEMBER
SHE HAD SPENT ALL HER SAVINGS BY MAY.

THERE ONCE WAS A NURSE NAMED MIN
WHOSE UNIFORM SEAT WAS QUITE THIN,
HER PURPLE LACE PANTS, COULD BE SEEN AT A
GLANCE
AND MAY ACCOUNT FOR THE ORDERLY'S GRIN.

THERE ONCE WAS A NURSE NAMED PAT,
WHO WAS SCRATCHED ON HER WRIST BY HER CAT,
THEY PUT HER TO BED, EXAMINED HER HEAD,
AND ORDERED A DELTA SCAN STAT.

OF ALL LIFE'S BITTER IRONIES,
PEEING IS AT THE TOP,
AFTER 60 , MEN CANNOT,
AND WOMEN CANNOT STOP.

CHRISTMAS ON FOURTH FLOOR

(Written in 1978 as a Christmas tribute to the nursing staff of the
50-bed, Medical-Surgical Unit where I was Head Nurse.)

'Twas the night before Christmas, when throughout Fourth Floor,
The night shift was busy, there were patients galore.

Some patients were snoring, asleep for the night,
But most had one finger pressed hard on the light.

Pulses and blood pressures, wavered and tilted,
The night shift continued to run 'til they wilted.

When the night shift was over, they grabbed coats and purses,
Willing to leave all, to the oncoming nurses.

Report was in progress, all the details were told,
Of each patient's symptoms, the tale would unfold.

Of the eight hours previous, no fact was concealed,
Whose wounds were recovered, whose wounds were unhealed.

After breakfast was served, all the bed pans were loaded,
Size, color and shape of the contents were noted.

The pills were poured out in the cups on the tray,
And dispensed with great care, the pains to allay.

When what to our wondering eyes should appear,
A covey of doctors in white-coated gear.

The R.D.C. doctors, they always come early,
There was Schwassenbach, Perris, Patcher and Burlee.

There was Creedly, Calvin, Zuy, yes and Newell,
Come to listen to heart beats and examine a stool.

White coats a-flapping, in split-T formation,
Checking pulses and chest rales and gut inflammation.

No sooner departed, when who should appear,
Tepello and Whitson to check eyes, nose and ears.

Next come Marshall and Sowell, so perky and quick,
Come to smoke up the station and visit the sick.

The "bone men" are coming! Roll out the cast cart!
Before somebody's fracture starts falling apart.

Dr. Ridlow arrives to pour over charts,
With meticulous work-ups so dear to his heart.

We don't call him "Jesus" as some people would,
Although we admit that he's almost that good.

The urologists three, so different in mien,
All ask the same questions, "Are my patients all peein' ?"

Out in the hall there arose such a clatter,
Nurses sprang from the lounge to see what was the matter.

We call them the "brain men", so different in manner,
Their mutual devotion, that fancy CAT scanner.

One partner so handsome, so natty, soft spoken,
But his legs bow out back, as if they were broken.

A "being" approached, his eyes how they glowered,
His pants above shoe-tops, should have been lowered.

Gruff and abrasive, but oh, what is worse,
He stands at the station, yells, "I WANT A NURSE!"

All but one scampered to get out of sight,
She was caught charting, no way out of her plight.

Dr. Hibbs is approaching, he's always "in training,"
He asks of the staff, "Are my patients still draining?"

About noon time each day, Dr. Phipps will arrive,
To see if his patients are dead or alive.

"I hurt," says the patient, "Doc, what is the matter?"
Dr. Phipps says, "You have, an infected gall bladder!"

Dr. Hackwell appears, so dapper, so mighty,
Nurses know that his bark, is worse than his bitey.

We've completed our duties, the report is now due,
We relinquish the reins, to the afternoon crew.

And homeward we go, work done for the day,
Our tasks on the floor, seem light years away.

There are husbands and children, our families to keep,
There are fun times and laughter and eight hours sleep.

At dawn the next day, we arrive on Fourth Floor,
Ready to care for our patients once more.

**SO ALL YOU KIND NURSES, YOU MUST KNOW THE
REASON,
GOD'S BLESSING IS YOURS, IN THIS HOLIDAY SEASON!
MERRY CHRISTMAS AND HAPPY NEW YEAR TO A
GREAT STAFF!**

THE CONCURRENT YEARS

1975 – 2005

The Viet Nam War had polarized our nation and affected our lives politically and personally. Joe who served as a Marine in Viet Nam sustained battlefield injuries that nearly cost him his life. Mark had been drafted into the army and served as a medic in Turkey. Fifty-eight thousand young men gave their lives fighting an undeclared political war at the wrong time, in the wrong place for the wrong reasons. In spite of its ignominious end, the people of the country felt great relief when it was over. The men who were called upon to fight this undeclared war are deserving of their country's undying gratitude and praise.

There had been a regional ingathering of our family and it seemed right that we were back in Texas, settled and pursuing our preferred interests. Norman seemed relieved to be in Texas and I fully realized that he would never voluntarily live outside its boundaries again. Being Texan is a state of mind and Norman's state of mind was: I am here and here I will stay, forever and ever, amen.

There were events going on in my life outside of my career. Because I wanted to devote a chapter to my nursing years, I will write separately about events that ran concurrently with the time I was working outside the home.

On our return from California, John, our youngest child, enrolled as a tenth grader at Harlingen High School. After Joe graduated from Texas A & M in 1973 with a Bachelor of Science Degree in Fisheries Biology, he and Fara moved back to the Rio Grande Valley and were living in Harlingen. After discharge from the army in 1974, Mark attended the University of Texas at Austin and graduated in 1978 with a Bachelor of Science Degree in Biology.

Following the purchase of another farm, Norman busied himself with leveling the various parcels of land and dealing with the concerns that go with the obligation of land ownership. He also dabbled in real estate sales and taught two years at the secondary school level.

My dad had been diagnosed with leukemia and with minimal chemotherapy, managed to enjoy relatively good health during the ten years of remission. But inevitably the balance tipped. In spite of his admirable strength and fortitude, the disease he had kept at bay for so long overcame all efforts to ward it off. After entering the hospital in November he did not respond to the usual medical intervention and he died on the 31st of December 1975.

I flew home when I was told he had been asking for me. I went directly from the airport to the hospital in Vermillion and when I entered his room, he appeared unresponsive. He had been alert and had talked earlier in the day. I said, "Daddy, it's Margie, I'm here." He didn't open his eyes but he said quietly, "Margie's here." Mom was sitting by his bed holding his hand. A few minutes later he said softly, "Anna, Anna." He never regained consciousness.

I had arrived too late to have one last conversation with my dear, wonderful daddy. To this day, if I allow myself to think about it, I feel the urge to cry. To lose a parent is a milestone in a person's life, and knowing you will never see them or hear them speak to you ever again, some little part of you never stops missing them. My loss was made sadder because of having been unable to spend much time with him through the years. Yearly visits just don't cut it. My folks would come to visit occasionally but as they grew older the 1400-mile trip was not an easy drive for them. I loved my dad. He was kind, gentle, decent and caring. Never one to verbally declare his love, he demonstrated in countless ways that he loved me without reservation. I was my father's child in so many ways and was told all my life how much I resembled him.

Fara was expecting a baby in two weeks and could not make the trip, but Norman, Mark and John made a hurried trip up to South

Dakota to be with the rest of the family for Dad's funeral. My eulogy to my dad is in the Commentary section of this memoir.

Stanuel Emerson Jones, our first grandchild, was born in 1976, followed by Jeffrey Norman Jones who was born the following year, so there were two little babies to enhance our lives. In addition to having babies, the Joneses were buying a home and making a major career change. Joe left his job with Texas State Parks and Wildlife Department and opened a State Farm Insurance Agency. His business prospered and their family grew by one more member, William Avery Jones, born in 1981.

In 1979 Norman spent seven weeks on an archaeological trip to Israel where he served as paleo-botanist for the consortium that conducted the dig at Tel El Hesi in the Negev Desert. It was a great experience for him and he returned with a full beard, wearing a leather necklace and looking for all the world like your garden-variety archaeologist.

While he was in Israel, I purchased a citrus grove on the west side of town. Norman was a bit shocked at my action and vowed he would never leave the country again without me, because he faced too many surprises when he returned. We soon learned there was not much profit in raising grapefruit, unless the owner did the grove care himself. After a devastating freeze a few years later, which left us with tons of rotting fruit on the ground and a grove of dead citrus trees, we bulldozed the fruit trees and thereafter the property was planted in vegetable crops, mainly cabbage. In spite of intermittent setbacks, we realized a nice return on my investment when we sold the property several years later.

We built a home in the Treasure Hills area of Harlingen in 1981 and settled into our new neighborhood. John graduated from the University of Texas with a degree in Journalism that year; our nest had emptied but was filling up with little grandsons. Being a working grandma cut into the time I could spend with them, but we enjoyed them when we could.

Late in the fall of 1983, Dolores Flados and I visited Venice, Florence and Rome, Italy. There were only two other people on the tour with us and we were fortunate enough to have an Italian woman with a Ph.D. in Art History as our tour guide. The other two people on the tour were an elderly Jewish couple from New York City.

Dolores and I pondered the irony of touring the holy sites of Christendom in the company of an avowed atheist and two Jews, but as it turned out each one added a special dimension to our travels in Italy. We became a group of compatible fellow travelers who developed a mutual admiration and appreciation for each other. The tour guide was quoted as saying "I've never done Texans before!" As an architect, Jack Levy furnished us with interesting information when we toured the ancient cathedrals and could explain everything pertinent regarding a flying buttress. Vickie, Dolores' daughter, was taking a semester of college work in Rome and we had the pleasure of her company, too.

I loved Venice, Florence and Rome; we reveled in what we saw and because it was so late in the season, we benefited from the absence of tourists. We climbed the Tower of Pisa, luckily, for now tourists are not allowed to do so. Dolores clambered quickly to the top, but not being fond of high places, I crawled the last few levels on my hands and knees. There is an account of an unforgettable evening in Florence in Section Four of this book

Norman was a great help with the housekeeping during my career days and he maintained our sizeable yard. We were blessed when Julie came into our lives as a domestic helper in 1984 and she remains with us to this day. When she was expecting her baby, I was her birthing partner, attended the prenatal classes with her and to my pleasure, Agatha was born on my birthday. Both have been very dear to us through the years.

Mark married Debbie Riggles Wire in August of 1984 at a Methodist Church in Austin. The wedding was a lovely event with Debbie's seven-year-old son, Brandon, serving as her escort. There was not a dry eye in the church at the sight of that little boy walking beside his mother down the church aisle. Debbie was a lovely bride.

The family wedding party stayed at the Villa Capri, a grand old motel long since demolished to make room for more urban sprawl in Austin, and we had a great wedding weekend. After smoking for over thirty-five years, I had given up cigarettes nine months previously and in the celebratory wedding party atmosphere, I lit up a proffered cigarette. I grew pale, nauseated, weak and thought I would have to retire to our room to recover, or die. That was the last time I ever considered smoking a cigarette.

We had acquired a cabin at Delta Lake in 1985 and spent our weekends fixing and working to get it in shape. Our family had many great times at the lake; we kept a sailboat and paddleboat at the lake and Joe would bring his boat up on family weekends. I loved being at the lake, but Norman never really developed a feel for it. We would work until we dropped and about the time we had accomplished what we set out to do and I felt like curling up on the deck for a good lakeside sit, Norman would say, "I am ready to leave when you are!"

We would take our grandsons with us at times and they would spend the entire day in the water, putting out trot lines and rowing the kayak from one end of the lake to the other. After about five years of hard labor and many thousands of dollars spent on repairs, the place looked great, or as great as two mobile homes placed end to end can look.

We had begun the tradition of having a Family Weekend every year at which time our kids and the grandkids would all gather in a designated location and enjoy a weekend of rest and recreation. We have varied the locations, far and wide, but some of the most enjoyable Family Weekends were held at the Delta Lake house.

Three nursing friends and I toured Spain and Portugal in 1985. The tour group numbered fifty-five people from all walks of life and various cultures. Many hilarious things happened on the tour. With a group that size, there are always a few people that others would like to throw off the bus, and we had one particularly obnoxious man who was a real thorn. We arrived at the Alhambra in Granada, Spain and visited the amphitheater within that magnificent edifice. Because of the unusual acoustical quality of the structure, concerts continue to be presented in its amphitheater even today. Considering King Ferdinand and Queen Isabella occupied the building in 1492, it was in remarkably fine condition. Irmgard, our German tour guide with an attitude, asked if there was anyone in our group who would like to speak or sing up near the raised section in order to

235

demonstrate the acoustics. Mr. Awful said, "Oh yes, I will be glad to sing something." At that announcement most of us looked at our feet and thought, "Oh No!"

Surprise, surprise...he hobbled up to the front of the area opened his mouth and sang "Memories" from the musical, Cats, in a pure, well trained, baritone voice. One never knows where talent lies. I forgave him a lot after that, but not everything!

Then there was the eighty-year-old Arab, on the tour, who became smitten with Dolores. A resident of Canada, he had been a representative to the United Nations from a Middle Eastern country and was present in the General Assembly when Russia's Khrushev took off his shoe and pounded it on the table. We thought he wanted to take Dolores back to his harem and we went to great lengths to protect her from his attempts to sit by her at every meal. How we laughed about this dilemma!

We toured Gibraltar and the city of Algiers. I disliked North Africa, and felt no admiration for its people; I couldn't wait to leave the country. It was Ramadan and the locals didn't eat or drink all day until the sun went down and needless to say they became a little grouchy. It didn't help that I came very close to being abandoned by the tour group on a hilltop in Algiers. We had been driven to a high point above the city where a camel tender would, for a small fee, allow tourists to climb up on his camel's back and be led around for a short camel ride. Watching my colleagues as they rode the camel, I stepped to one side of the bus and into a fresh pile of camel dung. I walked off a distance to a grassy spot to clean off the bottom of my shoes and while I was so occupied, the bus driver proceeded to drive off, leaving me there amidst the camel poop. My travel mates yelled for the bus driver to stop, this he did, and I ran to the bus, climbed aboard with my heart racing and my shoes smelling.

Fara Lynn Flados, our only granddaughter was born in March of 1987. She was a beautiful little girl with large blue eyes and an abundance of hair. Not living in close proximity, I regret that we have been unable to spend much time with her. I firmly believe that grandparents should be an integral part of a grandchild's life. Both generations benefit.

My sister, LuIda, and her husband had been spending winters in the Valley and it was wonderful to have them living in Harlingen. We saw them often during the months they lived nearby. Olaf died of stomach cancer in 1987, he was a good man and we loved him. Lu Ida continued to winter here in the Valley for several years after his death and I would help drive her down to Texas in the fall and then drive her back home to Iowa in the spring. We had some very enjoyable trips, traveling up and down the country from Texas to Iowa.

Because I lacked so few hours of credit, I decided to finish work toward my degree; both of my sisters had graduated from college and I didn't want to be the sister who hadn't. I took extension courses presented by Mary Hardin-Baylor University and at the age of 62 received my baccalaureate degree in 1988. Through the years I had attended five different colleges in my pursuit of a degree and I finally had it.

My dad's death had left an additional set of problems for my mom over and above the loss of her husband of more than fifty years. Because of Mom's paralysis it was necessary for her to have some assistance in her home. After my dad died, she stayed with Lu Ida and Olaf for a temporary time, then decided she wanted to live in her own home. She wrote to Fred, a man who had once worked for Daddy on the farm, and asked him to consider employment as her helper, to live in her home, keep the yard, shop for groceries and assist her about the house, in exchange for room, board and $125.00 a month.

Fred had never married, was close to Mom's age and was a neat, attractive man. He agreed to come on a temporary basis. So Fred moved in and took over the yard work, tended the flowers, planted a garden, did the vacuuming and became a permanent resident in her home in Spink.

Mom fed him vitamins, made sure he ate vegetables with his meat and "taters" and kept his clothes neat and pressed. Fred represented a great solution for everyone involved. He was accommodating and helpful beyond our expectations at the time. He and Mom liked the same T.V. shows and were very compatible. They grew very fond of each other. On visits home I could hear them early in the morning, laughing and talking in the kitchen before I got out of bed.

It never occurred to my mom that this arrangement might look less then proper, until one of her friends who seemed more curious than others, asked if he helped her put on her bra. (He didn't.) My mom had the use of one arm only. It was then she realized that some of her friends might have suspected hanky-panky. Fred helped her with her full-length brace each morning and she didn't have a problem with that, apparently neither did he.

They flew down to Texas twice to visit us and they came off the plane, Mom in a wheel chair, and Fred walking at her side carrying her purse. They were obviously fond of each other and enjoyed each other's company. Lu Ida routinely washed and set Mom's hair, and on one occasion when she was unavailable to do it, Fred washed and rolled Mom's hair, and did a fine job of it.

He was treated as a member of the family, and shared in all the family gatherings for birthdays and Christmas. When he had a birthday, it was celebrated as well, and he told Mom he had never had a birthday party in his entire life until he lived there in her home.

She fell to the floor one afternoon while Fred was running an errand in town and there was no one to help her, so she lay on the floor unable to get up or reach the phone. She was also in the process of making bread. She had mixed it and left it to rise on the kitchen counter before she fell. As she lay on the floor, she watched her bread rise over the top of the bowl. Her credo was always "waste not, want not" and she was not about to waste that bread! She was lying near the stove and by using her cane, she pulled the oven door down, pulled the bowl to the edge of the counter, let it fall onto the oven door and thence onto the floor. She kneaded it down, then lay back and watched it rise again. In the meantime, she scrootched over to where she kept her bread loaf pans and pulled them out onto the floor, the Crisco was kept low in the cupboard nearby, she reached it, and greased the loaf pans. When the bread was ready, she pinched the dough into three sections and placed each into a pan, gave them a punch and set them on the oven door to rise. And rise they did. When the loaves were ready to bake, she reached up, turned on the oven, waited until it was heated, placed her bread in the oven and lay back and waited for it to bake.

Just before the bread was ready to come from the oven, help arrived on the scene and picked her up off the floor. She was not hurt, her bread was safe and the three loaves were removed from the oven, all of them beautiful with golden brown crusts. My mom's bread was always great and that batch was no exception. This scenario depicts my mom as the plucky lady that she was.

To her, serving food to her family or guests was her way of expressing her love. She didn't feel the need to say it, she showed her love by making sure she had the people she cared about around her dining room table or in her kitchen for coffee and home-made baked goodies.

Having Fred live in her home was a workable arrangement for six years, then one day while driving in his car he became stuck in the mud. As he went to assess the damage, he fell dead of a heart attack. Once again, my mother faced a great loss and some decision-making. Because she could not stay alone, it was arranged for her to move into a new assisted-living facility in Akron, Iowa. She was satisfied there as she had her own furniture around her and she could entertain, be safe and receive assistance when she needed it.

Agnes, Berdell and I dug up all seven of her little evergreen fir, spruce and pine trees at the Spink house and received permission to re-plant them in strategic places around the new six-plex where she lived. Each time I go to Akron I visit Mom's trees, which are now enormous, beautiful evergreen trees.

After several years and too many falls it was decided that she needed to be in a facility that had around-the-clock care. She chose a nursing home in Alcester near where she grew up, twenty miles from Akron, where so many of her friends from her youthful days were now in residence. It was a harking back in time, to a locality where hers and Daddy's friends were now spending their last days, playing cards, doing jigsaw puzzles and discussing shared memories.

By this time she had a motorized wheel chair and she was a fast driver. Mom never did anything slowly. When cautioned to drive more carefully, her comment was, "you would think they could see me coming and get out of the way!" She continued to be a prodigious reader, maintained a journal until she could no longer write. She had published her first memoir in 1972, a sequel in 1982, and to our surprise, after her death we found that she had contributed an essay that was included in a published manuscript called, <u>The Dirty Thirties.</u>

Mom pieced over 100 quilts in the years after her stroke in 1962. All children, grandchildren and great grandchildren received quilts when they were born, when they were married and sometimes at other times too. Those of us who have them, treasure them. Because she entertained, traveled, wrote letters, baked bread and continued to cook good meals or give a little party at the slightest excuse, she became a wonder to her friends and neighbors. She accomplished more with only one useable arm and leg, than most of us do with a full complement.

In July of 1990 Fara accompanied me to South Dakota to visit my Mom. They spent many pleasant hours together. Mom's health was deteriorating and in conversation she expressed the desire to see her sister Abbie who was terminally ill, living in a nursing facility fifty miles away in South Sioux City Nebraska. I said, "Let's go!"

As luck would have it, Agnes and Berdell were visiting at the time and Berdell had a license to drive a bus. We arranged to rent the handicapped-equipped nursing home bus and we all piled in with Mom and drove to South Sioux City to visit Aunt Abbie.

On arrival, Abbie was sitting in a chair, all dressed up, with make-up applied, beaming, looking pretty as a picture. Her daughter, LaDelle, was there with her, and when we wheeled Mom into the room the joy on the sisters' faces on seeing each other was like an emotional slam in the gut. They wanted to just sit close, smile at each other and talk. Those of us observing the two found we had a problem stemming our tears. We took turns leaving the room to lean back against the wall in the hallway to regain control of our emotions. We would go back into the room until overwhelmed with emotion once again and take turns repeating the hallway recovery process. I'm not sure either of them was aware of the poignant picture of sisterly love they presented. They weren't crying, they were smiling; we were the ones with the problem.

After a wonderful visit, we headed back in our bus, feeling emotionally drained but very glad we had made the effort to arrange a reunion between Mom and her dear only sister. Aunt Abbie lived just two short weeks after that visit. But Mom had taken the steps necessary to ensure closure in her loss.

It was shortly after this visit with her sister, that Mom was diagnosed with inoperative cancer of the cecum and the cancer was unrelenting. When I went up to South Dakota in October, Mark and his little daughter, Fara Lynn, accompanied me so Fara Lynn could meet her great-grandmother for the first time. During this visit she reminisced with me about her and Daddy's courtship. She was sitting in a chair, looking so fragile, but she wanted to talk. She had a twinkle in her eye when she related this story. She stated that when my Dad was drafted into the army in World War I, they had been "keeping company" for a good while, but didn't feel they should get married before he went into to the army. As she put it, "we had an understanding that we would be married when he returned." She went on to explain that before Dad left, he told his best friend, Alfred, to look after her and not let any guys get any ideas about taking her out while he was gone. She looked up at me with a smile, and said in her slightly Norwegian-accented English, "You know what that stinker did? He was the first one to ask me for a date!" Then she laughed and said, "but I never told Emil."

She entered the hospital for a final time when she began presenting symptoms of intestinal blockage and an ileostomy was done. The doctor was heard to say it was palliative, for sure, but he would not allow this wonderful woman to feel thirst or hunger during her last days.

I flew back up in December to spend time with her and to relieve those who had borne the main responsibilities during her illnesses. Her mental acuity never waned. She continued to laugh aloud at T.V. sitcoms and could say some rather strangely funny things. One day with a twinkle in her eye, she said, "I hope no one thinks I have been puttin' on all this time." (A commonly used Norwegian saying that if you weren't as sick as you said you were, you were "puttin' on.") A niece had visited her and as she was leaving, said, "Goodbye,

Auntie" and my mom replied, " Goodbye, I'll see you soon, I hope-a-hope-a-hope-a!" (A comedian used to say that on the radio.)

On the afternoon of her death, I sat and held her hand, laid my head close to her and we both dozed off. Earlier she had said very matter of factly that she didn't know "why it was taking so long." She had periods of intense pain but was medicated and kept as comfortable as possible. When I awoke, it was to the realization that she was dying. I asked a nurse to notify Lu Ida and Leverne of the change in her condition. I leaned over her to hold her more closely, telling her how much her family loved her, naming them all, one by one; telling her what a wonderful mother and wife she had been, how we would always love her and that God loved her most of all. Leaning near her ear, I softly recited the Lord's Prayer and when the prayer was ended so was her life on earth.

This life, so well lived, so blessed with mothering talents, wifely love, joy and faithfulness, this mother...my mother... was dead and I had a big painful hole of sorrow in my heart. This admirable woman left a legacy of integrity and decency. By her influence and example she has anointed the generations that have followed her. I cherish her memory and after all these years, each day some event, some thought, some action transpires that brings her memory vividly to mind. Her funeral was a celebration of her life and as the minister read passages from her autobiography we were laughing through our tears.

Another milestone in my life; I fulfilled all the criteria of... orphan. I have never stopped missing the sharing of an event or the pleasure of a gab session with my mom When things happen in my life or my families' lives, I still miss the pleasure of writing to her to tell her all about it.

I was always told I resembled my dad, but as I grew older I began to be a spittin' image of my mother. On a nurse-recruiting trip to Mitchell, South Dakota, I visited a cousin whom I hadn't seen in many, many years. When I rang the doorbell, her husband looked out, turned to his wife and said, "What a surprise, Anna is here." Upon seeing me for the first time in 35 years he must have had a flashback to an earlier time when my mom was my age.

A friend had encouraged me to become a Certified Aerobics Instructor and I began teaching classes at Valley Baptist Medical Center for staff members who had minor infirmities or arthritis. I taught the classes for two years previous to my retirement. During this time I had become very interested in fitness for the mature adult and honed my skills as a fitness instructor and teacher.

Predicated on a personal conviction that I was performing at optimum, after sixteen gratifying years in the nursing profession I chose to retire at a time when I could go "out at the top." I had already given up the time consuming activities of bridge and golf and I was eager to take on new challenges and explore different interests.

Shortly after my retirement in 1991, we sold the lake house, which had become something of a money pit, sold our home in Treasure Hills and bought a townhouse at the Harlingen Country Club in Palm Valley. We chose Palm Valley because Joe and Fara had moved there and we wanted to be near our grandsons. Norman had grown weary of keeping a large yard and willingly agreed to try townhouse living. It was our twenty-first move since our marriage. After completion of that move it became apparent that our antique furniture needed to stay put or it could possibly collapse in a heap. Living in a townhouse is very convenient, our houseplants gradually turned to silk and when we left on a trip, it was just a matter of locking the door and taking off.

One month after moving into our townhouse, this area received 13 inches of rain, which caused some local flooding. We had just installed new carpet and the water rose to within one inch of our front threshold. We were lucky; one family in Palm Valley had a ten-inch fish swimming around in their family room.   The local weatherman had predicted "possible chance of scattered showers." Two weeks later, we had a hailstorm, which resulted in new roofs for the whole town of Palm Valley, but since that time there has been very little excessive rain and no damaging storms. Two hurricanes caused minor damage locally but we were spared a major hit, both times.

I began presenting talks at civic organizations, seminars and banquet meetings on the subject of the Relationship of Laughter to

Physical Well-Being. I enjoyed performing, believed in the topic and over a period of several years accepted many, many speaking engagements locally and from various parts of the country.

My routine was a humorous one and I took great pleasure in making people laugh. I added the topics of The Healing Power of Touch and Dealing with Stress to my repertoire of motivational talks, but always preferred the Laughter-Wellness topic. I receive great satisfaction from public speaking/teaching. It satisfies the desire to perform that I have always harbored deep down within my being.

I spent four years as a mentor for Mothers of Preschoolers (M.O.P.S.) and particularly enjoyed advising the young moms with their parenting skills. I detected great changes in the approach to rearing children. In some cases I was quite surprised at the extent to which young mothers would go to shelter their children from the ordinary disappointments of childhood. These moms are the offspring of the baby boomer generation, which in turn are the offspring of my generation, and I wondered how and why these changes in parenting had come about.

My biggest concern was the inability or reluctance of young parents to inculcate in their children a respect for authority. It started with allowing very small children to make decisions that should be made by parents, secondly, the unwillingness to assume the role of authority figure in their children's eyes and thirdly, a willingness to take their children's side against anyone or anything that presented the prospect of disappointment, delay of gratification or accountability to someone in authority. I could easily predict that the result of this attitude would be teens and adults feeling no deference to any figure of authority: parent, civil or social. Conditions in our schools already bear out the result of these parenting attitudes.

I have yet to see a shopper under 40 years of age return a supermarket shopping cart to a cart corral. I do however see little old gray-headed men and women hobbling about complying with the sign that says "Please return shopping carts to cart areas." To the younger generation, voluntary requests for compliance are to be flaunted if they happen to be inconvenient.

I taught a six-week course on handling the grieving process, which I found most gratifying. Somehow during the study, I realized my folks had, without consciously knowing it, done a rather remarkable job of teaching their children coping skills and how to handle grief.

In 1991 Norman and I took a battlefield tour of the Ardennes in Belgium in the company of members of the 99th Infantry Division, which had participated in the Battle of the Bulge in the winter of 1944 during World War II. We had a World War II historian as our tour guide, but I actually didn't understand the significance of what I was seeing.

This tour triggered my interest in the European Theater of Operations during World War II and particularly the Battle of the Bulge. I went on a reading binge and fifty-five books later, I feel I have become well informed on the subject. So much so, that I wanted to take another tour in order to appreciate what I had seen the first time. So in 1997, I went on a battlefield tour without my husband. It was made more memorable by the Belgian contingent of W.W. II archaeologists who were with our tour the entire time. One of them personally led two of us to parts of the Ardennes that held particular interest for me. This team of "diggers" have, in recent years, found the remains of eight soldiers designated as "missing in action" since December, 1944. After proof of identification the soldiers' remains have been honored with appropriate interment in a cemetery of their family's choice.

I schlepped around German and American foxholes for the better part of a week. Unfortunately due to the wet pine needles covering the forest floor, I took a bad fall into a German foxhole and sprained my ankle and spent the last three days of the tour hobbling around with a cane.

Because I had done my homework and knew the history of the battles that had taken place in the areas we visited, this trip was memorable for me. World War II continues to hold my interest and I would like to make one more trip to the Ardennes. We have come to know many veterans of the 99th Infantry Division and we have assisted in holding three mini reunions on South Padre Island for members of the Division. We have attended several national conventions and have made some dear friends among the membership.

Deplaning from my last overseas trip, Norman said, "Why is it you always come home from these trips limping and looking sick?" That isn't far from the truth since I slipped and sprained an ankle in Rome in 1983, and not only limped off the plane with a swollen ankle, but in a rather bathless state, since getting in and out of the deep, narrow bath tubs in Italy was impossible after I sustained my sprain.

I have a problem with European bathtubs; they are narrow and deep and once in, I have trouble getting out of them even without a sprained ankle. I had a private room in a little hotel in St. Vith, Belgium and had taken a nice hot bath only to discover there was no way for me to get out of the tub. There was no handhold and the tub was very narrow and deep making it impossible for me to turn over and crawl out. Since I was traveling as a single, my thought was that I could stay in the tub for days before someone would break my door down and find me, naked and "pruny" in the tub. So I struggled.

At the head of the tub was a little washstand with a very sharp, protruding, square corner and as I finally rose from the tub like a phoenix, (not really), I slipped and hit my head on the sharp corner and sustained a dent in my forehead that I carried for weeks. OSHA would have a field day in Europe.

I have traveled extensively in Mexico; I have done the resort bit, the tourist bit and have gone with tour groups into the interior, but my favorite way to see Mexico is by utilizing the national bus services. Traveling into the rural areas and meeting the native population is very heart warming, and I have seen the country as few tourists ever see it.

Traveling with Julie and her daughter one summer up in the Sierra Nevada foothills, we visited remote villages, prowled through an old abandoned hacienda and ate tortillas (fresh from a brick oven) that were covered with homemade cheese. We climbed down a rope to the canyon floor, soaked our feet in the coolness of a little stream and drank the water as it poured from the rock face of the cliff....that is traveling in Mexico as I like it. Norman doesn't always accompany me on my travels, I like to say, "I go, he goes and we go."

As a member of the graduating class of 1944, I was asked to present the address at the graduation ceremonies of the Elk Point Class of 1994. We were the "Fifty-Years-Class." A merger was in the offing and this class was the last to graduate from E.P.H.S., as we knew it. I kept it short and to the point. A draft of the 7 1/2 minute talk can be found in the Commentary section. I was struck by the demeanor of these young graduates when compared to our class of fifty years ago.

To celebrate our fiftieth wedding anniversary in 1996 our children and we hosted an all-family reunion in Branson, Missouri. Sixty-eight strong, we gathered at beautiful Cedar Lodge near Branson for an enjoyable weekend. The family wore their Marge and Norm T-shirts to two Branson shows but the family dinner on Saturday evening was the highlight of the event. Fara, who has a gift for it, planned the lovely decorations. With the help of her siblings and spouses they decorated the dining room with arrangements of family photos, gold mesh ribbon and candles. The program was a compilation of reminiscences, poetry and humor. I walked into the dining room that evening and burst into tears at the sheer beauty of it all. It is a wonderful memory of being with the Klemme families, Flados families and friends of many years.

I have taught fitness classes at a local R.V. park, for the past fourteen years. I have run a full program of aerobics, strengthening, toning, stretching and hand weights, teaching as many as eight classes each week. Because of the large numbers in the classes during the winter months, it was necessary to train people to assist me which makes it possible for the classes to reach fifty-five in number and still receive the necessary coaching and attention needed to ensure that proper form is maintained. I am fortunate to have an excellent facility, eager participants and willing assistants. I take a summer respite each year from teaching. Mainly to travel, write and re-coup.

I have written a manual, "Teaching Physical Fitness to the Mature Adult," which I use in the training seminar for fitness instructors that I present on alternate years. I train women from other R.V. parks who wish to start fitness programs and also those who wish to teach classes in their home communities after they leave the Valley and return in the Midwest. Since the Rio Grande Valley welcomes thousands of tourists to this area for the winter months, the need for fitness classes is great and I consider it my ministry. There is no mistaking the benefits from regular exercise, for after participants have been in class for a few months, tighter, stronger bodies are easy to detect.

I developed sciatic pain in my legs during the 2001-2002 year and found it necessary to turn the aerobics classes over to an assistant, however, I continued with the other classes until June at which time I realized there was something seriously wrong with my back. I gradually went to using a cane and on a trip to Iowa for Lu Ida's 80th birthday party, I went in a wheel chair, an experience that convinced me that I couldn't cure myself.

Upon returning home and after diagnostic tests, my one thought, was "Let's Cut!" I had surgery in July 2002 to repair four lumbar vertebrae and the relief was instantaneous. I have been relatively pain free since the surgery. With the exception of the aerobics classes which I delegate to a competent assistant, I returned to teaching my exercise classes three months after my surgery.

Upon purchase of a new computer, John made me a gift of his old one with the comment, "Mom, it is time to enter the 20th century and become a "compu-granny." This I have done by taking classes and hiring tutors. I consider myself computer literate and spend hours at what I call my working computer.

Writing has always given me pleasure. We have published The Flados Flag each Christmas since 1958, however, I also do some serious writing with the hopes of getting my manuscripts published. The Journal of Nursing Administrators and Imprint) have published three of my short manuscripts. The Checkerboard, the official newspaper of the 99th Infantry Division, has published an article I authored for one of its members, entitled Memoir of a Medic. I edited a history, A Call To Valor, written by a member of an ASTP unit and my brother's memoir, Memoir of an Army Pilot.

I love the English language and appreciate its strangely interesting nuances. When reading the works of the wordsmiths of the literary world, their well-written sentences seem like music to me, and I waller them around in my mind for the pure enjoyment of their structure.

Through the years I have cartooned and written poetry, limericks and "rhymie" prose. Interestingly, all three of our children have tried their hand at writing poetry and do quite well at it. There is an outline of a book filed in my office and the story is firmly implanted in my brain; whether I have the self-discipline to write it, is another consideration. The story is based on fact and if I can make my words sing, maybe it will be published. That should be my next obsession.

Through the years, while moving from one literary obsession to another, I became interested in Jewish history and read everything I could on the subject; from there I went to Russian history and buried myself in it for a time. The World War II obsession was the last of many and it hasn't waned as did the others; I still want to learn more about it.

Agnes and Berdell spent several winters here in the Valley and we enjoyed seeing them frequently when they were here. After a game of golf one January day in 1998, Agnes died suddenly of a heart attack. She was the first and the youngest of my siblings to die and we were greatly saddened by her death. After a memorial service in McAllen, Norman and I accompanied Berdell back to Springfield, South Dakota where her ashes were interred. I think of her often and cherish the memory of her unique persona. She was my "little sister" and it seemed so odd that she should be the first of the siblings to die. Berdell died of lung cancer in 2005.

Jeffrey married Heather Lidgey in 1998 in a Las Vegas ceremony with the Joneses, Norman, me and several of the Lidgey family in attendance. The wedding was held in the Bally wedding chapel, and I was the most surprised of all that it turned out to be so meaningful and so lovely. We had a good time and proved that a formal wedding with all the required accouterments can be arranged in six days with family in attendance, including three grandmothers.

Since that time in 1998, Kaitlynn Marie, Jeanna Ann and Lauren Avery have joined the Jones family, beautiful babies whom we love and enjoy. Heather has been a blessing to Jeff; she has demonstrated good parenting skills and we are grateful for her presence in our family.

Our three grandsons, like their father, skilled hunters and fishermen all, are grown and pursuing their own chosen paths. While they were young boys, Norman and I gave them their first instructions on the protocols of playing golf. In addition to their jobs, Jeff and Will are members of the U.S. Marine Reserves; Stan is in the insurance business.

After preliminary training in urban warfare, Jeff and Will, both members of the 1st Battalion, 23rd Regiment, 4th Marine Division were deployed to Iraq in August of 2004. They completed their tour of duty and returned home March, 2005, battle-hardened by their experiences and grateful to be back in the USA. Their morale seemed admirably high; but the stiff upper lips here at home were sometimes hard to maintain.

It is interesting how some families have offspring that are oddly aligned with the nation's wars. In our immediate family, my dad served in World War I, my husband in World War II, my brother, Leverne, in World War II and the Korean Conflict, son-in-law, Joe, in Viet Nam, son, Mark, drafted and deployed to Turkey and two grandsons, Jeff and Will served in Iraq.

Our granddaughter, Fara Lynn, at age eighteen, has been accepted at Texas A & M University for the 2005 school year and has been granted a full scholarship for her freshman year. Mark's family lives in Austin, John lives in Houston, Fara and Joe live here in Harlingen, as do Jeff , Heather and daughters. All blessedly well.

Fara had successful removal of an ovarian malignancy in 2001, which in spite of the possibility of dire consequences turned out to be what we consider something of a miracle. Removing an eleven-pound tumor, intact, with no detectable signs of metastases was nothing short of the Lord's gift to a Child of God. At least I like to think of it in that light.

Last April we moved down the street from our condo into a lovely home that borders the 13th fairway of the Harlingen Country Club. Living on one level became a necessity and the location is conveniently near Fara and Joe. We have a great view from our patio and enjoy watching the wild life, mainly of the rodent variety, true, but interesting nonetheless. Some of the passing golfers can be interesting, as well. Our native birds abound, and every now and then we see strange birds that have strayed from their normal migratory pathways and its binoculars to the fore!

My husband has been diagnosed with Parkinson's disease, and at eighty-two years of age, is an avid reader and enjoys a rather comfortable lifestyle lunching with his friends and attending monthly meetings of the Rhinos, a discussion group of learned men.

At seventy-nine, I still find excitement in my activities and our friendships. We have enjoyed touring from one coast to the other and many places in between. I have come to grips with my mortality, but try to laugh about it and give death the names it deserves, such as "croak," " bite the dust" or "kick the bucket."

Pretty expressions for death seem pointless to me. People go to great lengths to avoid saying "die" or "dead," preferring to use expressions like "expired," "passed on" or "went to be with the Lord." I like the word "croak" when discussing my own demise (oops, there it is again) and why can't we "croak and be with the Lord?" It gives the whole sorry prospect of dying a sly, wry twist of mirth that makes the thought bearable. Laughter always makes the unbearable, bearable!

In my Funeral Folder, those whom we will leave behind when we "cross the bar," (hear how silly that sounds?) will find all pertinent information needed; our obituaries with just the dates required to make them complete, instructions as to funeral arrangements, disposition of body and personal effects. I enjoy working in my funeral folder and have laughed at some of the things I have placed in it, but in some cases, laughed, and later removed them for propriety's sake.

My life has been blessed with a loving, loyal husband and three children, who in the process of growing up, gave their parents minimal stress or frustration. I can pass the wand of family responsibility to them, comfortable in their ability to assume the roles of living representatives of their father and me and their grandparents who have gone before.

Life has been good. I firmly believe we should look toward the future with laughter in our throats; it tends to make our God greater and our demons smaller. It is said that love makes the world go 'round, and so it may, but laughter keeps us from tipping and slipping as we navigate our life-road, however bumpy it may be.

I still maintain a list of long-range goals and I know perfectly well I must hurry! I am making the most of every minute; I am laughing whenever I can find something humorous to read, watch or do. I watch no movies, plays or T.V. shows with depressing subject matter, except for the news!

We make a choice each morning; to be bitter or better, to feel gloomy or glorious, to cope or mope, to be joyful or mournful and the choice isn't always easy. Striving for perfection presents an incredible burden: perfect wife, perfect mother, perfect housekeeper, perfect this, perfect that. Sooner or later we deal with it; a late meal, a little dust on top of the refrigerator, a new wrinkle, three pairs of abandoned shoes by a favorite chair, so what? Blame gravity! Shoes fall, so do dust particles.

Because joy is mentioned over two hundred times in the Bible, I must conclude that the Lord meant for us to be joyful. Of all the blessings we enjoy, laughter is for free. It is subtle, precious and it comes with no identifying characteristics of nationality, politics or religion. Laughter is an equalizer that has no equal, and when we make of it a gift to those around us, it is wonderfully transformed into a gift we give ourselves.

WHATEVER ELSE YOU DO

By Max Ehrmann

Whatever else you do or forbear, impose upon yourself
the task of happiness
And then abandon yourself to the joy of laughter.

And however much you condemn the evil in the world,
Remember that the world is not all evil;
That somewhere children are at play, as were you
Yourself in the old days;
That women still find joy in the stalwart hearts of men.
And that men, treading with restless feet their many paths, may
yet find
Refuge from the storms of the world in the cheerful house of
love.

SECTION FOUR
COMMENTARY AND REFLECTIONS

WHAT NOURISHES ME

When I consider nourishment, NURTURING MYSELF, I think of:

Hibiscus flowers, breakfast with Norman, facing east toward a rising sun.

Whole wheat toast and humming birds feeding outside my window. Polished wood.

Marching bands preceded by our country's flag. Writing newsy letters. Soft music and stained glass windows. Teaching exercise classes, watching white clouds and green trees interacting with the breeze.

Birds singing. Softly falling rain.

A letter from someone dear. Butterflies and crossword puzzles.. Home made jelly...Acting in a skit or play, tall trees, a dinner out with friends, and laughter.

Monday mornings, pillows that have aired all day and e-mail. Praying as I drive.

Our family around our table, fresh coffee, Norman's smile, his "Hi, Keed" on arrival home from anywhere.

Family weekends.

Whistling, poinsettias and Christmas time.

I encourage all who read this, to make a list of what nourishes YOU!

THANKSGIVING IN FLORENCE, ITALY – 1983

After touring in northern Italy, our four member tour group joined up with a tour group of six for the trip south to Florence where we were to spend three days. The other group was made up of two Australians in their early sixties and two couples from New York who could only be described as loud, uncouth and assertive. However, they had a marvelous tour guide who kept us laughing en route to Florence and gave Francesca, our guide, a much-needed rest.

The combined groups were to separate on the fourth day, with their tour going to southern Italy and ours going to Rome, but it was Thanksgiving Day and the two tour guides indicated they had a surprise for us that evening.

At 7:00 p.m., we congregated for our bus trip to a restaurant and our "surprise." We were taken on a circuitous route to a monastery on a hill. As I remember there were some tight squeezes for the bus en route to the former monkery that had been converted into a restaurant.

The dining room was very spacious and after being seated, we were invited to the hor d'eurves table, which held delicacies such as smoked sausages, beef tongue and a myriad of vegetables. We had wine aplenty and a serenading orchestra dressed in breeches, sashes, flowing sleeves, reminiscent of somewhere, (Who knows where!) many violins and a bosomy contralto with a big, well trained voice and body to match.

There was a trumpet fanfare and in marched our tour guides followed by the waiters carrying aloft on a large platter, a most gloriously golden, roast turkey, decorated with red, white and blue paper flags; both drum sticks were waving flags, as well. There was much "oohing and aahing," cheering, stamping of feet, hugging, kissing and expressions of appreciation and surprise. The wine, you know! And it was Thanksgiving Day!

The chef had obviously tried to make the traditional Thanksgiving menu...and did an incredible job of it although I mentally made note that I should perhaps share my recipe for southern cornbread turkey stuffing with him! It was late by this time; the Italians eat late, and we were having a marvelous time.

The Australians were delightful. The men in the band kept coming back for requests and the subsequent tips that ensued. At our request the musicians played Waltzing Matilda for the Australians, Deep In The Heart of Texas for the Texans and some Broadway songs for the New Yorkers. When they played the Chicken Dance Song, Dolo, I and two people from New York performed the dance. Then surprisingly, the band played the Hora...the traditional Jewish dance. I knew how to dance the Hora, and Sylvia and Jack Levy, our Jewish travel companions did too. Jack was too busy eating, so Sylvia and I danced the Hora to a round of applause from the others in the room. But Jack grew nervous because he thought Sylvia would have a heart attack dancing the Hora so soon after eating, with her history of heart trouble!

The other diners in the restaurant consisted of a large tour group of Americans who sat quietly and didn't seem to be having any fun when compared to our rather noisy, rowdy bunch. The only other group in the dining area was a table of twelve Japanese tourists on the far side of the room who never indicated or acknowledged that they were aware of our presence or shenanigans during the entire time. There were many, many Japanese tourists vacationing in Italy.

About this time the band struck up a nice American type waltz and the lead violinist walked over and asked me to dance. Was I surprised? Oh yes, but I readily accepted. He was rather short; his eyebrows were on a level with my collarbone but we did a rather graceful, proper waltz, nonetheless. Or so I thought at the time. I was grateful that he didn't nestle his head on my bosom, it was right there!

The evening was winding down and we beckoned to the orchestra, who never sat, but just kept strolling and playing, albeit the other table of Americans had begun shooing them away. We asked them to play something for the Japanese! Something from the Mikado! The musicians promptly launched into the most widely known aria from the Mikado and the female vocalist walked over to where the Japanese were seated and sang it to them most beautifully. It was the only time, up until that moment, that they glanced in our direction, for they were aware that we had requested the song for them. We applauded with gusto when the song ended. The Japanese nodded slightly.

Shortly after this, the Japanese group began preparing to leave, and we asked the band to play the beautiful, farewell song, Areviduci Roma. As they proceeded to walk in single file toward the door at the far side of the room, everyone at our table, noisy to the last, waved and called out "Areviduci, Areviduci!" When they were even with our table, they all stopped, as if on cue, turned toward us and bowed low, very formally, then straightened and continued on their way out the door. Our group was touched emotionally by their unexpected tribute and for the first time that evening we grew very quiet. It was one of the most touching moments of my life. I don't think it was the wine!

I wanted to run after them and say, "Hey you guys, that was lovely, I'm sorry about the bitterness of World War II, but dad-drat-it, you shouldn't have bombed Pearl Harbor!!

SHRINE OF OUR LADY OF FATIMA IN PORTUGAL

(Note: Written in 1985 after a visit to the Shrine of Our Lady of Fatima in Portugal. This essay won a Valley By-Liners Award in 2004.)

Only the roadside pilgrims marred the pristine beauty of the woodland highway. For them, there was no air-conditioned glass-encircled bus from which to peer in wonder at majestic trees and verdant undergrowth. For those of us visiting this impoverished country for the first time, the cork trees and the flowering shrubs offered pleasing contrast to the dilapidated settlements that abounded on the outskirts of Lisbon.

In worn, dusty clothing, clinging to their meager belongings and carrying their young children on back or bosom, the pilgrims trudged along the roadside on tired feet. Their destination and ours was the Shrine of Our Lady of Fatima.

We arrived early in the morning and discovered there were no crowds; there were only rain-washed trees and water puddles dotting the enormous pavilion of the Shrine. Surrounded by the unadorned, stark vats and candle racks where the ailing, desperate pilgrims could light their tapers and dip their maimed limbs, it seemed no place of miracles to me. A cynic's thoughts suffused my mind.

As the gray scudding clouds rushed past overhead, I stood transfixed. I was surprised to find I was alone; most of the group had returned to the bus or the souvenir shop. As I walked past the dipping vats and faded candles with their entangled rivulets of wax, I bent forward to touch them with my fingertips. My mind's eye

261

saw the throngs who had in days past worshiped and prayed upon this spot. I thought of those in transit headed toward this place of hope and expectation. I was an intruder here, in cynic's stance. If this be a place of miracles, why did I feel such sadness?

Before retracing my steps toward the empty bus, my mind and heart sent forth a prayer to Almighty God, to grant, this day, the fervid hopes and needs of dusty pilgrims making their tedious journey toward the healing grace of Our Lady of Fatima. Ah, Portugal!

MAKING JELLY

(This was written as a "gotcha" piece for my sister, Agnes. ALMOST all of it is true!)

Every weird trait our family has is blamed on the depression of the thirties, which took place when we were growing up. A waste not, want not, attitude was instilled into our psyches from the cradle on. If Mom made an apple pie, she made jelly out of the peelings. In fact the female members of our family could make jelly out of the bark of a tree or weeds, if impelled. Me, I didn't make jelly, I bought jelly, that is, until I had a daughter that began growing every kind of fruit tree imaginable in her back yard.

What goes around, comes around. My daughter grew grapes, loquats, blackberries, figs, oranges, peaches, grapefruit and limes, but Fara doesn't make jelly, either. This activated my waste not, want not syndrome BIG TIME, and a deal was cut; I would make the jelly and we would split it 50/50. It was then that I embarked upon a sea of jelly.

One day in May, a five gallon bucket of grapes arrived in my kitchen. I cleaned off the spiders, dust, removed the stems and placed all the grapes into two big kettles, then I started cooking. It boiled into a beautiful purple liquid and after about 20 minutes, I turned off the heat and started "rendering" the grapes. Sounds easy, it isn't. I never had such a mess in my life. All that straining, bursting, squirting, splitting, squeezing and dripping left my kitchen flecked with purple from ceiling to floor. After multiple strainings, I ended up with magenta colored hands and a clear, wine-colored

263

juice that warmed my heart. I poured it into quart jars and sealed it. I then found the Clorox bottle and began the task of bleaching out the kitchen and myself.

Not long after this experience, I decided to MAKE THE JELLY! I carefully read the Sure Jell instructions, dumped in my ingredients and began to cook my juice. When it began to boil, I panicked; the jelly was like water, no way would it jell, I thought. Agnes!, I will call sister Agnes, little Miss Jelly Maker from South Dakota! I ran to the phone and dialed her number.

The Voice, "Kinsleys," she said.

"This is Marge. I am making jelly."

"So?"

"I don't know how to make jelly, I have never done it. I'm scared."

The Voice, " An idiot can make jelly!"

" I know that," I say, " but I'm not an idi-"

"Don't get cute, just tell me where you are in the process. Are you serious? You have never made jelly? But how did this happen?"

" I don't make jelly, I eat Smuckers," I said.

"Smuckers, Schmuckers. You're a Klemme, aren't you? Or maybe you are a 'schmuck'. Get it, Smuckers, schmuck! Isn't that a hoot?" (Laughter)

"Yes, I'm a Klemme, I'm feeling insecure, that's all."

"You have never felt insecure, that I ever remember."

"Could we cut out the psychological analysis and get back to the jelly? I am here with two caldrons of grape juice threatening my safety and you are making comments about my psyche and my Smuckers."

"Did you say 'caldrons', you are cooking in caldrons? What kind of caldrons?"

"Pots, Agnes, metal pots, but right now they look like caldrons to me."

" Well, Yah,..... so okay...... Gad, I can't believe you never made jelly before. It is so easy... Okay, so what are you doing now, as we speak?" She sighs, an obvious attempt at tolerance of my ignorance.

"I have added all the ingredients and I am boiling it, right now, 'as we speak'."

" What does it look like?" she asked.

"IT LOOKS LIKE GRAPE JUICE BOILING IN A KETTLE!" I say, my panic barely under control.

"Will you calm down? You're just making jelly, after all."

"Okay, Okay. It's foaming and bubbling."

"Foaming and bubbling? How many 'caldrons' are foaming and bubbling?" (More laughter)

"Both big pots are foaming and bubbling.....and rising...just climbing right up the sides of both kettles."

"How far from the top of the kettle?" she asked patiently.

"About a half inch," I say.

"A HALF-INCH? A HALF-INCH? MY GAWD, THIS IS AWFUL," she yells, "WHY DIDN'T YOU SAY SO. WHERE ARE YOU STANDING? CALL 911, NOW!! I SAID, NOW!! ARE YOU WEARING ANY KIND OF PROTECTION?"

"Shouldn't I turn off the burners first?" I ask.

"STOP FOR NOTHING, SEEK SHELTER, STAND IN A DOORWAY, GET IN A BATH TUB, DO IT NOW!!"

"Agnes," I say meekly, "the jelly seems to be going back down the insides of the kettles, I turned off everything. It looks shiny on top, and a little thicker. I think I have jelly here, by jibbers. What do you think?" After a moment of silence, in a calm, controlled voice, she says, "As I said at the outset, it really doesn't take any brains to make jelly!"

And I have been making jelly ever since. I think I could make jelly out of apple peelings or the bark of a tree. It's easy, an idiot could do it.

THE FINAL DANCE

The semester was coming to a close in my college Modern Dance Class and my grade up to that point was not going to enhance my grade point average. The mid-term had not been easy; required as we were, to move in single file diagonally across the gym floor incorporating all the steps and movements we had been taught. The Final was to be an original dance using specified moves and steps to the music of our choice and in whatever sequence we chose, but all the prescribed steps and movements had to be included in the performance routine. The dance could be done singly or in groupings of two or more students.

At an age of forty-seven I was not a typical dance class member and I began to have rather child-like feelings of insecurity about who would dance with me, or indeed, who would choose me to dance with them. I certainly didn't want to do a solo.

As the voluntary selection process began, I watched from the sidelines as the boisterous, young coeds selected their partners and squealed and hugged at the knowledge that they had the team of their choice. I was resigning myself to a solo Final performance when I spotted a young girl on the sidelines like myself looking a bit anxious and ill at ease. I remembered her mid-term had been something of a disaster. Throughout the semester she had appeared very shy and withdrawn in class.

Time for action! I walked over to her and asked if she would consider being my partner in the Final scheduled for the following week. She smiled, in obvious relief, and said she would be happy to be my partner. She lived forty miles up the Valley and commuted each day so we would have to work out our practice sessions in the interim, after her and my classes were over.

I set about planning for our presentation. From our player piano, I taped some rinky-tink, honky-tonk music with stripper over-tones. Our costuming criteria was that it must be minimal. We could wear one or two items to indicate the theme of the dance, however, all must wear the standard black leotards as were worn in class.

This charming little dance partner had a slender, lovely figure and no self-perception of her latent beauty. She had grown up in a Hispanic household with very strict rules regarding her conduct and activities. At eighteen years of age, she had never had a date and was always accompanied by an older member of the family when she attended social events. She was not comfortable wearing a leotard because it seemed so revealing. Compared to some of the other bold young women in our dance class she was a person of wonder and beauty.

I found a length of figured material to drape around the hips and tie in a saucy bow on the side. The single other part of our costume was a headband with a feathery poof above the right ear. We had the costume. Now for the dance! Choreographing came easy as we worked out a routine using the required steps and moves but reminiscent of a honky-tonk, hootchy-kootch dance. Our theme was a "mother-daughter turn of the century dance hall routine." And we practiced at our home until we had it perfect. The required moves did not come easy for my young partner but as we practiced and laughed together she became more relaxed and was beginning to dance energetically and look great in the process.

Wearing our costumes, we arrived in class on the day of the Final and found a place in the semi-circle sitting on the gym floor. We took note of our confident fellow classmates. As the instructor called out the groups and the theme of their dance, each group made their way to the center of the gym and performed some very slick and impressive dance routines! There was the Choctaw Indian Dance, the Budding Ballerina Dance, the Broadway Show Dance and the Cheerleaders Dance. All were impressive, practiced routines that used the required moves and steps. We were last. When the instructor announced the Mother-Daughter Turn of the Century

Dance Hall Performers there was a stillness in the room. We stepped to the middle of the gym floor, our outrageous music began and Yolanda and I seemed transported! We danced the required steps with far more abandon than I thought capable for us. The applause and whistles started before the dance ended. Some who had their purses threw pennies and the instructor was smiling from ear to ear. Frankly speaking, we brought down the house and the end result was I aced the course and Yolanda brought a dismal mid-term D up to a B.

THE GENDER THING

Being fully aware of the diversity in human beings, these stated opinions are the result of many decades of observed behavior while traveling the by-ways and highways of life. They are privately held generalizations regarding gender, and contain no scientific evidence to justify their veracity or their usefulness. I am aware of the significance of a normal distribution curve in a population, as well as the on-going effect of the women's liberation movement on these general assumptions. These are my personal opinions drawn from my observations of the interaction between men and women..

Wisdom comes late in life, and the young are destined to bumble along not knowing what they need to know, because 1) they rarely ask for advice 2) they seldom recognize good advice from bad, and 3) once advice is received it is rarely applied. As generations before them have done, they look back and ponder why they didn't learn some of the rules for living when they could have used them as a positive influence in their lives.

It all starts with the school years when everyone yearns to be popular and well liked. Some are, some aren't , and those who somehow never attain that goal, look back with a gnawing anxiety on why they missed out on that particular state of being. Peers mercilessly categorize each other, and this applies to both boys and girls. For purposes of identification, the categories, hereinafter, will be referred to as the "hunks," the "beauty queens" and the "wanabees."

As time goes on, interesting social predilections occur. Hunks go hunking around and usually marry rather plain, grateful women, not the beauty queen, for hunks are accustomed to adoration and a beauty queen is usually incapable of providing this, because that is her major need, as well. However, Jane wanabee will feel blessed to have hunk and adore him. His husbanding talents are apt to be scanty, but he needs to be adored and she is grateful for the privilege of playing the role of admirer.

Beauty queen is the female counterpart of hunk, she needs adoration and will marry someone who will adore her. She will choose her mate from the ranks of the less beautiful wanabees. She will marry someone who will spend his life being grateful that she accepted him as her mate; indeed, she will insist on this gratitude.

The wise female, plain or beautiful, will avoid marrying hunk; she searches out the achiever and she places great importance on intelligence, ambition, innate kindness and good humor, for she is concerned with security and good parenting instincts. She is most apt to find these traits in the wanabees. Women marry for security and affection and tend to find it in the fellows who never made a touchdown or were homecoming king.

The male, who is ambitious, kind, motivated, good-natured and honest is the most sought after and the luckiest of men. His outward appearance is of little concern to women. He may go through life wishing he could have been hunk in school, and may never learn that it was of little importance to women who were seeking husbands. Loving relationships come easy to most male wanabees.

Women who make a special effort to appear sexy, usually aren't. The mousy ones are the sexpots, and ironically, sexually driven males chase the wrong girls. Men should look to the girl that smiles easily and is kind and considerate with physical beauty being a minor consideration.

Men marry primarily to ensure regular sex. However, men prefer the uncomplicated company of men in whose presence they can belch, cuss, scratch, fight and pass gas with abandon. Men are rather basic creatures with only a thin veneer of civilization's refinements. Historically men were the primary colonizers and mated with whomever or whatever, was in close proximity. When the women (wives) of their own kind and nationality were imported, it was then and only then that rules of courting and marriage were promulgated that precluded mating with those considered a threat to race, creed or culture. It was only then that their prejudices and discriminations concerning socially acceptable alliances and behaviors were rigidly enforced.

Women love the company of men, but unrealistically expect men to relate to how they feel, how they think and what they consider important. They expect to find a mutual involvement in the male-female relationship, but men are rarely capable of providing this type of emotional fulfillment. Truth be known, most men don't give a flying fig about reactions or feelings resulting from their behavior in any given situation. Men and women marry with different expectations and for different reasons. Women are the nurturers, civilizers, the tamers, and the keepers of the culture, race and faith. They embrace that role wholeheartedly. Men resist, but achieve a trade-off of sorts, each bartering what they are innately capable of offering. Women offer sex in exchange for security and the expectation of emotional support.

Women are capable of maintaining a friendship with a member of the opposite sex. Men find this difficult, if not impossible. A heterosexual male can rarely maintain a relationship with a female based solely on a feeling of friendship. She will think of him as a friend, he will have difficulty keeping his, consequently her, sexuality from intruding into the framework of the friendship.

Men and women struggle to find fulfillment and gratification in the arena of life looking for the wrong mate, in the wrong places and for the wrong reasons. We breed our animals most carefully, but our children are seldom taught the finer points of mate selection, or what can be logically and realistically expected from the male-female relationship. Sadly they bear the consequences of their/our folly.

This driving force, this mystery of eternal attraction whose answers are withheld for too long, entices us to stumble and fall, live and learn, laugh and love, to reach for the unreachable and strive for the unattainable. Acting on instinct, relying on our less than perfect intellects, caught up and held captive by emotion and self-indulgence, each succeeding generation will continue to seek, but seldom find, the solutions to the gender thing.

A TRIBUTE
EMIL FRITZ KLEMME 1895 – 1975

One of the fondest memories of my father was etched in my mind during an annual pilgrimage to South Dakota a year before his death. He was 78 years old at the time and as I watched from a kitchen window, I saw him in the field, south of the house. He was driving a big tractor, cultivating a field of corn. His yellow shirt billowed out behind him in the gentle breeze, and the rich soil that he loved with all his heart and soul, turned easily when prodded by the cultivator blades. His back was straight and his head was held proudly. He was doing what he loved best: working the land. He was a son of the soil and no one loved the sight of a straight furrow, a weedless field or a stand of corn any more than he. Making the land produce bountifully was his labor of love.

He had suffered from leukemia for many years and there were times when he was tired, ill and dispirited; but always a day on the tractor at work in the fields raised his spirits and rejuvenated his body. Until the very last, this was the magic medicine.

He was a beloved husband, a kind and loving father, a man who to my knowledge never committed a petty or spiteful act toward friend or neighbor.

On the day of his funeral with a brisk wind blowing, snow drifting and a chill factor of minus 39 degrees, the church was filled to overflowing with those who came to pay last tribute to this kind man, this plower of straight furrows.........my Dad.

A TRIBUTE
ANNA MARIE KLEMME 1899 – 1990

This dear, Christian lady who took such joy in living, planted young trees, clipped new recipes, wrote in her journal and remembered birthdays of friends and relatives throughout her life. In her later years, she continued to read the daily newspapers, several periodicals, made 100 pieced quilts, took joy in holidays and played cards daily until past 90 years of age. She wrote long newsy letters to her distant children each week and felt a phone call was a totally inadequate way to communicate with her family. She was courted by her husband in a horse and buggy and lived to see men walk on the moon. What a life to live!

Last December we knew she was dying, but she continued to amaze us with her clear thinking, her smile and flashes of wit. Her funeral service, at her children's request was to be a celebration of her life, and so it turned out to be. The pastor read passages from her autobiography, My Life As I Remember It, which had us all laughing through our tears.

A letter I received, during the last year of her life, ended with this statement, "I really must close now, for I want to watch the Belmont Sweepstakes on TV!" She taught her children to expect gratification in hard work, rewards in a Christian attitude and joy in love and laughter. We were blessed to have her as our mother.

A TRIBUTE
AGNES KLEMME KINSLEY   1928-1998

A TERRIBLE SADNESS GRIPS THE HEART WHEN BELOVED SISTERS DIE
AND AS I SIT AND REMINISCE, I CANNOT HELP BUT CRY.

I FEEL HER TIME WAS PREMATURE, SHE HAD SO MUCH TO LIVE FOR
BUT TRUTH BE KNOWN, I MUST ADMIT, SHE NOW HAS EVEN MORE.

OH HOW TENUOUS OUR CLAIM ON EARTHLY LIFE CAN BE
COULD MY GRIEF BE SELF INDULGENCE? AM I THINKING JUST OF ME?

REMEMBERING THINGS I SHOULD HAVE DONE, AND WORDS I MEANT TO SAY,
OVERWHELMING MEMORIES OF LAUGHTER COME TO PLAY.

RECALLING ALL THE FUN AND JOY WE SHARED THROUGHOUT THE YEARS,
DELIGHTING IN THE MEMORIES, I'LL LET LAUGHTER DRY MY TEARS!

I THANK GOD FOR ALL THE YEARS, SHE WAS OURS TO KNOW AND LOVE,
AND KNOW WITHIN MY HEART OF HEARTS, SHE IS WATCHING FROM ABOVE.

(Note: Written after the death of sister, Agnes)

COMMENCEMENT ADDRESS

(Note: I was asked to give the commencement address to the graduating Class of 1994 at Elk Point, South Dakota. Our class had graduated 50 years before that date and there was an impending merger of two local high schools into one entity. This was to be the last class graduated from Elk Point High School before the merger.)

COMMENCEMENT ADDRESS

THE ELK POINT HIGH SCHOOL
GRADUATING CLASS OF 1994 - MAY 22, 1994

Two score and ten tears ago, almost to the day, the Class of 1944 was graduating from Elk Point High School and like you, we were 18 years old and anxious to get on with our lives.

We began first grade in 1932 when Franklin Delano Roosevelt was president of the United States, and we graduated in 1944...and Franklin Delano Roosevelt was still president. No other classes can make that claim, but then no other president can make the claim of a third term either. During those same twelve years we also had the same superintendent and the same janitor, Jonas Leyman and Andy Sorenson, who became legends in their own time, at least, in our eyes.

We were children of the depression and as we entered high school, we traded a time of economic depression for the all out mobilization of World War II. Did this affect us? Of course, we were greatly affected by these two national calamities.

281

Many of us had brothers, cousins and in some cases, fathers, serving in the armed services. Most of us were poor, by today's standards.....Money? What was that? We faced shortages you would find difficult to believe; film for our camera, razor blades, chewing gum. Food and meat were rationed. Sugar was scarce and so was gasoline. Would having no gasoline affect your young lives? I remember substitutes for most things like coffee and candy, but they weren't very good. A wartime chocolate bar tasted like paste mixed with something brown.

A date could cost as little as 50 cents, provided it took place on Thursday night, which most of mine did. Two movie tickets cost 20 cents, two malted milks cost 30 cents....There you have it, the 50 cent date!

But with the EGO OF YOUTH, we coped with it all rather well. We were poor and didn't know it; in fact, we didn't realize we had been disadvantaged and underprivileged until we were in our forties.

We laughed a lot, we partied, we played Spin-the-Bottle, we danced, we jitterbugged and we walked to where we were going. No gas, you remember!! At our Junior-Senior prom, Eddie Texol and his Hay Stackers furnished the music and incidentally, it wasn't country western music although it sounds like it should have been!

It took very little to amuse us. On Skip Day, we went to Sioux City where we visited the Fairmont Dairy, a Fire Station and toured a home for orphaned children. But we were the lucky ones; my sister's class went to Sioux City on Skip Day and visited the Swift Meat Packing Plant. No one in that class ever ate weiners again.

Football games were held in the afternoon and there were no fancy A, Double A or Triple A classifications. The team played where they were told to play, with teams in closest proximity to Elk Point, no matter what category of "A" they were. Most of us were there, yelling and cheering them on with such inspiring cheers as " Strawberry shortcake, Gooseberry pie, ELK POINT HIGH SCHOOL , AYE, YI, YI!!! My classmates sitting out there in the audience told me that particular yell never happened! But it's my memory against theirs. Then they proceeded to say and sing some of the cheers and songs that I had forgotten!

We grew close as a class, we were supportive of each other, cared for each other, our school and our community; and we still do.   I think we have the record for holding class reunions.

Graduation was a very emotional experience for us. We wept. Down deep, where we lived with ourselves, we knew that in spite of wartime uncertainties, we had been blessed with a great four years, protected by caring families and a free nation of laws.......and we had an insatiable desire to show our self-reliance. Some members of our class had left school to enlist in the armed services; others faced induction shortly after graduation and would be carrying a gun within a short time. And they did.

Many of us in the class of 1944 have grandchildren graduating from high school and /or college this month. But as I look at you out there in your graduation robes, I find that the 50 years that divide us seems like the blink of an eye. We have run the course; it is now your generation's turn. It is a mighty challenge to fulfill the expectations and hopes of the generations that have preceded you. And it is a splendid calling to inspire and guide the generations that will follow after you.

If you wonder whether I am going to offer you free advice. YOU GOT IT! Consider these guidelines a gift from the Class of 1944 to the Class of 1994. Try to remember them:

SO IF IT'S WORTH DOING, IT'S WORTH DOING RIGHT.

OPEN YOUR EYES AND EARS TO THOSE FOR WHOM EVERYTHING SEEMS TO GO RIGHT, THEN DO LIKEWISE. IT IS CALLED   EMULATING SUCCESS. THERE IS NO SUCH THING   AS GOOD LUCK; WE MAKE OUR OWN LUCK.

LISTEN TO YOUR "INNER ADVISOR," WE ALL HAVE ONE.

LEARN TO RECOGNIZE GOOD ADVICE,   AND THEN TAKE IT.   THIS SOUNDS EASY, BUT THE FIRST PART IS THE HARDEST TO LEARN.

SHOW ENTHUSIASM FOR WHAT YOU DO.

REMEMBER TO LAUGH. LAUGHTER HEALS THE MIND, SPIRIT AND BODY. THERE IS A MIND-BODY CONNECTION THAT PROMOTES WELLNESS.

With those pearls of wisdom, you should all soar like eagles!

You will be the last graduation class of Elk Point high School, as we know it today. You are unique, already............The Class of 1944 wishes you well; we congratulate you. We are honored to have shared this occasion with you.

End of talk.

(Note: There were 36 members of the graduating class of 1944 and a similar number in 1994. A classmate said that the brevity of my talk would determine the length of his applause. The applause was appropriate so I must have met his expectations.)

Commentary: There was a sizable crowd in the auditorium, however there was no invocation given, no flowers on the stage and no indications that the event was special. The parents and guests seemed to relate to my message and laughed in all the right places. The graduates sat quiet and dull-eyed, slouched in their chairs, their shorts and tennis shoes under their blue graduation robes in obvious display, their mortar boards pushed back on their heads or cocked to one side. I came away somewhat saddened. In my mind's eye I was seeing my graduation class of 50 years ago, whose reaction to the graduating experience was quite different.

ON SAYING GOODBYE

Saying goodbye is my least favorite activity and I am not good at it. Throughout my adult life I have said too many goodbyes to the people I love. I have stood in too many airports waiting for the unwelcome emotion of farewell. Having grown up in a family that doesn't approve of blubbering farewells, or tears in general, I stand convicted of both.

Having lived away from my home community, visits home were wonderful, but there was always the dreaded goodbye, knowing many months, sometimes a year might pass before I would see my family again. It has not become easier through the years. The image of my aging parents in the airport waiting area has been replaced by the figures of my dear siblings, ever present, ever willing to meet me on arrival and deposit me on departure.

I find returning to the Midwest and visiting the scenes of my childhood psychologically necessary and as long as I have family to visit, I will continue to return as often as possible. Even though our children and grandchildren live in Texas, saying goodbye to them is a bummer and saying goodbye to friends isn't easy, either

I choose to make my departures as simple as possible; leave me at the curb, make the farewell fervent, but brief, and allow me to do my coping in a waiting area where if I should weep into my hankie, the travelers of the world will be too occupied talking into their cell phones to notice my tears.

THE "GRAMMIES" YOU MAY HAVE NEVER KNOWN

(Note: This is an addendum chapter written for those generations who will follow after me, descendants, many generations from now, who will know me only in conversational reference).

When writing one's life story, the author may be reluctant to share information that future generations may find incredible. Because I always wished I knew more about my great-grandparents, this chapter is written for those of my descendants who may have wondered about me as a young person, long before my hair was white and I became known as "Grammies."

As a young girl, I loved to laugh and had what my mom called "silly streaks." These silly spells would come unbidden, by people or events, at which time I would act out and say and do silly things, oftentimes laughing until I couldn't stop, ending up crying in sheer exhaustion. During these times I felt an urge to make other people laugh and no act was too ridiculous or off the page.

Because I grew up in a family that loved to laugh, but was not particularly driven to demonstrate humor in behavior or speech, I purposely set about developing the comic side of my personality at an early age. I felt duty bound to fill that void since I loved the nuances of the English language and the expression of day-to-day events in a humorous manner,

I have an aversion for inflicting pain of any kind, physical or emotional, on man or beast. Tactlessness on anyone's part upsets me, and I have never understood what motivates it. People should be kind to one another. Abandonment of people or animals has always appalled me.

My relationships with others were honest, and I dealt with disagreement up front and as kindly as I knew how. This was particularly true in relationships I had with members of the opposite sex in my youthful years. If I liked a fellow, but had no desire for the relationship to go further than friendship, I would say, "be my friend, that is what we have here." Then I would be one. Maintaining relationships under false assumptions gave me no pleasure, so I didn't do it.

Physically, I would have been considered pretty, but not beautiful. My hair was reddish dark blond and I had an abundance of it. Mine was a great head of hair and I enjoyed wearing it in many different styles. I had a clear, Nordic complexion with rosy cheeks, a trait inherited from my forebears. My eyes were grayish blue; my nose was small and straight (I always wished it were larger.). My teeth were small and straight (I always wished they were larger, as well.). I was 5 feet 6 ¾ inches tall, with high firm breasts (I wished they were larger.), long-waisted and well proportioned. My husband said I was "willowy." Gad, I don't know a female on the planet who wouldn't enjoy being called willowy. My legs were long, (could have been shapelier) and I had pretty feet with short toes. My best features were probably my hair, arms, hands and blemish-free skin. I made a special effort to look my best and knew that my folks and later, my husband, took pleasure in my appearance.

Since there was the inhibiting factor of my Norwegian upbringing, my taste in clothes required an evolution of style that evolved over many years. As I matured emotionally and intellectually, I gradually developed my own style of dress that was uniquely ME. I consider my clothing style to be 1/4th American Indian, 1/4th Gypsy, 1/4th Hippie and 1/4th Nun. I liked things that flowed, glowed, shimmered, glimmered, dangled, jangled, rippled and trailed and I loved black, which is the nun part. I knew just how much was too much and how much was ME. Of course I loved jewelry and big earrings .

I was late settling into my own personality. Molded and reared to think and behave in a certain way, there were forces within me crying out for expression. I gradually allowed the inner me to become my normal, natural persona: garrulous, gutsy, humorous, joyful, outspoken, assertive, opinionated and tolerant of diverse opinions. I think!

I fail to understand people who have no opinion on topical subjects. I have an opinion on everything and don't give a flip whether anyone agrees with me or not. I have always enjoyed discussions where opinions differed, although I find most people are uncomfortable participating in them. I value people who are considered eccentric or what I call "prickly," as long as it is accompanied by a sizeable intellect.

Having been taught to acquiesce to my husband in all things, it took me years to work through the fact that my opinion was as valuable as his and acquiescence in all things was not particularly admirable. My husband went through the motions of protesting my indications of growing independence but I sensed he did not object to my autonomous thinking since he had encouraged it in our children and usually respected the thought processes of others. Through the years, the little dependent wife he married became an independent thinker that dared to disagree on many matters of importance, great or small.

The dynamics of our marriage have undergone great changes over our fifty-eight years together; in some areas there are indications of minor role reversal. I have become stronger in a relative sense to the degree that my husband has become dependent. This has been neither damaging nor injurious to our relationship. There is still mutual love and respect for the other's viewpoint, there is still resolution of differences after healthy, sometimes very volatile discussions.

My husband's "love language" would most assuredly be the need for physical touch. He has always reveled in the touching, intimacy of our physical relationship. Although age dictates its evolution and transformation into a less acrobatically challenging exercise, sexual intimacy remains an integral part of a marriage even one that has lasted for fifty-eight years.

We were of the generation that considered showing affection in public as tasteless and inappropriate. Looking back, I think that may have been a serious mistake in the parenting of our children. Since we chose not to demonstrate that side of our personal relationship, they rarely saw us touching or being affectionate. In retrospect, I firmly believe children learn to conduct their personal relationships by observing how their parents conduct theirs, by that I mean, the touching, kissing, hugging, the making-up and saying, "I'm sorry" after disagreements.

I have had the joys of a satisfying marriage; I have borne children and seen them to adulthood. I have watched my grandchildren grow up and have taken great pleasure in my great-grandchildren. I have known the satisfaction of a comfortable life, diverse interests in one intellectual pursuit after another, which would wax and wane as I moved through the years. I regret that I will not have the time to read all the books I want to read, or pursue the many interests that I have left unexplored

Time is a most precious thing. Blessedly given, once expended we cannot retrieve it. When we are young, our lives follow a seemingly bountiful pathway of time and we feel little need to guard, cherish or protect it. When the obvious signs of our mortality become apparent, we began to wish we had used every living minute of that gift of time more judiciously, that we had tasted and savored more fully all the rich blessings and experiences that made up our life journey.

Dear ones, be joyful and savor the meaningful relationships that shape your life. Sleep only as necessary to maintain good health, nourish and maintain your body sensibly. Take time to be thankful to God, thoughtful and kind to those you love and who love you. Remember to laugh, for laughter will make bearable whatever unbearable moments you may experience. When embraced as a lifestyle, these attitudes and behaviors inevitably generate their own rewards. MLF

THE ROAD FROM SPINK

1926	Union County South Dakota
1930	Spink Township
1944	Sioux Falls, South Dakota
1944	Baraboo, Wisconsin
1945	Jacksonville Florida
1946	Miami Florida (married Norman)
1946	Jacksonville, Florida (Navy)
1946	Cape May, New Jersey (Navy)
1947	Rehoboth Beach, Delaware(Navy)
1947	Charleston, South Carolina(Navy)
1948	New London, Connecticut(Navy)
1948	Groton, CT, U.S. Submarine Base Housing(Navy)
1948	U.S. Submarine Base Housing, Locona, Panama(Navy)
1948	Military Housing Farfan, Panama (Navy)
1949	Pensacola, Florida (rehab)
1949	Corona, California (rehab)
1949	Long Beach, California (rehab)
1950	Corpus Christi, TX(rehab) Discharged from the Navy
1950	Austin, TX (re-entered U of T) (Fara was born)
1952	College Station ,TX (Attended A & M) (Mark was born)
1957	Huntsville, TX (John was born) (Norm receives Ph.D.)
1965	Denison, Iowa (taught Midwestern College)
1970	McAllen, TX (L.R.G.D. Consultant)
	(Fara married Joe Jones)
1972	Bakersfield, CA (Norm Taught at Cal. State Bakersfield)
	(Marge in Nursing School. Received R.N. degree)
1975	Harlingen, TX (Flynn St. for 5 years.) Harlingen, TX
1980	(Cypress St. for 10 years) (Mark married Debbie)
1991	Palm Valley, TX (Town House for 12 years)
2004	Palm Valley, 5424 Palm Valley Drive. S., Harlingen, TX

MOVED - 28 TIMES
LIVED IN 20 TOWNS/CITIES, 10 STATES AND THE PANAMA CANAL ZONE

ABOUT THE AUTHOR

M. Flados relates to the history and lifestyles of a former era with the knowledge of one who walked the walk and talked the talk of her Norwegian Lutheran heritage. Being a child of the Great Depression did not preclude her finding joy in the challenging and momentous events taking place during her lifetime.

A South Dakotan by birth, a Texan by marriage, her experiences as motivational speaker, registered nurse, fitness trainer, college professor's wife and mother of three, add a special depth and perception to her writing.

She is a resident of Harlingen, Texas. Describing herself as a "nice kid and a peachy dancer," M. Flados provides the gift of laughter in this informative, historical, sometimes hilarious, life journey on The Road From Spink.

Printed in the United States
51993LVS00004B/97-153